Web Development Solutions

Ajax, APIs, Libraries, and Hosted Services Made Easy

Christian Heilmann
Mark Norman Francis

friendsof

DESIGNER TO DESIGNER™

an Apress® company

Web Development Solutions: Ajax, APIs, Libraries, and Hosted Services Made Easy

ISBN-13 (pbk): 978-1-59059-806-1

ISBN-10 (pbk): 1-59059-806-7

Printed and bound in the United States of America 9 8 7 6 5 4 3 2 1

Distributed to the book trade worldwide by Springer-Verlag New York, Inc., 233 Spring Street, 6th Floor, New York, NY 10013. Phone 1-800-SPRINGER, fax 201-348-4505, e-mail orders-ny@springer-sbm.com, or visit www.springeronline.com.

For information on translations, please contact Apress directly at 2560 Ninth Street, Suite 219, Berkeley, CA 94710. Phone 510-549-5930, fax 510-549-5939, e-mail info@apress.com, or visit www.apress.com.

The source code for this book is freely available to readers at www.friendsofed.com in the Downloads section.

Credits

Lead Editors	**Assistant Production Director**
Chris Mills, Matthew Moodie	Kari Brooks-Copony
Technical Reviewer	**Production Editor**
Ian Lloyd	Kelly Winquist
Editorial Board	**Compositor**
Steve Anglin, Ewan Buckingham, Gary Cornell, Jason Gilmore, Jonathan Gennick, Jonathan Hassell, James Huddleston, Chris Mills, Matthew Moodie, Jeff Pepper, Paul Sarknas, Dominic Shakeshaft, Jim Sumser, Matt Wade	Lynn L'Heureux
	Artist
	April Milne
Project Manager	**Proofreader**
Sofia Marchant	April Eddy
Copy Edit Manager	**Indexer**
Nicole Flores	John Collin
Copy Editor	**Interior and Cover Designer**
Liz Welch	Kurt Krames
	Manufacturing Director
	Tom Debolski

CONTENTS AT A GLANCE

CONTENTS

CONTENTS

ABOUT THE AUTHORS

Christian Heilmann is a German web developer stranded in London after a journey around the world working for various web agencies and dotcoms. With a background in social work with disabled people and radio journalism, he sees the Web as a perfect media to allow access for everyone and keeps a pragmatic view on how to convey information. He currently works as a lead developer and trainer for Yahoo!, writes for .net magazine, and blogs at http://wait-till-i.com.

Mark Norman Francis is a Londoner, born and bred. He spent many years doing various IT jobs for City University, including working on the support desk and systems administration. After tiring of the relaxed environment and long holidays, he entered the real world. In 2000 he joined Purple Interactive, a commercial web company with clients such as Barclays, IBM, and Honda. One site produced there was an unofficial F1 site, later acquired by Formula One Management. After leaving the world of motorsport, he joined Yahoo! in June 2004. He blogs at http://cackhanded.net/.

ABOUT THE TECHNICAL REVIEWER

Ian Lloyd runs Accessify.com, a site dedicated to promoting web accessibility and providing tools for web developers. Ian works full-time for Nationwide Building Society in Swindon, UK, where he tries his best to influence standards-based design. He is a member of the Web Standards Project, contributing to the Accessibility Task Force, and is the author of *Build Your Own Web Site the Right Way with HTML and CSS*, published by SitePoint (in which he teaches web standards–based design to the complete beginner). He has also been technical editor on a number of other books published by Apress, friends of ED, and SitePoint. Standards stuff aside, he's got a real thing for classic VW vans ("You know, the 'hippie bus'") and is also looking forward to the day that his puppy terrier calms down for longer than 5 minutes.

Layout conventions

To keep this book as clear and easy to follow as possible, the following text conventions are used throughout.

Important words or concepts are normally highlighted on the first appearance in **bold type**.

Code is presented in `fixed-width` font.

New or changed code is normally presented in **`bold fixed-width font`**.

Pseudo-code and variable input are written in *`italic fixed-width`* font.

Menu commands are written in the form Menu ➤ Submenu ➤ Submenu.

Where I want to draw your attention to something, I've highlighted it like this:

> *Ahem, don't say I didn't warn you.*

Sometimes code won't fit on a single line in a book. Where this happens, I use an arrow like this: ➡.

```
This is a very, very long section of code that should be written all ➡
on the same line without a break.
```

1 STOP THE WEB . . . YOU'RE GETTING ON!

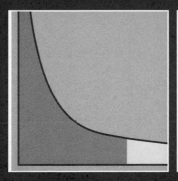

By Norm Francis

At the beginning of our journey, let's take a moment to think about why the Web is so interesting and why having a web site is so useful, or as some would argue, essential. This is where we will start, before we even begin to immerse ourselves in all of those technologies you've heard about. This chapter will cover the reasons for starting a web site, look at some success stories of people just like you who have already done so, and give you the kind of positive feel-good vibe you need to walk into the rest of the book with confidence.

Let's get started!

Web presence

Have you ever tried to look up a company or service on the Internet, only to be frustrated? You asked some friends, but they didn't know where to find it. Then you tried using a search engine such as Google (http://www.google.com/), Yahoo! (http://search.yahoo.com/), or Windows Live Search (http://www.live.com/?searchonly=true), only to find no relevant results. Then you tried using a directory listing such as those compiled by Yahoo! (http://dir.yahoo.com/) or the Netscape/AOL-sponsored open directory (http://dmoz.org/). However, it was all to no avail and you gave up, annoyed that they didn't think to offer details of their services, catalog, prices, or what-have-you in the widely accessed and low-pressure environment of the Web.

Why stop at just companies?

You're trying to get in touch with an old friend, but the phone number you have for them in your diary is now out-of-date. You run through the same rigmarole. You might find them on Friends Reunited (http://www.friendsreunited.co.uk/) or Classmates (http://www.classmates.com) if they were a school or college friend. But what if you met them outside of education? You might find it difficult to track down a Drinking Buddies Reunited, Tae-Kwon-Do Class Reunited, or First Met Each Other At Ibiza Reunited site to help you out.

Curses.

Now imagine it's someone else trying to find **you**.

You can see where this is leading—whether you simply want to keep in touch with old friends, share your music or other form of art with others, or let people know about your business, it's becoming increasingly important to set up your own web site.

Why set up your own site?

There are many reasons to have a personal web site:

- You have a burning passion for a particular subject and think other people might be interested in what you know.
- You might want to sell things without setting up a physical shop.

- You have an artistic flair and want to share your creations with the world.
- You are part of a band and need a place to share news and gig information.
- And many, many more (as they say on compilation albums).

Whatever the reason, there has never been a better time to start your own site. So much community knowledge is now wrapped up and shared in easy-to-use packages that you no longer need to be an expert at web development to create sites that look professionally created, with compelling content and rich media experiences.

By leveraging easily available software templates, libraries, and APIs (don't worry, we'll be explaining these terms throughout the book if they mean nothing to you right now), you can be up and running with your own web site in a matter of days or even hours.

And it's cheap! Web hosting is now a commodity, most web services are free (and the rest are quite inexpensive), and there is no reason to buy software to create your online masterpieces with—free programs are available just for the asking.

The root of all evil (making money from the Web)

In an article he wrote for *Wired Magazine* in 2004, Chris Anderson coined the term the "Long Tail" to describe products and services that aren't high in demand or high in volume, but nonetheless can be a significant part of a business's turnover (as illustrated in Figure 1-1.)

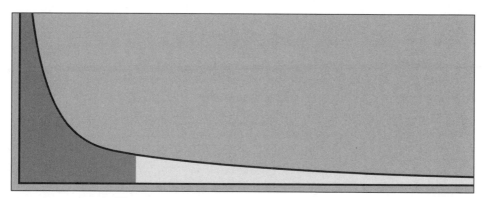

Figure 1-1. A visualization of the "Long Tail"

The Web is the perfect illustration of the Long Tail brought to life. Anyone can make a name for themselves on the Web, because there is an entire world of people looking for the services, skills, or discussions you can offer them. And the less "mass-market" or more obscure your offering is, the more likely you are to find a passionate, dedicated audience simply because no one else is covering that area.

Let's have a look at a couple of examples to show you what others have already done.

Steve Pavlina—personal productivity guru

Steve Pavlina started his web site in October 2004 (see Figure 1-2) and has turned it into one of the most highly trafficked sites on personal productivity on the Web. In a recent article on his site, he stated

> *StevePavlina.com was launched 19 months ago. 12 months ago it was averaging $4.12/day in income. Now it brings in over $300/day (as of 7/31/06). I didn't spend a dime on marketing or promotion. In fact, I started this site with just $9 to register the domain name, and everything was bootstrapped from there.*

–http://www.stevepavlina.com/blog/2006/05/
how-to-make-money-from-your-blog/

Figure 1-2. http://www.stevepavlina.com/

Now, not everyone is going to turn into a such a success overnight, but it's worth thinking about. If you are passionate about something, just by blogging about it you can turn a hobby into a career, or at least a valuable second source of income. And even if you don't manage to make a large second income, even say $50 a month in advertising revenue is enough to pay for hosting fees and whatever, so it is not to be sniffed at.

Daring Fireball

In June 2004 John Gruber, author of the site Daring Fireball (see Figure 1-3) tried something bold. He created a membership system for his site devoted to "Mac Nerdery, etc." giving people who signed up for a yearly fee a T-shirt and access to full syndication of his content. This proved so successful that in April 2006 he left his job to start publishing his site full-time instead.

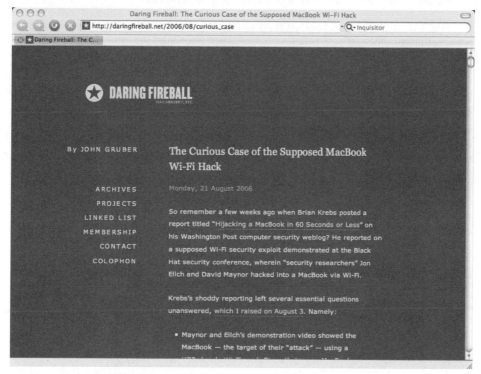

Figure 1-3. http://daringfireball.net/

Of the people who use computers in the world, a small fraction are Mac users. Of those, only another small fraction are going to care enough about their experience to subscribe to a site devoted to discussing at length the Mac's user interface. With articles claiming how selecting items from a list using the keyboard is flawed, debunking apparent flaws in the wireless networking, and debating whether the Safari engine is called "Web Kit" or "Webkit," you must agree that this is a very niche site.

And yet, with enough people reading it around the globe, it can turn into a full-time job and income generator.

Shameless self-promotion

So as you've already seen, money can be a big factor in choosing to start a web site… but it is not the only motivation. In this section we'll look at some other reasons why people are creating new sites all the time.

Your résumé/curriculum vitae and portfolio

You might want to promote yourself for a variety of reasons. Some people use the Web as a marketing tool for getting freelance work or when applying for a new job. If you can talk passionately about your work, it can give potential employers more information about you and your skills.

You can put up more details about previous projects and fill out your personal history; putting in more information on everything you have worked on than you can normally fit into a normal résumé. Many people, especially those who work in web development and design (and other kinds of art and design fields) tend to create an online portfolio, containing several examples of their work (such as links to sites they've designed or coded, or images of their art) for would-be employers to scope out.

And by listing your personal hobbies with links to pages of personal recollections, photos, and videos, you can easily make people see you are a real person, not just a list of facts and figures.

Archive your hobbies

Do you have a hobby? You might think about using your web site to create an archive of your work, either simply for safety or to share with friends, family, or the whole world.

For example, if you love to create watercolor pictures, you could use a flatbed scanner or a digital camera to take copies of your work for publishing on the Web. Then you can create a site that allows the audience to browse your work by chronological order, related themes, or even just by the primary color in the work! The same applies to people who like oil colors, cross-stitch, crochet, or amateur photography.

Or, if you're a musician, you can share copies of your songs and compositions and encourage others to play and remix your music for you.

The scrapbook of your memories

You could also just approach your own site as a scrapbook of your life—either dedicated to an event or just an ongoing "brain dump" of stuff that matters to you.

If you are going to get married and want to share the event online, you can create a site keeping people up to date about the progress toward the event. Then, once the actual day arrives, the site can transform into a central location where people can share and store the photographs and video clips they take.

As another example, suppose you and your spouse are about to have a baby. You can share this with your friends and family by creating a site in which you share pictures of the ultrasound scans, stories of cravings and back pain (and pictures and video of the actual birth if you must). Then, after the birth, use the site as a scrapbook for all of the baby pictures you intend to embarrass your children with later in life.

Summary

So, from this chapter, you've seen that there are many reasons why people create web sites. A lack of ideas and inspiration is not usually the reason that's stopping many people from creating one. Normally it's their lack of ability, or perceived lack of ability. You may be a great artist, but that won't automatically translate into being a great web developer.

In the rest of this book, we'll take you through all the steps you need to set up your own dynamic web experience, from the philosophy of how modern web sites are built, to the technical details of building the pages: integrating things like photos, video, and maps; animating your site; and adding search.

> *What you need*—an idea, purpose, or just a desire to experiment

Into this mix, you need to bring an idea—either the central core of what you want to build, if you already know, or just a desire to play and experiment with making web sites.

> *What you don't need*—any previous skill or experience with making a web site

Let's continue on our journey.

By Chris Heilmann

In this chapter we'll talk about different ways you can participate on the Web. We'll start with the various services you can use to take your first steps:

- Homepage services
- Hosted blogging solutions
- External help in the form of a "knowledgeable buddy"
- What You See Is What You Get (WYSIWYG) editors

We then go on into what you need to know about web development in order to create web sites without relying on third-party services or products:

- Basics of web development
- A crash course in web development and the technologies and languages that drive it

And last but not least, we'll talk about the people who make or break your site—your visitors and what you can expect from them.

All of this will give you a thorough insight into what it takes to create a successful and easy-to-maintain web site that invites visitors instead of ordering them around. The chapters that follow will then provide you with perfectly legal and surprisingly easy ways to achieve some of the things that might baffle you in this one.

You in the limelight on a shoestring budget

Taking part in the Web is exciting—no doubt about that. It is also amazingly easy, compared with other media (it is much harder to get on radio or television, or into the newspapers—unless you do something illegal and get caught).

The Web also means immediate publication and reader feedback, 24-hour availability, and worldwide distribution and reach without shipping overhead. But we talked about that in the first chapter already and (we hope) sold you on the cause.

In this section we discuss some solutions you can choose to create your own space on the Web. We'll examine the problems and limitations you'll have to deal with when going this route. In the rest of the book we'll introduce you to a different way of approaching your own part of the Web—one that will result in a site that is easy to find, maintain, and extend without you having to know all the ins and outs of web development.

Homepage services

Traditionally the first thing a new "netizen" tries out is so-called "homepage services." These are free offers of web space that come with preset designs or step-by-step generators (sometimes called wizards) for you to generate your site. In the past, they were the only way to take your first steps as a web publisher as web space was too expensive and you paid for traffic.

Among the first homepage services were Homestead (http://www.homestead.com/), Tripod (http://www.tripod.lycos.com/), Angelfire (http://www.angelfire.lycos.com/), and Geocities (http://www.geocities.com).

Nowadays almost every Internet connection you get at home comes with free web space, and lately Google joined the market of homepage services with their Googlepages (http://pages.google.com/). Generating your first web site with homepage services is very easy: almost of all of them offer tools to write text, upload images, and create new pages linked with the other ones. Figure 2-1 shows the interface for Googlepages.

Figure 2-1. Page maintenance and creation interfaces

The main snag you soon run into is that these generators limit you in your ways of expression: there are upload restrictions, and you can either choose from several preset looks or you get no presets at all. The latter might make it hard to maintain a consistent look and feel, and the former makes it tough to achieve anything outside the ordinary.

The final code generated by these tools is seldom clean and optimized, and results in large documents that make it hard for search engines to index your site and allow people to find it. It might even make it impossible for some visitors to surf your site at all. Later on in this chapter (and in the rest of the book) we will talk about the possible diversity of visitors to your site. Some visitors are, for example, not able to see your site and rely on software that reads it out to them. These software packages, called screen readers, don't work too well with HTML that is not clean or properly structured. As a lot of homepage service tools are built to produce a visual outcome, with little regard to properly structured page code, this can lead to inaccessible sites.

Not all of these services offer an easy way to upload a lot of files—like FTP access—but instead use upload forms. Depending on their cleverness, these services make it a pain to upload a lot of files as you have to go through them one by one.

Another big issue with homepage services is that there simply is no such thing as a free lunch. In exchange for the web space and the traffic, you'll normally have to display banner ads or frames that link back to the service. Most services don't allow you to use advertising on your site to make some extra money.

> *It is pretty hard to make a professional first impression when your site is full of advertisements for free smileys or ringtones.*

While homepage services have become a lot more advanced in the recent years—Googlepages creates surprisingly clean code (although not always semantically valuable)—they are still quite cumbersome to use and smack of "cheapskate" web design, which is something you might not want your portfolio to be associated with.

Hosted blogging services

If all you want to do is to write and distribute your thoughts and poems about how grim the world is (please, don't), then blogging services are the right solution for you. Blogger (http://www.blogger.com), Yahoo! 360° (http://360.yahoo.com or http://uk.360.yahoo.com/), MySpace (http://www.myspace.com), and all the others out there make it easy to set up your blog. Some even allow you to choose your own domain name (like www.yourname.com) and choose from several predefined designs optimized for publication of your text. Figure 2-2 shows the Blogger homepage indicating the three steps you need to take to set up your blog, and surprisingly this is really everything you need to do.

Figure 2-2. Blogger.com makes blogging easy.

Many of these services come with design libraries from which to choose your design. These libraries are maintained and regularly updated, like the "Select a Theme" page of Yahoo!'s 360°, shown in Figure 2-3.

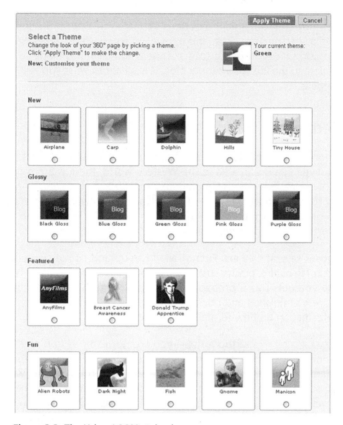

Figure 2-3. The Yahoo! 360° style chooser

Reproduced with permission of Yahoo! Inc. © 2007 by Yahoo! Inc. YAHOO! and the YAHOO! logo are trademarks of Yahoo! Inc.

Once you want more, you'll run into limitations of services or options of the blogging applications—which means you have to deal with them or consider setting up your own blog on a server, using a solution such as WordPress (http://www.wordpress.org) or writing your own, instead of choosing a hosted blogging service.

> This doesn't make using blogging services a bad option. A well-kept blog with the out-of-the-box blogger design is much more appreciated in the "blogosphere" than one that is interspersed with cobbled-together HTML and imagery that doesn't need to be there in the first place.

The idea of blogging is to quickly put some thoughts on the Web and invite readers to comment on them. Blogging systems like WordPress are amazingly easy to set up on your own server—we will use one in this book—and they have become a de facto standard of participation on the Web for individuals and even small companies.

Hosted services, however, do limit the options you have to extend the simple publishing idea with extras or personal touches, and a lot of bloggers start hacking inside the blogging systems to add that extra touch to make them stand out. In doing so, a lot of them mess up the code and the idea of a simple blog. It is all about what you write, and not necessarily how it looks.

The "knowledgeable buddy solution"

Another common happening is turning to a "knowledgeable buddy" to help you with your web site. If you live in an urban area in the Western world, there is a pretty high possibility that you know somebody who is "into computers" and can help you with a web site. As you don't want to spend much—or any—money, this person will be either a very altruistic expert with no social life or more likely a new web developer who tries to get something for his portfolio to show to possible clients.

This solution poses several dangers. First of all, if the up-and-coming web developer does become successful in pulling paying customers with your demo, then later he may have little time to help you out. This is probably the biggest reason for the existence of a lot of web sites that are half-finished and don't get maintained any longer—there was simply no handover of information on how to maintain the site.

Web developers are a bit like tattoo artists—you are not likely to find one who does "do-overs" of half-finished sites. We take pride in what we do, and it is bad enough to have to do things we hate for money, let alone a "freebie" for a friend. This is why when we offer you a free web site, we also expect you to listen to advice in terms of what to avoid and what a "good" web site is. Since this information might clash with what you think a "good" web site is and what you want to achieve, a lot of these collaborations end up in arguments where both parties leave annoyed—and the outcome is a half-finished web site.

Another problem is that the knowledgeable buddy will be likely to create a solution with the tools and technologies that he considers fit and hip at the moment—or ones that he's not quite sure about and wants to train himself on.

This means that the final outcome may not work properly or reveal its problems once you want to scale up the site. It also means that most of what you want to achieve is coming in second to the technological challenge. Furthermore, it means that if the original developer doesn't have time any longer to help you and you are lucky to find another person to take on the job, it is likely that that person gets into "mechanic mode." This is the behavior pattern you see a lot in mechanics—bad-mouthing anything an earlier mechanic has done and replacing everything with yet another solution to end all your problems (see http://www.evolt.org/node/38850). Sadly enough, this solution might turn out as buggy in the eyes of yet another helper once this one gets too busy with paid work. It is a vicious circle.

In summary, keep that pal in case you get stuck, but don't jump into web development without knowing what is possible and blindly following the advice of someone else. Other people may be too busy to help you—or you may fall out with them one way or another—and in the end your web presence is your show. This is why you cannot rely exclusively on the knowledge of others but need to know at least the basics of web development yourself. Later in this chapter you'll get to know the basics, and having this information in your head makes it a lot easier to talk to other developers and to spot what is quality work—and what is not.

WYSIWIG—What You See Is What You Get solutions

WYSIWYG rang loud in the ears of everybody who was around when the Web was young and a lot of people wanted web sites quickly and without much in terms of budget. WYSIWYG editors mean you edit the page as it is displayed; you can drag and drop new elements onto the page and generally have an easy way to create your site. The only problem is that unless the audience you're trying to reach will also look at your page in this editor—which is not very likely—WYSIWYG turns quickly into "What You So Intensely Wished You'd Gotten."

Different user agents, a term used to describe software or hardware people use to surf the Web—including browsers—will display your web page differently, and different users will also have different settings on their computers according to their likes and needs. Therefore, the concept of WYSIWYG is flawed from the start—you can't conclusively say that how it looks in the editor will be how it looks in your browser, or your users' browsers. Far from it.

Probably the first WYSIWYG editors were Microsoft FrontPage and Netscape Composer (part of the ill-fated Netscape Communicator Suite). Others included Adobe PageMill and NetObjects Fusion. The Cadillac of WYSIWYG and the professionals' choice is most probably Macromedia (now Adobe) Dreamweaver, which can be used both in WYSIWYG (known as Design Mode) and code view (or even a split mode showing both). Figure 2-4 shows Dreamweaver 8 in action.

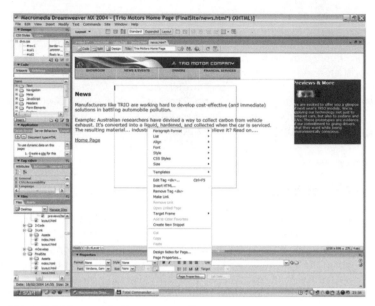

Figure 2-4. Macromedia Dreamweaver 8

The snag about WYSIWYG is that it promotes web development as a visual skill. However, because the Web and HTTP (Hypertext Transfer Protocol)—the protocol that defines how computers talk to each other— are text driven, this is just not the case. In short, you need good visual *and* code skills to be a successful web designer.

> *Web sites are text that has been structured with a certain language to tell user agents what to do with it. In the case of browsers, this means displaying (or rendering) them as visual constructs. Other user agents, however, may only display text or even read out the site to the visitor.*

WYSIWYG editors are likely to create markup that is bloated. This is partly to allow for full flexibility in designing the page but also to make sure that the site can be changed with the same settings and options when you load it again at a later stage. Good editors like Dreamweaver might provide an option to optimize this bloat and create a "live" rather than a "development" version that does not feature the extra code sections needed for the editor to keep parts of the document editable.

One thing that is problematic about WYSIWYG editors is that a lot of them offer too many options—possibly to stand out in a competitive market—so that taking the first steps is pretty easy but it becomes rather trying to use the editor to its full potential. The number of "Web Design with Editor XYZ" books out there is probably larger than the publications on how to create web sites with the web technologies involved. The difference is that any publications tied to a certain version of an editor become pointless rather quickly, whereas the ones talking about the technologies that drive the Web are less likely to become completely obsolete. The same applies to your skill as a developer should you have any aspirations to go down that path—what is hot right now in terms of editing tools may cause a dry chuckle in employers checking your résumé in six months' time.

> *WYSIWYG editors are the overly friendly used car salespeople of the Internet—you think you got a bargain and leave with a flashy-looking model, and some miles down the road you realize that the covered-up rust is starting to show through and the car slowly but steadily falls apart, translating to more and more small—but costly—repair jobs.*

Basics of web development

Here are some facts about web development that might be hard to swallow:

- You have to face code, and you have to write cryptic commands with your keyboard in order to create a web site.
- You must become familiar with characters on your keyboard you haven't used before—like all those different braces ({, }, [,]) and other weird keys like ^, <, >, and |.
- You have to learn a lot more about computers than you thought you would have to.

However, the good news is that over the last few years developers have not been idle and have come up with such a vast amount of publications and solutions to choose from that you can get by only knowing about the technologies and using and following examples of others. The danger there is, of course, that you might follow outdated and even wrong advice, but there is a filtering mechanism for that: feedback mechanisms and a lot of people who care about web design.

A crash course in technologies and languages that drive the Web

This section provides some high-level explanations of the major technologies you need to know about in order to participate on the Web. The explanations are kept to a technical minimum; it is more important to understand the ideas and the logic behind these technologies. This also means that some of this information will be not what you expect or what you may have encountered in other "beginning web design" tutorials. We won't go into all the details of what you need to set up and know to run your own web site right now; the following chapters will show you that some technologies may not be necessary any longer.

First we discuss the various aspects of web development that you would have to deal with if you were to create a web site in the traditional way. We will go into more detail in other chapters when we start going through some practical examples.

Protocols and file naming gotchas

A protocol is a definition of how different systems communicate with each other. The one that drives the Web is called Hypertext Transfer Protocol (HTTP). When you open a browser and you type in http://www.yahoo.com, the browser initializes a request in HTTP to get the address of the location http://www.yahoo.com, retrieve the first document this server offers and show it to you.

Servers are computers connected to the Internet and don't define themselves exclusively by the location you type in. For example, http://icant.co.uk, http://wait-till-i.com, and http://onlinetools.org are all on the same physical computer, while http://www.yahoo.com is not on a single computer but hundreds. To identify each computer on the Internet (and also on local networks), the computer gets a number, known as the Internet Protocol (IP). If you are running Windows and you want to know your IP, you can open your Start menu, select Run, and type in cmd. You'll get a black box with text, which is the DOS console. Type in ipconfig and you'll get information about your computer, which looks something like this:

```
Windows IP Configuration
Ethernet adapter Wireless Network Connection:
Connection-specific DNS Suffix  . :
IP Address. . . . . . . . . . . : 192.168.0.3
Subnet Mask . . . . . . . . . . : 255.255.255.0
Default Gateway . . . . . . . . : 192.168.0.1
```

There are many protocols other than HTTP—for example, the encrypted, safer version HTTPS, Simple Mail Transfer Protocol (SMTP) for email transfer, Lightweight Directory Access Protocol (LDAP) for authentication, or File Transfer Protocol (FTP).

The latter was invented to allow for quicker file transfer between different computers compared with HTTP. By using an FTP client instead of a browser, you can quickly upload or download a lot of files from your computer to a server without having to use an upload form or save links one by one. Figure 2-5 shows how a visitor sees your web site accessed via HTTP and how you can reach the same web site on a file level via FTP.

Figure 2-5. Same server, different protocols

Different protocols have different restrictions when it comes to file names. On your computer you can use spaces and special characters in file names; however, when you want to reach files with names like these via HTTP, you'll have to replace the spaces and special characters with numbered entities, as shown in Figure 2-6.

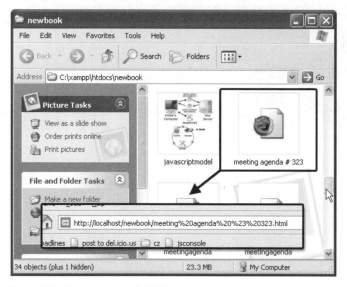

Figure 2-6. File system versus HTTP

The easy-to-read file name meeting agenda # 323.html is turned into a rather cryptic meeting%20agenda%20%23%20323.html in order to be available on the Web.

Another problem with file names is that Windows as an operating system doesn't differentiate between uppercase and lowercase, whereas other operating systems do. On Unix-based operating systems, BaaBaaBlackSheep.txt and baabaablacksheep.TXT are two different files, but Windows sees them as one. If you were to download both from a Linux FTP server, you'd end up with one instead of two files in your download folder. The other, more likely scenario is that when you link files from a web page using the wrong case, you can click and follow the link on Windows but a Linux server would not be able to find the file and you'd have a broken link on the page.

We could bore you now with lots of details about different file systems and details of protocols, but instead we'll give you a list of rules to follow to make sure your files can be read on all operating systems and transferred via any protocol:

- Don't use any spaces or special characters in your file names. Valid characters to use in file names are a–z, A–Z, 0–9, dashes, periods, and the underscore.

- As the period is also the separator for file names and file extensions, it is a good idea to avoid using periods in the file name itself.

- Because Windows is not case-sensitive but other operating systems are, try to keep all file names lowercase.

- If you need to separate words in file names in order to keep them readable, you can either use CamelCase notation (starting each word with an uppercase character), underscores, or dashes. As an example, baabaablacksheep.txt can be made more human readable as BaaBaaBlackSheep.txt, baa_baa_black_sheep.txt, or baa-baa-black-sheep.txt. Be consistent with the formatting you use.

- Try to keep file names as short as possible without becoming too cryptic. The reason is that some operating systems have length constraints in file names, and long file names also result in long URLs that might be hard to bookmark or follow. When linked inside an HTML document, long file names also add unnecessarily to the overall page weight of the document.

> *The "page weight" of a document is the sum of the document's file size and all of its dependencies, like scripts, Cascading Style Sheet (CSS) files, and images. Although it seems superfluous to consider this data in the days of fast servers and broadband connections, smaller files also mean less server traffic and a faster experience for the visitor. The time the document needs to load is not necessarily the time the visitor "feels," and quick-loading documents that start pulling the dependencies as soon as they've finished rendering get a lot better feedback than large documents that load all at once.*

Image optimization

When browsers started supporting images, web development and the Internet really started engaging the mainstream market. Before images, the Web was linked texts and not everybody likes to read. When it became possible to embed images in web sites, a lot more people started creating sites, and a lot of companies started getting interested in the Web as an advertising platform—after all, a product picture says more than a thousand words, right?

The problem with images was, and still is, that you just cannot upload raw image material to the Web. The reasons are file size and picture dimensions. You need to resize images dimensionally to fit the rest of the page layout or even to fit in your visitors' browsers without them having to scroll around, and you need to reduce the file size of the images in order to make them download quickly and not take ages to show up.

The first step to putting images up on the Web is to know what image formats are supported by browsers. These are currently JPEG, GIF, and PNG (and not all options of PNG are supported by Microsoft Internet Explorer 6 and earlier versions).

> *Another image format that will become important in future browsers is Scalable Vector Graphics (SVG). This format is not universally supported yet, but it is very powerful. Unlike the other image formats, SVG is vector based, which means it is totally scalable without quality loss. You can reduce JPEG, GIF, or PNG in size, but when you artificially make them bigger they lose quality and appear pixelated.*

JPEG is a format that retains the original number of colors when you optimize the image but reduces the quality. The image appears to be cut up into lots of very small rectangles that overlay each other on their edges. The resulting images tend to have blurred shapes, and some of the rectangles are still visible. These glitches are called artifacts. Figure 2-7 shows the difference between an uncompressed image and the compressed JPEG.

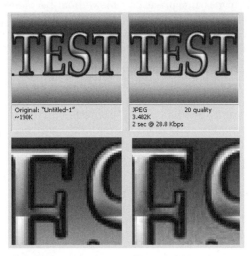

Figure 2-7. Images lose quality and clarity when you compress them as JPEGs.

GIF images use a different way of reducing file size: they cut down on the number of colors (maximum of 256) in the image before packing the rest of the data. That way, they are very efficient with images that have large areas of a single color, and both PNG and GIF retain the crispness of shapes. Figure 2-8 shows what the same test picture looks like as a highly compressed GIF.

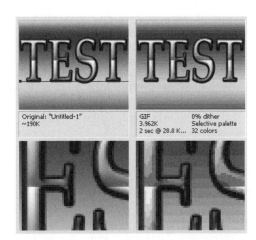

Figure 2-8. GIF reduces the file size of images by cutting down on colors. This can result in ugly-colored areas rather than smooth gradients.

One trick to work around the issue of lack of colors is to use dithering. Dithering means that you mix the colors by putting pixels of colors that are close matches next to each other in an irregular but close pattern. Because the human eye fixes smaller problems like these for us, we get the impression that there are a lot more colors in use. Figure 2-9 uses the same number of colors but looks a lot more detailed.

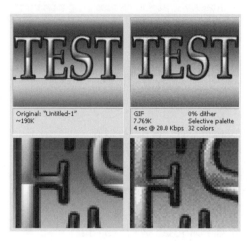

Figure 2-9. Using dithering to simulate more colors

The downside of dithering is that shapes get a bit more blurred and the file size increases as the packing does not work that smoothly any longer.

Some differences exist between GIF and PNG. For starters, GIF can store several frames and show them in an animation. Supporting alpha opacity is one thing that PNG does that GIF does not do. You can define one color of the GIF image as transparent, which means the page background will shine through. PNG, however, allows you to store a whole layer that defines how transparent or opaque different parts of the image should be. IE 6 does not support that, but on a browser like Firefox it is pretty impressive what PNG can do. Figure 2-10 shows the difference between alpha opacity (above) and transparency (below).

Image optimization for the Web is a skill in itself, and it takes years of experience to find the right balance between small file size and quality. Here are some rules of thumb:

- If the image is a photo or has lots of gradients in different colors, use a JPEG.
- If the image is a geometric structure or an application screenshot, or has large areas in one color, use GIF or PNG.
- If retaining a certain shape and quality of outlines is important, use GIF or PNG.

Figure 2-10. PNG (top example) allows you to blend an image smoothly into a background color via alpha opacity. GIF, on the other hand, only allows for a single transparent color (bottom example).

HTML

HTML (Hypertext Markup Language) is the language web sites are written in. This is a statement you read a lot, but it is not entirely true. A more accurate explanation is that HTML describes what a certain document is and contains information for user agents as to what to do with different parts of the document.

Say you have the following text excerpt:

Meeting Agenda

What to do with web standards

On Friday, the following attendees will meet to discuss the importance of standardization of web communication:

Steve Jobs
Tim Berners-Lee
Linus Torvalds
Bill Gates
Tantek Çelik

If you wanted to tell a person what the different parts of the text are, you might say the following:

"It starts with a headline called *Meeting Agenda* and another headline called *What to do with web standards*. Following is an introductory paragraph and a list of names of people who are scheduled to attend the meeting."

In a text-editing program like Microsoft Word, you'd use the different formatting styles to turn the text into these elements, as shown in Figure 2-11.

Figure 2-11. Structuring a document in Microsoft Word

To communicate to a user agent to do the same, you'd embed all the different parts of the text in HTML "elements." These are instructions embedded between angle brackets (<>). You start with one instruction (called the opening tag), then the text you want to define, and then you repeat the instruction with a preceding slash (called the closing tag). In this case the instructions would look like this:

```
<h1>Meeting Agenda</h1>
<h2>What to do with web standards</h2>
<p>On Friday, the following attendees will meet to discuss the➡
 importance of standardization of web communication:</p>
<ul>
  <li>Steve Jobs</li>
  <li>Tim Berners-Lee</li>
  <li>Linus Torvalds</li>
  <li>Bill Gates</li>
  <li>Tantek Çelik</li>
</ul>
```

These instructions are HTML elements and are defined in a web standards recommendation by the W3C. You can find all the recommendations that the W3C has defined and that user agent developers have implemented on the W3C web site: http://www.w3.org.

The elements in use here are

- **Headings Level 1 and Level 2 (h1, h2)**—You have six levels at your disposal (h1 to h6) and h1 is the most important. You can use them as often as you want to in a document, but it is good practice to use only one h1 and keep a logical order (h1, h2, h3, h2, h3, h4, h2, h3... and not h1, h6, h3, h2...).

- **Paragraph (p)**—Tells the user agent that this text is a paragraph and a single logical unit. You can have several sentences in one paragraph.

- **Unordered List (ul)**—Indicates that all the elements in between the opening and the closing tag belong to the same list.

- **List item (li)**—Indicates that the embedded text is a list item.

HTML elements can contain other elements (like the unordered list does) and may also contain attributes, which are instructions in the opening tag (never in the closing tag) in the format attribute="value".

To make a user agent understand and show or read out this document as HTML, you need to take two more steps. The first one involves embedding the document in more HTML elements and instructions.

```
<!DOCTYPE HTML PUBLIC "-//W3C//DTD HTML 4.01//EN"➡
"http://www.w3.org/TR/html4/strict.dtd">
<html dir="ltr" lang="en">
<head>
  <meta http-equiv="Content-Type" content="text/html; charset=utf-8" />
  <title>Meeting Agenda for Friday, 30.07.2006</title>
</head>
<body>
  <h1>Meeting Agenda</h1>
  <h2>What to do with web standards</h2>
  <p>On Friday, the following attendees will meet to discuss the➡
importance of standardization of web communication:</p>
```

```
      <ul>
        <li>Steve Jobs</li>
        <li>Tim Berners-Lee</li>
        <li>Linus Torvalds</li>
        <li>Bill Gates</li>
        <li>Tantek Çelik</li>
      </ul>
    </body>
  </html>
```

There's a lot here, so let's go through it step by step:

- The first line is a DOCTYPE, which explains to the user agent what the following instructions are. Notice that there is a web address in this line that points to the W3C web site. At this location the user agent (most probably a web browser) will find instructions as to what the different elements are and what other elements they can contain. Without this line, the document could be anything.

- The html element starts the instructions describing the document. In this case it has two attributes, one called dir for reading directions with a value ltr (which is short for "left to right") and one called lang with a value of en (which defines the document's language as English).

- Following is a head element, which contains information about the document rather than the document's textual content.

- Within the head element is a meta tag that describes the content type (text/html) and the charset in use (utf-8). This is necessary as browsers can understand more than text and using utf-8 ensures that you can display special characters of international languages (for example, the Ç in Tantek Çelik). Notice that the meta element has no closing tag as it is not meant to enclose any content. Therefore, you add a slash at the end of it.

- The title element contains the title of the document (which is different from the main heading of the text!).

- Next is the body of the HTML document, which contains all the elements we defined earlier.

- After the last bit of content in the body, you have to close both the body and the html element by adding the closing tags.

If you now save this document in a text editor (like Notepad) with the file name meetingagenda.html, you can double-click it and it will open in your user agent that handles HTML documents—in most cases, your browser. Figure 2-12 shows how that looks in Mozilla Firefox.

Notice that the HTML elements are not displayed but instead the browser shows the text as defined in an internal display instruction called a style sheet. Also notice that the text defined in the title element of the head is displayed as the text on the browser bar and not in the main document.

Figure 2-12. Mozilla Firefox showing an HTML document

Many different versions of HTML are available, each of them allowing for different elements and with syntactical differences. The currently most modern and rather future-proof versions require that

- All elements be in lowercase (`<li>` instead of `<LI>` or `<Li>`)
- Attribute values be embedded in quotation marks (`lang="en"` instead of `lang=en`)
- Each element be closed (`<p>text</p><p>text</p>` instead of `<p>text<p>text`)

Following these simple rules will ensure that your HTML can be rendered by older and newer user agents as well as those to come in the future.

> *In summary, HTML describes what a certain text is and gives user agents instructions as to what to do with this text. It gives the text **structure**.*

CSS

Figure 2-12 showed that user agents have built-in definitions of how certain HTML elements should be displayed (or *rendered*, which is the correct term). They do the job, but you may not necessarily agree with their look and feel and want to come up with your own one. You can do this by creating your own CSS file and applying it to the HTML document.

CSS is an acronym that stands for Cascading Style Sheets. Style sheets are already used in other software like Microsoft Word templates. Out of the box, Word has some preset styles, as shown in Figure 2-13.

You can define your own styles and apply them to the document—for example, the styles used in the friends of ED template shown in Figure 2-14.

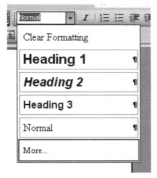

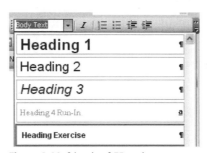

Figure 2-13. Microsoft Word's preset styles

Figure 2-14. friends of ED styles

To style different parts of the document in Word, you highlight them and apply that style. If you have a document that is already structured and you want to apply a new style, you can highlight one structure item—such as a heading—and choose Select Text With Similar Formatting from the menu. Then you apply the style. In a sense, this is what CSS does with an HTML document.

The syntax of CSS is relatively easy:

```
selector {
  attribute : value;
  attribute2 : value2;
  /* more attribute/value pairs */
}
```

- You define a selector, which retrieves the corresponding elements from the document.
- You group all the settings for these elements inside curly braces ({}).
- Each setting consists of an attribute and a value pair divided by a colon and ending in a semicolon.
- If you need to add a comment that describes what something is, you keep it inside a /* */ construct.

For example, if you wanted to define the styles for the main heading and the paragraphs, you could write the following:

```
h1 {
  font-family : Arial,Sans-Serif;
  color : navy;
  background : beige;
  font-size : 1.2em;
  padding : .5em 1em;
}
p {
  font-family : Arial,Sans-Serif;
  color : black;
  font-size : 0.8em;
  padding : 0 0 .5em 0;
}
```

As you can see, the values can differ from property to property. Some are numbers with measurements, some are words, and some are lists with optional values. For example, the font-family setting applies Arial as the font if it is available but will apply Sans-Serif as a second choice.

If you were to apply this style sheet to the HTML document (we'll come back to this later), the heading and the paragraph would be displayed differently, as shown in Figure 2-15.

Figure 2-15. A style applied to an HTML document

You can extend the style sheet now to add styles for the other elements in the HTML document—for example, the second level heading:

```
h1 {
  font-family : Arial,Sans-Serif;
  color : navy;
  background : beige;
  font-size : 1.2em;
  padding : .5em 1em;
}
h2 {
  font-family : Arial,Sans-Serif;
  color : dimgray;
  font-size : 1em;
  padding : 0;
}
p {
  font-family : Arial,Sans-Serif;
  color : black;
  font-size : 0.8em;
  padding : 0 0 .5em 0;
}
```

As you can imagine, this can become quite repetitive and result in large CSS documents, which is why CSS has "Cascading" in it. Cascading means that when you define certain style attributes (like the font family) for one element, the same font will be applied to all the elements that are contained inside this one. This means that when you define settings that should be applied to all elements in the body selector they'll be applied:

```
body{
  font-family : Arial,Sans-Serif;
  font-size : 0.8em;
  color : black;
  background : white;
}
h1 {
  color : navy;
  background : beige;
  font-size : 1.2em;
  padding : .5em 1em;
}
h2 {
  color : dimgray;
  font-size : 1em;
  padding : 0;
}
p {
  padding : 0 0 .5em 0;
}
```

Although we haven't defined any settings for the `ul` or `li` elements, they will be rendered in Arial and in the same font size as the paragraphs when you apply this style sheet, as shown in Figure 2-16.

Figure 2-16. Cascading in action

Other features of CSS include nesting and grouping of selectors. For example, if you wanted to apply the same padding styles for both the paragraphs and the list elements, you simply add the `li` selector preceded by a comma:

```
p, li {
  color : black;
  padding : 0 0 .5em 0;
}
```

You can also use selectors to style elements differently according to what other elements they are in. To achieve this you simply add a space in between the selectors:

```
ul li {
  color : black;
  padding : 0 0 .5em 0;
}
ol li {
  color : black;
  padding : .5em 0;
}
```

This means that list items inside an ol element (which is *ordered list*—numbers instead of bullets) will have a different padding than those inside a ul element.

Classes and IDs

There are two more options that allow you to style HTML elements: classes and IDs, which are both HTML attributes. For example, if you wanted to single out the name of Tim Berners-Lee as the chairman of the meeting and both Steve Jobs and Bill Gates as commercial advisors you could do that in the HTML with an ID and two class attributes:

```
<!DOCTYPE HTML PUBLIC "-//W3C//DTD HTML 4.01//EN"➧
"http://www.w3.org/TR/html4/strict.dtd">
<html dir="ltr" lang="en">
<head>
  <meta http-equiv="Content-Type" content="text/html; charset=utf-8" />
  <title>Meeting Agenda for Friday, 30.07.2006</title>
</head>
<body>
  <h1>Meeting Agenda</h1>
  <h2>What to do with web standards</h2>
  <p>On Friday, the following attendees will meet to discuss the➧
importance  of standardization of web communication:</p>
  <ul>
    <li class="commercial">Steve Jobs</li>
    <li id="chairman">Tim Berners-Lee</li>
    <li>Linus Torvalds</li>
    <li class="commercial">Bill Gates</li>
    <li>Tantek Çelik</li>
  </ul>
</body>
</html>
```

Both class and ID can be applied to any HTML element. The difference between the two is that ID is unique to the document (you can only use the ID once per document) whereas a class can be applied to any element any number of times in the same document—even different elements. In CSS you reach IDs with the #name selector and classes with the .name selector—for example:

```
body{
  font-family : Arial,Sans-Serif;
  font-size : 0.8em;
  color : black;
  background : white;
}
h1 {
  color : navy;
  background : beige;
  font-size : 1.4em;
  padding : .5em 1em;
}
```

```
h2 {
  color : dimgray;
  font-size : 1.2em;
  padding : 0;
}
p, li {
  color : black;
  padding : 0 0 .5em 0;
}
#chairman{
  font-weight:bold;
  color:#363;
}
.commercial{
  font-weight:bold;
}
```

The result (see Figure 2-17) shows the participants with an ID or a class, respectively, in a different style than the other list items—as defined in the last two selectors.

Figure 2-17. Different styles according to ID and class

That is more or less the core syntax of CSS and what you can do with it (there's a lot more such as more complex selectors, pseudo-selectors, all the different attributes that allow you to really style the text), but the question remains how to get the user agent to use the style sheet to render the page.

First of all, save a document with all the styles in the previous code listing with the file name meetingagenda.css. Then tell the user agent to pull this file in when the page loads by adding a link element to the head section of the document:

```
<!DOCTYPE HTML PUBLIC "-//W3C//DTD  HTML 4.01//EN"➡
"http://www.w3.org/TR/html4/strict.dtd">
<html dir="ltr" lang="en">
<head>
  <meta http-equiv="Content-Type" content="text/html; charset=utf-8" />
  <title>Meeting Agenda for Friday, 30.07.2006</title>
  <link rel="stylesheet" type="text/css" href="meetingagenda.css" />
</head>
<body>
  <h1>Meeting Agenda</h1>
  <h2>What to do with web standards</h2>
  <p>On Friday, the following attendees will meet to discuss the➡
importance of standardization of web communication:</p>
  <ul>
    <li class="commercial">Steve Jobs</li>
    <li id="chairman">Tim Berners-Lee</li>
    <li>Linus Torvalds</li>
    <li class="commercial">Bill Gates</li>
    <li>Tantek Çelik</li>
  </ul>
</body>
</html>
```

Keeping the styling in a separate file like this has several benefits:

- You keep one central point for the whole look and feel. That way, you keep maintenance easy—one file changed means a whole site (consisting of many documents that all link to this CSS file) gets a new look and feel.

- The style sheet will be loaded once from the server and from that point on will already be cached on the visitor's computer—which saves loading time and server traffic.

> In summary, CSS describes to the user agent how to render different HTML elements. CSS describes the **presentation** of the document.

JavaScript

The first thing to know about JavaScript is that it is not Java; all they share is the name and a bit of syntax. The second thing to know is that no web site *needs* JavaScript, and also shouldn't rely on it. However, you can use JavaScript to make your web site a much smoother and quicker surfing experience.

The basic Internet surfing experience can be pretty frustrating. HTML is a fixed state; the page gets loaded, the user agent renders it, and that is that. Every time you interact with the page, such as clicking a link or submitting a form, the user agent sends a request to the server, the server responds and sends a new HTML document back, and the user agent needs to render that again. Figure 2-18 illustrates this model.

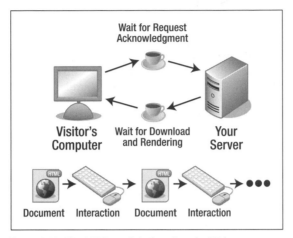

Figure 2-18. The HTTP model of surfing the Web

JavaScript is a programming language that describes functionality that executes in the browser on the visitor's computer. This is a great thing, as the visitor does not need to reload the page and wait for your server to answer. It is also great as you don't necessarily need to be online to experience this functionality. You can change the page after it was loaded and react to user interaction without having to reload the page, as illustrated in Figure 2-19.

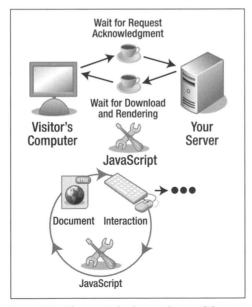

Figure 2-19. The JavaScript interaction model

Probably the most common examples of this are forms that check that visitors entered something in the right format and make them aware of their mistakes before sending the data to the server. Using JavaScript cleverly prevents the visitor from having to reload the page and discover something is in error.

> *In a time where broadband connections seem to be a given (at least in the Western world) this seems superfluous, but there are two things to consider. The first one is that not having to reload the page also means one less hit for the server—thus less strain on it and a faster overall surfing experience for all your visitors. Second, the speed of your Internet connection is only a part of how quickly visitors consider your web site. Depending on how busy the computer is with other things, rendering the page can take a long time.*

Lately another use of JavaScript has become fashionable and established itself as a de facto standard for web applications: Ajax. Ajax stands for Asynchronous JavaScript and XML and in a nutshell means that you don't reload the whole document when the visitor interacts with it but only the parts that change. That way, the visitor will not have to wait for the whole page to change, but can still read and use the rest of the document while the part that he requested to change loads and changes in the background. Figure 2-20 shows that model.

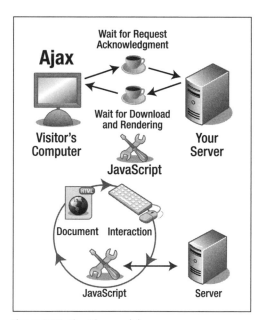

Figure 2-20. The Ajax model

> *If you search online for tutorials about scripting and JavaScript, you are likely to find a lot of flashy effects labeled Ajax. If there is no server interaction involved, this is a misnomer, and it is sad that a lot of these tutorials are still around.*

We hope you can see the usefulness of JavaScript. The problems with it are that support for certain functionality differs from user agent to user agent and that it may be disabled on the visitor's machine or removed by security software like firewalls. The good news is that JavaScript is a programming language, which means that good JavaScripts test if the current user agent can support certain functionality, and apply themselves after this test has been successful. This idea is called *progressive enhancement* and that type of scripting *unobtrusive JavaScript*.

There is more to unobtrusive JavaScript and if you are interested, check out the self-training course at http://onlinetools.org/articles/unobtrusivejavascript/.

JavaScript files have the extension .js and are embedded in the head of the document with a script element. In this example, we have a JavaScript inside a file called meetingagenda.js and can apply it to the document in the following way:

```
<!DOCTYPE HTML PUBLIC "-//W3C//DTD HTML 4.01//EN"➥
"http://www.w3.org/TR/html4/strict.dtd">
<html dir="ltr" lang="en">
<head>
  <meta http-equiv="Content-Type" content="text/html; charset=utf-8" />
  <title>Meeting Agenda for Friday, 30.07.2006</title>
  <link rel="stylesheet" type="text/css" href="meetingagenda.css" />
  <script type="text/javascript" href="meetingagenda.js"></script>
</head>
<body>
  <h1>Meeting Agenda</h1>
  <h2>What to do with web standards</h2>
  <p>On Friday, the following attendees will meet to discuss the➥
  importance of standardization of web communication:</p>
  <ul>
    <li class="commercial">Steve Jobs</li>
    <li id="chairman">Tim Berners-Lee</li>
    <li>Linus Torvalds</li>
    <li class="commercial">Bill Gates</li>
    <li>Tantek Çelik</li>
  </ul>
</body>
</html>
```

Explaining the syntax and elements of the JavaScript language is out of the scope of this book, but you'll learn in upcoming chapters how to use, change, and work with JavaScripts.

*In summary, JavaScript allows you to execute small programs in the user agent and on the visitor's computer. This gives you, among other things, the power to change the document without having to reload the page. The browser reacts to user interaction and gives feedback, which is called the **behavior** of the document.*

Server-side languages

There are many so-called server-side scripting languages. This means that functionality you program in these languages gets executed on the server and not on the visitor's computer. This makes it a lot safer to use them and therefore these languages have far wider reach than JavaScript—you can access databases, create files, read and include other files, create images, and even send emails or connect to other servers to retrieve data from them.

We've chosen PHP as an example of a server-side language as we will be using it in this book as it is pretty easy to learn the basics of it when you know JavaScript and HTML. The other benefits of using PHP is that it is free, it works with other free software like Apache Servers, it comes installed on most cheap web servers, and the amount of great free software available on the Web written in PHP is staggering. In order to use PHP, you need to install it on your server and give files the correct file extension to make the server execute the code.

Like all other server-side scripting languages, PHP gets executed when the server reads the document. Then the document gets changed according to the functionality described in the PHP script before the server sends the altered document back to the visitor's user agent. Figure 2-21 shows this cycle.

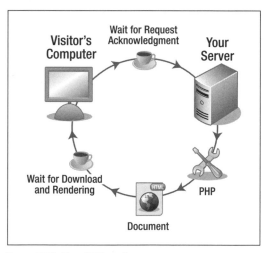

Figure 2-21. How PHP works

You start PHP code with a <?php command and end it with a closing ?>. Everything in between these two will be analyzed by the PHP processor and executed. If we go back to our HTML example, we could add a line that states when the document was last changed to tell the visitor if the data she's seeing is still up-to-date.

```
<!DOCTYPE HTML PUBLIC "-//W3C//DTD HTML 4.01//EN"➡
"http://www.w3.org/TR/html4/strict.dtd">
<html dir="ltr" lang="en">
<head>
  <meta http-equiv="Content-Type" content="text/html; charset=utf-8" />
  <title>Meeting Agenda for Friday, 30.07.2006</title>
  <link rel="stylesheet" type="text/css" href="meetingagenda.css" />
</head>
<body>
  <h1>Meeting Agenda</h1>
  <h2>What to do with web standards</h2>
  <p>On Friday, the following attendees will meet to discuss the➡
importance of standardization of web communication:</p>
  <ul>
    <li class="commercial">Steve Jobs</li>
    <li id="chairman">Tim Berners-Lee</li>
    <li>Linus Torvalds</li>
    <li class="commercial">Bill Gates</li>
    <li>Tantek Çelik</li>
  </ul>
  <?php echo '<p id="footer">&copy; Awesomemeetings.com 2006,➡
Last modified:' . date ('F d Y H:i:s.', getlastmod()) . '</p>' ?>
  </body>
</html>
```

If you save this document as meetingagenda.php and open it on a server that supports PHP via HTTP, you'll get the output shown in Figure 2-22. The date is the last modification date on the server, which is the time you uploaded it.

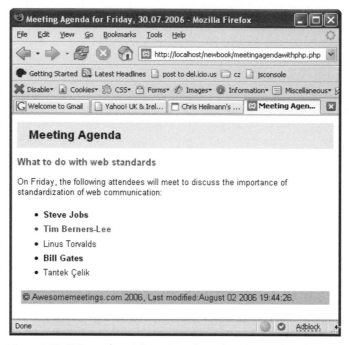

Figure 2-22. PHP-generated data—inserting a date shows when the page was last updated on the server.

If you look at the source code in your browser, you won't see the original PHP code, but instead you'll get the HTML returned from the PHP code:

```
<!DOCTYPE HTML PUBLIC "-//W3C//DTD HTML 4.01//EN" ➡
"http://www.w3.org/TR/html4/strict.dtd">
<html dir="ltr" lang="en">
<head>
  <meta http-equiv="Content-Type" content="text/html; charset=utf-8" />
  <title>Meeting Agenda for Friday, 30.07.2006</title>
  <link rel="stylesheet" type="text/css" href="meetingagenda.css" />
</head>
<body>
  <h1>Meeting Agenda</h1>
  <h2>What to do with web standards</h2>

  <p>On Friday, the following attendees will meet to discuss the ➡
importance of standardization of web communication:</p>
  <ul>
    <li class="commercial">Steve Jobs</li>
    <li id="chairman">Tim Berners-Lee</li>
    <li>Linus Torvalds</li>
    <li class="commercial">Bill Gates</li>
    <li>Tantek Çelik</li>
  </ul>
```

```
<p id="footer">&copy; Awesomemeetings.com 2006,➡
Last modified:August 02 2006 19:44:26.</p>
</body>
</html>
```

PHP allows you to conditionally hide HTML that—unlike solutions using JavaScript to hide text—will never be available to the visitors unless you want it to. If you hide text via JavaScript, all a visitor has to do to reach the text is to turn JavaScript off. A visitor cannot turn off your PHP, as it is outside of her reach. You will run into situations where you want to show different HTML output dependent on the visitors' access level, the date, or other parameters and keeping this logic server side ensures that visitors won't get any HTML they don't need or shouldn't be able to access.

If, for example, you wanted to hide the commercial meeting attendees unless there is a certain URL parameter provided, you can do that:

```
<!DOCTYPE HTML PUBLIC "-//W3C//DTD HTML 4.01//EN" ➡
"http://www.w3.org/TR/html4/strict.dtd">
<html dir="ltr" lang="en">
<head>
  <meta http-equiv="Content-Type" content="text/html; charset=utf-8" />
  <title>Meeting Agenda for Friday, 30.07.2006</title>
  <link rel="stylesheet" type="text/css" href="meetingagenda.css" />
</head>
<body>
  <h1>Meeting Agenda</h1>
  <h2>What to do with web standards</h2>
  <p>On Friday, the following attendees will meet to discuss the ➡
  importance of standardization of web communication:</p>
  <ul>
    <li id="chairman">Tim Berners-Lee</li>
    <li>Linus Torvalds</li>
    <li>Tantek Çelik</li>
    <?php if ( isset ( $_GET[ 'commercial' ] ) ) { ?>
    <li class="commercial">Bill Gates</li>
    <li class="commercial">Steve Jobs</li>
     <?php }  ?>
  </ul>
  <?php echo '<p id="footer">&copy; Awesomemeetings.com 2006, ➡
Last modified:' . date ('F d Y H:i:s.', getlastmod()) . '</p>'?>
</body>
</html>
```

Depending on whether the URL has a parameter called commercial, this will result in two different attendee lists, as shown in Figure 2-23.

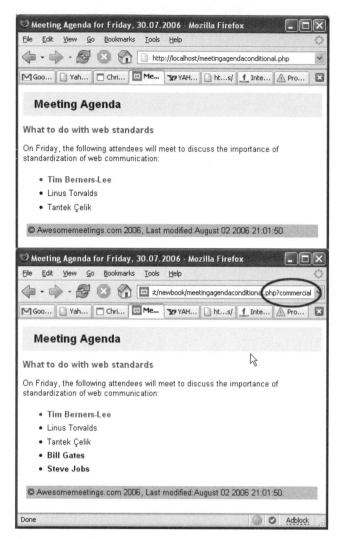

Figure 2-23. Conditional content dependent on URL parameters

Using PHP allows you as a web developer to create easy-to-maintain sites by templating them. Templating means that instead of creating static HTML documents for each page in your site, you extract parts of the documents that are the same on each page, or only differ following a defined logic, and put them in their own files. Examples are headers and footers and the page navigation. For example, the following PHP script would pull in different HTML and PHP documents, assemble them to one big document, and send that back to the user agent:

```php
<?php
  include( 'header.html' );
  include( 'header.html' );
  include( 'content.php' );
  include( 'main_menu.php' );
  include( 'footer.html' );
?>
```

This makes it a lot easier to change any of these sitewide without having to change all the documents separately.

> In summary, server-side languages like PHP allow you to reach beyond the limits of HTML and make sure that changing your content and HTML at a later stage is a lot easier than dealing with a lot of fixed-state HTML documents.

Who is on the Web

Here is the amazing thing about the Internet as a media: everybody is invited to join the party. You might have a fixed idea as to who is going to be visiting your site, but this is not necessarily who is going to end up there. Just consider this small range of possible visitors of your web site:

- Stephen (16), an online game fanatic with a whiz-bang computer and a fast connection
- Jessica (30), a secretary in an office with monitored Internet access and tight restrictions as to what she can install on her computer and JavaScript blocked by a firewall
- Maria (62), a grandmother with bad eyesight and arthritis who uses the Web to communicate with her children and grandchildren
- Sandeep (22), a passionate web developer who is very happy to tell anyone what is wrong with their web site
- George (42), a busy executive using a free Internet terminal in the airport waiting lounge
- Ben (23), a researcher with limited vision who uses a screen reader that reads out web sites to him, enabling him to experience and enjoy the worldwide access the Web offers him
- Peter (32), a home computer user who is very afraid of viruses and privacy issues on the Internet

- Maurice (35), a local government worker who cannot move his hands but uses speech recognition to surf the Web
- Jessie (20), who is on vacation checking her email and follows a link sent to her by a friend (she's wondering why she bothered paying for an Internet café terminal with a connection the speed of two cans connected with a string)
- Googlebot (who knows?), a program scrounging the Web for textual data to put in the search engine databases

All of these folks can arrive at your web site and expect to find what they were looking for. This is the main concept to keep in mind: nobody comes to your site because of your site. People get there because they have a certain goal: they want to find out about something you wrote about, they want to see nice pictures of a certain thing, they want to listen to a certain kind of music, or they heard about you and are interested to learn more about you. The web site is a medium, a means to achieve that communication, and the more you concentrate on the needs of your visitors and less on what can be technically achieved on the Web, the more people will find and use your site to communicate with you or enjoy what you have to offer.

There is a flipside to this beautiful concept, though: in addition to the people listed earlier, there are also a whole bunch of people on the Web we could do without:

- Spammers trying to enter any channel of communication you leave open to tell you about products you don't want and don't need
- Spammers trying to get their URL linked in comments on your site to get more inbound links for their own web sites—thus ranking higher in search engines
- Hackers trying to find a flaw in your scripts they can abuse to either use your computer as a relay for attacks on other web sites (so-called denial-of-service attacks) or to gain access to your server to use it as a storage facility (so-called dumpservers)
- Less malicious attackers like users of forums linking your photos from your site, thus causing you a lot of traffic without the benefit of people visiting your site (which is called hotlinking)

When you go online, these are all the people you have to consider. This can be a full-time job, which is why a lot of web sites don't get updated, fixed, or cleaned out—the maintainers are just too busy deleting spam comments, answering emails, or renaming images to cut down on server traffic.

Summary

In this chapter you learned about the free and nontechnical options you can choose to participate on the Web, and what their shortcomings are. We discussed the various aspects of web development should you choose to "roll your own" solution and need to know what is involved in creating a good web presence.

There is a lot more to creating a web site than having a pretty design and some ideas, and the annoyances of the Web—hacking attempts, spammers, and people with not much consideration for your free time (those sending unnecessary emails or hotlinking your content) sometimes make running and maintaining your own web site a very frustrating experience.

In the chapters that follow, we'll give you an alternative concept to this one: you'll use services that are on the Web to take on some of the frustrations and tasks and allow you to concentrate on what you want to do: publish and communicate. We'll help you along the way, showing you how to write for the Web, setting up your own local development environment, storing and retrieving media, and creating links.

2

3 WHAT YOU NEED TO GET STARTED

By Chris Heilmann and Norm Francis

In this chapter we will provide you with the tools and advice needed to start writing and collating the content for your web site. We will specifically look at

- Getting in the right mind-set
- Setting up a local development environment
- Setting up a simple content-management system as a basis for your site

If you work for a big company, the content for your company's site is probably handled by some form of commercial content-management system, but these are rather complex to install and may be overkill for the purpose of creating and maintaining a small web site. Therefore, we are going to use a free blogging tool—WordPress—and tweak it to meet our needs.

When you are finished with the chapter (and have followed the instructions in it), you will have a local server running (which means you can surf files on your local hard drive as if they are on a real Internet server and thus simulate the actual running of your web site without being online). You will have also chosen a nice WordPress look to alter to your needs and should be able to start writing content to export to a live Internet server at a later stage.

Before we delve into the technical details, though, let's take a step back and get you into the right mind-set for participating on the Web these days. Most of the failed web sites out there were not caused by technical issues or lack of ideas. The main cause was, and still is, that expectations of the people whose job it was to maintain the site didn't get fulfilled and they lost interest. The next section will help you ensure that you don't end up in that category.

The right mind-set

The credo of this book is to enable you to make content available to other people on the Web as easily as possible. It is not just another book about web design or development—it is all about the content.

> *Good books on web design include Jeffrey Zeldman's* Designing with Web Standards (2nd Edition) *(Peachpit Press, 2006), Dan Cederholm's* Bulletproof Web Design *(New Riders Press, 2005), or if you are very design/project management oriented, try Any Phyo's* Return on Design *(New Riders Press, 2003). Also, anyone who wants to participate on the Web by creating or maintaining web sites should—in my humble opinion—read the book* Don't Make Me Think: A Common Sense Approach to Web Usability (2nd Edition), *by Steve Krug (New Riders Press, 2005). It is a wonderful one-hour read about something that is lacking a lot in our daily lives when it comes to dealing with the Web—common sense and usability.*

We concentrate heavily on content since being a good web designer involves a lot more than just setting up a web site and creating some HTML and CSS. It means getting your head around the design as a whole—understanding the brand to create a relationship of trust with the consumer and promote what the product has to offer, understanding the people the site should reach, and analyzing the needs of the client who asks for a design. On top of all these skills, a good web designer also needs to know the limitations of the medium and how people use it. A good web designer knows what needs to be done to ensure the recipient understands the message or the product/service for sale as quickly and painlessly as possible.

We aren't striving to make you a web designer in this book—we are not designers ourselves. We will, however, give you a good insight into what tools to use to build up an effective site as easily as possible, and what to avoid. Our advice is largely based on personal (bad!) experience and information about what works best for others (based on our experience of working with good designers).

Things not to focus on

The biggest mistake to make is to think that the main reason people come to your web site is to experience and see your web site. That only works in two cases: when someone looks for a web designer to create a web site for them (and boy are you in for some competition then!) and when you have applied for a job as a web designer and the company takes a look at your site to check out your credentials.

In nearly every other case, people will find your web site because of the content of your web site, as this is what search engines see. Of course, there is also word of mouth and you can get lucky with a special design trick and one of the hundreds of "neat web design" showcase sites finding and promoting something you've done. This is, however, rare these days, as the design envelope has been pushed precariously close to the edge already.

It is pretty pointless to spend time on things you don't need, despite how much you see them in use in other places—this doesn't mean they will add value to your page. Here are some examples of needless devices:

- **Flash tunnel pages**: A Flash tunnel page shows an animated logo with a miniscule "skip intro" link before proceeding to the main page (yes, these tunnel pages still exist, as amazing as that may sound). They only keep people away from what you want to give them. They also stop search engines from indexing what your site offers.

- **Counters**: A counter showing that x number of people visited you in the last months is, depending on the figures, nothing to brag about and actually only of value to yourself. Statistics packages like StatCounter (http://www.statcounter.com) can give you interesting information about your visitors (and reveal interesting sites that link to you), but there is no need to share this information with all your site visitors.

- **"Welcome to my web site" text**: There is no "Welcome to this concert leaflet" text on concert flyers either, so why stop people from finding what they came for by making them read through unnecessary text?

- **CSS switchers that only change the look and feel of the site**: If you really want to offer site customization, consider offering multicolumn versus single-column layouts or a zoom style sheet instead (http://joeclark.org/access/webaccess/zoom/). The time you spend on all the various look-and-feel styles could be spent more valuably on a clever print style sheet (http://www.alistapart.com/articles/goingtoprint/).

- **Background music**: Just don't.

- **Protection scripts that stop visitors from right-clicking the page and saving images and other information**: These scripts are no protection whatsoever, as people who are out to get your data will simply turn off JavaScript and then save your data anyway. These scripts stand in the way of well-meaning visitors who might need right-click menu functionality to surf around your site.

- **Visual gimmicks like Java applets that reflect a logo in a lake or cover it in raindrops**: These gimmicks are nice to see for a few seconds, but the next time you have to wait for them to load and initialize you wonder if you couldn't have lived happily without them.

- **Your local weather information** (unless your web site is a local newspaper site): If you live in London it is very frustrating to learn how warm and dry it is someplace else...

If you want to know more about what not to do and you are interested in a light-hearted read, check out Vincent Flanders' web site: http://www.webpagesthatsuck.com/. *He explains good web design by showing bad examples. The whole thing is also available in book form. An especially funny and good read is "The Biggest Web Design Mistakes of 2004" series at* http://www.webpagesthatsuck.com/biggest-web-design-mistakes-in-2004.html.

Things to focus on

Let's not dwell on the negative—as easy and tempting as this may be—but instead look at what you should focus on in order to create a successful web site. There are not many surprises here, and most of it is common sense, but it is good to keep these ideas in mind whenever you start assuming that visitors are as interested in the technical part of the web site as you are.

The following are some concepts to remember if you want to have a great web site, attract happy visitors, and not work too hard to achieve that:

- **It is about content**: If you don't have any interesting content (or content that is also available on hundreds of other sites), you will not reach many people no matter how much you polish the surface of your site.

- **It is about sharing**: If you put content on the Web, it is there for people to see, download, and maybe use. You can protect your rights by choosing and displaying a license agreement and copyright information (you'll find a great "create your own license" tool at http://www.creativecommons.org), and there is simply no sense in trying technical tricks to prevent people from downloading your images or copying your texts. When you follow the instructions in this book, you will use a lot of content and programs other people developed. It is only fair to return the favor. Without people sharing their tools and content for free, the Web would have never grown as big and exciting as it is now.

- **It is about access**: If your content is made available to everyone on the Web regardless of ability and technical environment, you are much more likely to be found and talked about than when you try to block out groups of users or expect a defined technical environment. Your computer setup is not representative of everyone on the Web, and you simply cannot expect people to get a larger monitor or fast computer, or install certain browsers or plug-ins, just to access your site. If your content is interesting enough they may, but don't count on it.

- **It is about communication**: Allow people to communicate with you. Let them comment on your information and offer them easy ways to connect to you—for example, via an email link in the footer of each page or a contact form. Offer your information in easy-to-syndicate formats (like RSS—we will talk about this later in the next chapter) and links to other sites with similar information. This may sound counterproductive—after all, why should you send them visitors you want to have?—but these other sites are likely to link to you as well. The more sites link to you, the higher you will climb in search engine results.

- **It is about availability**: This may sound like a paradox, but spreading your content on the Web and different sites may be a much more efficient way to make it available than keeping it on one server. Of course, you need to use the right sites to do so. We live in exciting web times where you can upload your photos to http://www.flickr.com and connect to other picture enthusiasts, upload videos to http://www.youtube.com, and share links at http://del.icio.us and documents at http://docs.google.com (formerly Writely.com). All of these sites are backed up by large corporations with good servers; even if your site is down for a day, they'll still be out there. Advertising your site as the source of these pieces of data on the other sites will drive people back to it, and you can use the application programming interfaces (APIs) they offer to easily include the data in your site. APIs are tools that provide an easy way to reach the data stored in a system—like your photos in Flickr, for example—without needing a lot of programming knowledge.

- **It is about patience**: As with anything that is really good, you need to spend some time on a great web site. You may not appear in the search engine results in the first few weeks (sometimes not even in the first few months). Don't get discouraged by that, but instead try to increase your communication with other people in your area of interest—they will link to you and you will start to show up in the Googles and Yahoo!s of this world. Having a web site also means that you will get a lot of feedback that is annoying or plain rude. Don't dwell on that, but pick out information that may be related to real problems and solve these. However, it is your site, and there will always be people who don't like what you have to say or offer—you shouldn't try to please everybody.

- **It is about knowing your audience**: Your assumptions of how a web site in your area of expertise should look might be totally off the mark. Ask people who are interested what they expect, or ask them what they hate about other sites that offer similar content.

- **It is about playing to your strengths**: If you are not good with words, don't try too hard but stick to information and what excites you about the subject your site covers. You can also get help from a friend who can put your ideas into words. The same applies if you are good with words but bad with design or structuring information. Don't try to tackle everything yourself, but get some peer review and input to make the end product talk for itself.

- **It is about offering instead of pushing**: Don't force anything on your visitors. Videos and music should not start unless the visitor chooses to start them. In addition, offer such things as downloads. If you link to PDFs or other media formats, say so in the link because many people prefer to download them instead of reading them in the browser (or they may not follow the link at all, if it's a format they won't be able to read).

- **It is about keeping it simple**: Don't try to overcomplicate anything on your web site. Make it obvious what the menu is and what is available. Make it easy to search the site and to contact you. Make it obvious who is behind the site and what the purpose of the site is. Be honest about yourself and people will like you for it. There are far too many one-man-show web sites trying to appear as a whole corporation or network on the Web already. Read your content over and over again—any word that can be omitted or any sentence that could be clarified is a win. People on the Web are busy and not all of them are native speakers of your language. Don't make it hard for them. Furthermore, the Web is a secondary media. People do other things while reading your site and don't take all the content in—instead they scan for interesting words. Steve Krug explains this at http://www.sensible.com/chapter.html.

- **It is about advertising without annoying**: Make sure you pick an easy-to-remember URL and advertise it. With this we don't mean buying advertising space but doing simple things like adding the URL to your email footer, stationery, or other promotional material. Especially consider using email footers—these reach further than you think if you participate on forums and mailing lists.

Are you ready for this? We can promise you that you won't regret spending time on a web site if you follow these simple points. Because you need a good starting point for any race, let's now talk about making sure you can test your site without having to put it live by creating a local development environment.

Your local development environment

Strictly speaking, it's not necessary that you have a local development environment in order to have a good web site. You could just as well edit files directly on the server or have your editor set up to automatically transfer changes to the server once you change and save them.

There are, however, a lot of benefits to having a local server running:

- You can make mistakes without them showing up on the live site.
- You can make serious mistakes without losing data or rendering the site unavailable.
- You can try out things offline or on the move (if you have a laptop).
- You can use server-side languages (or products that need them) such as PHP or ASP, and technologies that only work with HTTP (such as Ajax).
- You can rapidly see changes without having to send files to a server and reload the pages from it—your hard drive should be faster to access than your server.

> *Your computer may already have a server running. To test this, just open your browser and enter* http://localhost *(without any www or .com). If the browser cannot find anything, proceed with the chapter.*

The good news is that while installing a local server was a painful and long-winded process on Windows and Macintosh operating systems in the past (Unix or Linux always came with a server), the process has become increasingly easier.

Next we'll explain how to set up a full local development environment using Apache, PHP, MySQL, and WordPress. We'll give instructions both for Windows and Macintosh computers.

> *Notice that these instructions are geared toward installing a local development environment and not a live server. If you're installing a live server you need to pay a lot more attention to detail because live servers have to be secured against hacking attempts.*
>
> *Although the following instructions are incredibly easy and will result in a server running on your computer, setting up a server that is secure and that can withstand a lot of users requires much stronger skills and should not be taken lightly. Far too many servers on the Web are abused as relay stations for spam and viruses because their maintainers didn't take server security serious. Don't become a part of the spam problem. Be sure that the hosting partner you choose to host your web site has spam-protection mechanisms in place. Most hosting companies these days won't allow you to change much in the initial setting of the server anyway, which is a good thing since it is their job to make sure your site is safe. Sometimes this means stopping you from doing things that would open your server to attacks. Trust the experts on security, and then you can concentrate on getting good content out.*

Installing a local server on Windows

These instructions are for Windows XP (Home or Professional), but shouldn't vary much on Windows 2000.

Although it is perfectly possible to download and install each of the components of a local server with PHP and a MySQL database, it can be quite tricky to make them all work and talk to each other, which is why we are going to be lazy and let other people help us.

By other people we specifically mean the maintainers of http://www.apachefriends.org, who offer a preconfigured server package under the name of XAMPP. The great thing is that the maintainers not only offer an easy installer but also keep the package up-to-date by releasing updates whenever one of the server components is itself updated.

> *Notice that not all hosting partners do the same, which means it can be that your local server configuration might be more modern than your real server. Also, be sure to test for different installed extensions and notify your hosting partner when you want to use software that needs something special, such as extensions to PHP.*

1. Go to Apache Friends, shown in Figure 3-1, and download the latest XAMPP package at http://www.apachefriends.org/en/xampp-windows.html. The easiest option is to go for the installer version (in the list on the XAMPP opening screen, scroll down and click the Method A: Installation with the Installer link).

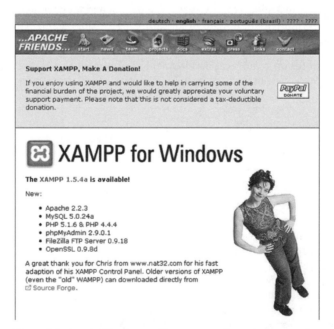

Figure 3-1. Apachefriends.org offers a preconfigured server package called XAMPP that is constantly kept up-to-date and offers upgrade packages. Download the latest version of XAMPP to start installing your local server.

2. Once you have downloaded the installer, double-click it to start. XAMPP comes in several languages—the original one is German. Here we'll use the English version.

3. When you click the Next button in the Setup Wizard, you will be asked where to install XAMPP. If you are OK with the server files being copied to C:\Program Files (choose a different location if you wish, although we'd recommend the default), just click the Install button.

XAMPP now installs a lot of files, which are listed in a scrolling box, thus updating you as to what is happening (see Figure 3-2). The installation can take several minutes, depending on the speed of your computer.

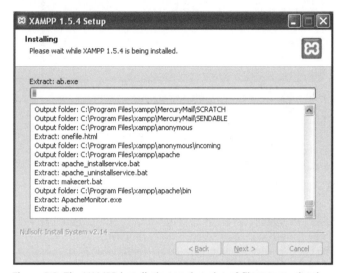

Figure 3-2. The XAMPP installation copies a lot of files to your hard drive and the process may take several minutes.

The installer will also cause some DOS window boxes (with black background) to show up during install. This is perfectly normal and nothing to worry about.

4. When XAMPP has finished installing, you are asked to click the Finish button to close the installer. Do so now.

5. XAMPP then asks you to install the different server components as services, which means that they'll start automatically when you start Windows. If you are not planning to use your local server a lot, choose No, as all of these programs will unnecessarily slow down your computer. You can change this easily later on.

6. Regardless of what you chose, you are then asked if you want to start the XAMPP control panel. Choose Yes to open the XAMPP control panel, as shown in Figure 3-3.

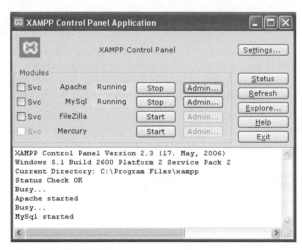

Figure 3-3. The XAMPP control panel allows you to start and stop each of the components and tells you the status of your local server.

The control panel allows you to start and stop each of the XAMPP components, check the status of the server, refresh the settings, and go to the administrative sections for each component.

For the development purposes explained in this book, you only need to have Apache (the server) and MySQL (the database) running. The other components are FileZilla (an FTP server) and Mercury (an email server). Keep both turned off.

7. Keep the boxes marked svc unchecked. If you check them, both Apache and MySQL will be installed as services and will start up every time you boot Windows. This is not what you want; you can start them manually without wasting resources and slowing down Windows.

8. If everything worked fine, clicking the Admin button beside the Apache entry should open your browser and show you the XAMPP installation page with all the information about your server installation, as shown in Figure 3-4.

> *One program that can interfere with your server is the telephone-over-IP and instant messaging tool Skype, as it uses the same resources to connect to the Internet as a local server. Be sure to shut it down if your Apache server does not start, and then try again.*

9. Notice that the information page is by default in German (and not in English as shown in Figure 3-4) regardless of the installation language. Simply switch to your desired language in the Sprachen (Languages) menu on the left.

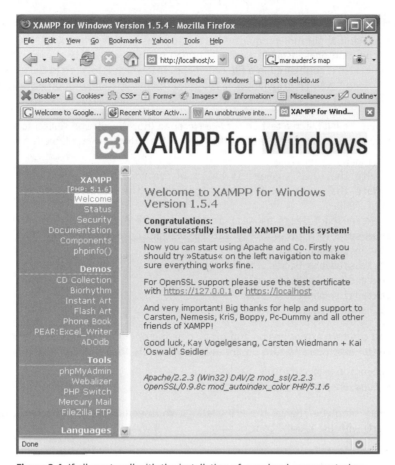

Figure 3-4. If all went well with the installation of your local server, entering
http://localhost in your browser should bring you to the XAMPP information page.

You can now explore all the options XAMPP gives you. You can check the status of your
server, see how secure it is, read documentation, and check the status of your PHP installation with phpinfo(). Also notice that XAMPP has some demos that you can click through
to check that all components have been successfully installed.

Your server home directory is the htdocs folder in your XAMPP installation (if you chose the
default install, this is located at C:\Program Files\xampp\htdocs\), and this is where you
need to copy the files you want to see on your server. When the server is running, you can
browse the files by accessing http://localhost or http://127.0.0.1 with your browser.

Under Tools, you'll find phpMyAdmin, which is an application that allows you to handle
your databases. You can create and modify databases, check their state, and create back-
ups. You'll need phpMyAdmin for the WordPress installation later on.

Tweaking PHP

Some scripts and applications require different add-ons to PHP. While XAMPP already has the most common ones installed, you might need to change the PHP configuration from time to time. PHP is configured in a file called php.ini, which is located in the apache/bin subfolder of your XAMPP installation. If you used the initial configuration install location, you can find it at C:\Program Files\xampp\apache\bin\php.ini.

1. Open the INI file in a text editor like Notepad (not Word!) and search for *Windows Extensions*. You'll find a section that lists all the extensions available for PHP:

```
; Windows Extensions
; Note that ODBC support is built in, so no dll is needed for it.
; Note that many DLL files are located in the extensions/ (PHP 4) ➡
ext/ (PHP 5)
; extension folders as well as the separate PECL DLL download (PHP 5).
; Be sure to appropriately set the extension_dir directive.
;extension=php_apd.dll
;extension=php_bcompiler.dll
;extension=php_bitset.dll
;extension=php_blenc.dll
... and so on...
```

2. You can turn extensions on and off by deleting or adding the preceding semicolon. Useful extensions to turn on are as follows (delete their preceding semicolons):

```
extension=php_curl.dll
extension=php_domxml.dll
```

3. Every time you change the PHP settings, you need to restart Apache (stop, then start) with the XAMPP control panel.

Installing a local server on the Mac

While Mac OS X does come with Apache installed by default, PHP is not included as a standard component. Various guides to downloading, compiling, and installing PHP are available, but the process can be quite involved and it is easy to make a mistake that you may not notice. Fortunately, there is a much easier option: MAMP, available at http://www.mamp.info/ (see Figure 3-5).

1. Click the Free Download button. Because the download is quite large, it is provided as a zip file.

2. After downloading this file, double-click it to extract the disk image within, then double-click that to mount it.

3. Drag the MAMP folder from the window that opens after mounting the disk image to your Applications folder (see Figure 3-6).

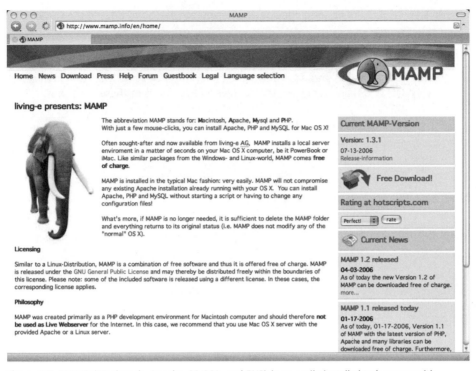

Figure 3-5. MAMP (**M**acintosh, **A**pache, **M**ySQL, and **P**HP) is an easily installed web server with everything you will need to run a local development environment on OS X.

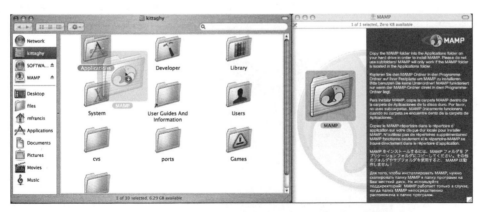

Figure 3-6. Drag the MAMP folder from the new window to the Applications folder of your computer's hard disk.

4. After MAMP has finished copying across, you can eject and discard the MAMP disk image.

5. Open the Applications folder, and the MAMP folder within. Among the other files installed in this folder you'll find the MAMP control application (Figure 3-7). Using this you can start and stop the web server (Apache) and the database server (MySQL) and change some of the configuration settings of these programs.

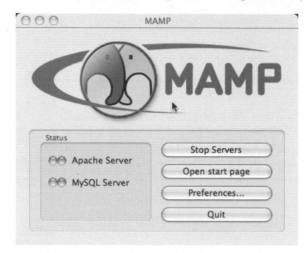

Figure 3-7. MAMP control panel application, found within /Applications/MAMP

If you have OS X version 10.4 or above, you could also double-click the file Mamp Control.wdgt to install the MAMP Control Widget onto your Dashboard (Figure 3-8). This widget allows you to start and stop the servers, but does not let you control their settings.

Figure 3-8. Installing the MAMP Control Widget into Dashboard

6. You should now use either the widget or the application to start up the web server and database. Once they have started, you should be able to point your browser at http://localhost:8888/MAMP/ to confirm that everything has installed correctly, as in Figure 3-9.

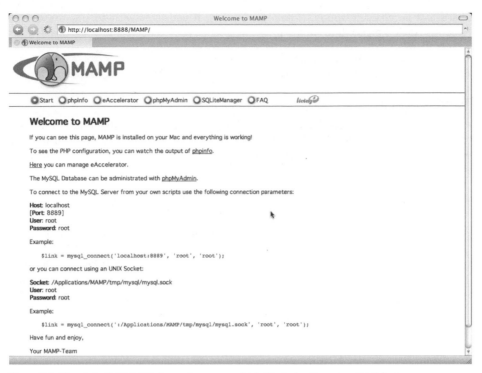

Figure 3-9. The default MAMP information page, which illustrates the current settings

From this page you can see the current settings of PHP using the phpinfo link, alter the structure of any databases using the phpMyAdmin link (you will need this link later in this chapter, when installing WordPress), and check the FAQ page for answers to some frequently asked questions about MAMP.

As standard, MAMP runs on nonstandard port numbers (the dialing code of the web server, if you will). If you would prefer to use the default ports so that you can use http://localhost/MAMP/ in preference to http://localhost:8888/MAMP/, then open the preferences of the MAMP control application (by default this is installed under applications/MAMP and the application is called MAMP—double-click it, and then click the Preferences button), and under the Ports tab choose Set to default Apache and MySQL ports, as seen in Figure 3-10. Note that this will require you to be running MAMP under an account that has Admin rights and that you'll need to enter your password every time you start the servers, as ports numbered less than 1024 are reserved for system services in OS X.

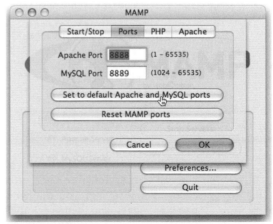

Figure 3-10. Click Set to default Apache and MySQL ports to access the web server more readily.

There is a companion option, Reset MAMP ports, if you later wish to use the default Apache installed on OS X, as found under the Sharing preference pane.

The files that you want to serve up as your web site are placed in a folder commonly known as the "document root"—this is /Applications/MAMP/htdocs by default.

Tweaking PHP

As with XAMPP on Windows, you might need to change the PHP configuration from time to time. This is stored in /Applications/MAMP/conf/php5/php.ini. To edit this file, you will need to use an editor that will allow you to change the file and save it in plain-text format:

- TextWrangler is a free text editor—you'll find it at http://www.barebones.com/products/textwrangler/.

- BBEdit is the most famous text editor on the Mac, and has been around since the days of System 6. It is quite expensive compared to some other products on the market, however. It's available at http://www.barebones.com/products/bbedit/.

- TextMate is a fairly new text editor that has a growing following among programmers on the Mac and is very reasonably priced; you'll find it at http://www.macromates.com/.

The default program in OS X for text files, TextEdit, is unfortunately configured by default to save files in formats other than plain text, even when they are plain text to start with. You can follow the instructions in the Apple Support document located at http://docs.info.apple.com/article.html?artnum=106212 to change its preferences if you would prefer not to install a different text editor, but we'd advise you to do so.

When you open this file, search for the text Dynamic Extensions in order to find the section that contains settings for the extensions loaded into PHP. By default, it will look like this:

```
;;;;;;;;;;;;;;;;;;;;;
; Dynamic Extensions ;
;;;;;;;;;;;;;;;;;;;;;
; [some explanatory text] ...

; Extensions
;extension=apc.so
extension=imap.so
extension=yaz.so
extension=pgsql.so
extension=pdo_pgsql.so
extension=pdo_mysql.so
```

You can turn extensions on and off by deleting or adding the preceding semicolon. After changing any settings, you will need to restart the web server using the MAMP control panel or widget, and then check the settings in the phpinfo link mentioned earlier.

Installing WordPress

Now that you have Apache, PHP, and MySQL running, you can start your own local blog installation using WordPress. The benefit of having a local install of WordPress is that you can try out different settings, create your own templates, and play around with the system without having to be online all the time. For example, you might want to change the look and feel or add things to the site but you don't want your visitors to see these changes as you make them. Therefore, it is smart to try things out locally instead of antagonizing real visitors.

1. Start by going to the WordPress site and downloading the latest build: `http://wordpress.org/download/`.

The installation of WordPress is largely the same across different operating systems. The only differences are the file locations. These instructions are based on the PC installation, and we will add the alternative locations for Macs when they apply.

WordPress is an immensely popular blogging tool that has several benefits:

- It has a very easy-to-use interface.
- It is easy to install—you don't need to know any PHP to install it.
- It is backed up by a huge number of developers constantly creating new themes and plug-ins for it.
- It is free.

2. When WordPress has finished downloading, unpack the zip file to the home directory of your XAMPP installation, as shown in Figure 3-11 (on your Mac, once the zip file has downloaded, uncompress it by double-clicking on the file; this will expand the contents into the folder wordpress).

3. Drag this folder into the document root at /Applications/MAMP/htdocs/.

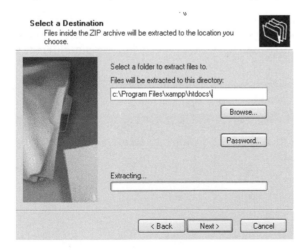

Figure 3-11. Unpacking the WordPress zip file to your local server home directory creates a new folder called wordpress and copies all the necessary files there.

WordPress consists of a fair amount of files, and unpacking may take some time. Once it has finished unpacking, you should have a structure of several folders and many files in the wordpress folder, as shown in Figure 3-12.

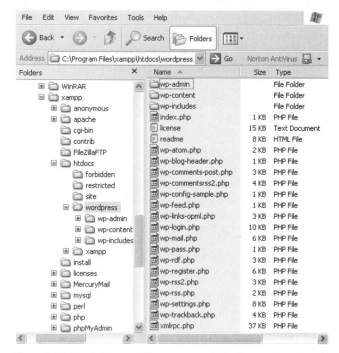

Figure 3-12. The folder and file structure of WordPress after unpacking.

The folder structure is pretty straightforward:

- wp-admin contains all the files of the admin interface. You are not likely to ever need to touch these.

- wp-content is more interesting, as it contains the content interface of WordPress. There are two subfolders inside this folder: wp-plugins, which is where all the plug-ins for WordPress go, and wp-themes, where you can put different skins for WordPress.

- wp-includes contains all the small tool functions WordPress uses. Again, you are not very likely to ever need to change anything there.

The most important file for now is wp-config-sample.php. This is where you tell WordPress the location of your database as well as the passwords to access it. You also configure your blog here.

4. Rename wp-config-sample.php to wp-config.php and open it in your chosen text editor.

All you need to change to make WordPress work on a local server are the following settings:

```
<?php
// ** MySQL settings ** //
define('DB_NAME', 'wordpress');     // The name of the database
define('DB_USER', 'username');      // Your MySQL username
define('DB_PASSWORD', 'password'); // ...and password
define('DB_HOST', 'localhost');     // 99% chance you won't need to ➡
change this value
```

5a. On your Windows computer, change the DB_USER to root and leave the DB_PASSWORD empty, as shown here in bold:

```
<?php
// ** MySQL settings ** //
define('DB_NAME', 'wordpress');     // The name of the database
define('DB_USER', 'root');        // Your MySQL username
define('DB_PASSWORD',''); // ...and password
define('DB_HOST', 'localhost');     // 99% chance you won't need to ➡
change this value
```

5b. On your Mac, change the DB_USER and DB_PASSWORD to root, and the DB_HOST to localhost:8888, as shown here in bold:

```
<?php
// ** MySQL settings ** //
define('DB_NAME', 'wordpress');     // The name of the database
define('DB_USER', 'root');        // Your MySQL username
define('DB_PASSWORD','root'); // ...and password
define('DB_HOST', 'localhost:8888');     // 99% chance you won't need ➡
to change this value
```

> *Never ever do this on a live system! The user* root *has access to all your server resources and leaving it without any password is like putting up a massive sign on your homepage inviting hackers. If you want to change the user and password for the database access you can do that in the* phpMyAdmin *link of your installation.*

6. You then need to create a new database for WordPress. Go to the phpMyAdmin install of your XAMPP install at http://localhost/phpmyadmin/ (or visit http://localhost:8888/MAMP/ and click the phpMyAdmin link on your Mac). You'll find a form field called Create new database halfway down the screen. Enter the name wordpress and click the Create button.

If all goes well, you get a confirmation message, as shown in Figure 3-13.

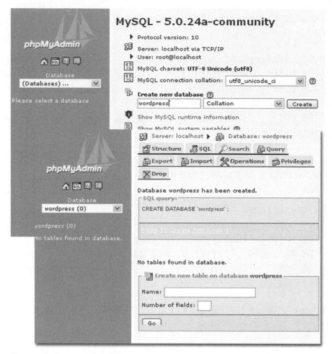

Figure 3-13. Creating a new database in PHPMyAdmin

Once the database is in place, you can start installing WordPress.

1. Go to http://localhost/wordpress/ wp-admin/install.php (use http:// localhost:8888/... at the start of the URL on your Mac). You should see the installation screen of WordPress, as shown in Figure 3-14.

2. Click the First Step link and enter the title of your weblog and your email. The title is the name of your web site, so make sure the details you enter here are the same as what you want them to be on the live system later on. The email address you specify is where WordPress sends information about what is happening on your blog. You

Figure 3-14. The WordPress installation screen

will also need it to retrieve your passwords when you forget them. Click the Continue to second step button and WordPress will create all the necessary database tables.

3. WordPress also creates a username and a password for you. Take note of this password, as you will need it in a second. This password is created randomly on the fly and you will be able to change it, but for now you won't go anywhere without it. Figure 3-15 shows our second-step confirmation page.

Figure 3-15. The WordPress confirmation screen with your login information

4. Follow the login link (wp-login.php) and enter the data on this screen into the form.

5. For added security, make sure the remember me box is unchecked and click the login button.

If all goes well, you will see your very own WordPress install in its full glory, as shown in Figure 3-16.

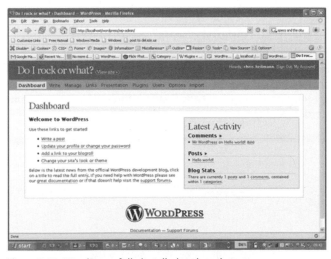

Figure 3-16. WordPress, fully installed and ready to go

The first thing you need to do is to change the temporary password to a real one and enter your personal data.

6. Choose Users from the main menu and enter all the details you deem necessary.

7. For starters, change the password to something more memorable. Don't change the username, though, as Admin will give you all the rights you need.

8. Click the Update Profile button and you are ready to have a stroll around your WordPress installation.

At this point, it is a good idea to read some of the documentation (see `http://codex.wordpress.org/`), check the different options of the system, and change some of the presets (like the links section), or try writing a post. You will use the WordPress admin Dashboard as your primary means of adding content to the site, which is why it is a good idea to get accustomed to it to the extent that you feel comfortable with it. If you ever get stuck and wonder what is going on, check out the WordPress codex at `http://codex.wordpress.org/` for help.

Tweaking WordPress

Now that you have installed WordPress and had a quick stroll through its options, it's time to learn about extending and tweaking it. There are two ways to change WordPress (omitting the obvious one, which is messing about with its PHP code yourself—we don't recommend this, unless you know what you are doing):

- Plug-ins, which are code extensions offering you more functionality than WordPress offers you out-of-the-box
- Themes, which are skins for the system changing the look and feel of it

Let's start with plug-ins. There are several web sites that feature different WordPress plug-ins:

- The plug-in section of the WordPress Codex: `http://codex.wordpress.org/Plugins`
- WP-Plugins: `http://wp-plugins.net/`
- Blogging Pro: `http://www.bloggingpro.com/archives/category/wordpress-plugins/`

The installation of these plug-ins depends on their complexity; some are as simple as unpacking them to the right folder, while others need database manipulation or require login data from third-party systems. Let's first run through a simple example to get you started with WordPress plug-ins.

1. Download the "No more dead links" plug-in at http://wait-till-i.com/ index.php?p=329 (follow the obvious download this plugin link at the top of the page).

This plug-in allow you to use a special syntax for links in your blog posts. The syntax is as follows:

```
[link:URL,Text,XFN data]
```

In other words, linking to Mark Norman Francis's site for us using XFN data would normally be

```
<a href="http://cackhanded.net"  rel="colleague met"> ➡
Mark Norman Francis</a>
```

Using this plug-in allows us to instead enter

```
[link:http://cackhanded.net,Mark Norman Francis,colleague met]
```

> *XFN is a microformat that describes the relationship you have to the person you link to. It is described in detail at* http://gmpg.org/xfn/ *and WordPress already supports XFN in the* Links *section.*

This in itself is not a big deal, but what the plug-in also does is check whether the URL is available at this time. If it isn't (in other words, the page linked to is no longer there), the plug-in replaces the link with a DEL element. That way, you will never offer a broken link to your readers.

2. Once you've downloaded the plug-in, unpack it to the plugins folder of your WordPress install—in the case of the default location, this is C:\Program Files\xampp\htdocs\wordpress\wp-content\plugins\ (or /Applications/MAMP/ htdocs/wordpress/wp-content/plugins/ on your Mac). In this case, it's a single PHP file—make sure this file is in the root of the plugins folder. Other plug-ins are more complex and have their own subfolder consisting of several files, so make sure you follow the instructions of each plug-in before you install it.

Copying the plug-in files to the correct folder is just half the work. You also need to activate them to tell WordPress to use them.

3. To do this, simply choose Plugins from the main menu, scroll to the plug-in name in the list of all available plug-ins (they are sorted alphabetically), and click the activate link.

WordPress will tell you that the plug-in was activated and changes the background color of the plug-in's entry to mark it as activated, as shown in Figure 3-17.

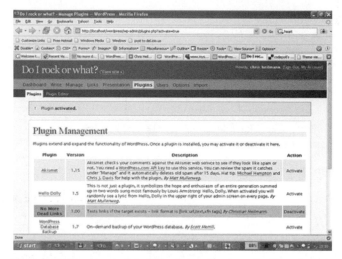

Figure 3-17. The plug-in list of WordPress showing a freshly activated plug-in

Next, let's move on to altering the look and feel of WordPress using different skins, called *themes*. Once you've installed different themes, you can change the look of your blog by selecting the Presentation entry in the menu. You'll get to a page that shows the available themes currently installed and a link to the WordPress Themes folder at `http://wordpress.org/extend/themes/`, which showcases several available themes.

A better place to go to for themes than the link is `http://themes.wordpress.net/`, which features hundreds of themes for download (at the time of this writing, 808 different ones).

> On the ThemeViewer homepage you can specify the different options you want your theme to have (colors, rounded corners, defined or fluid width, and so on), and you can test-run each of the themes before downloading them.

Let's run through the process of installing a theme.

1. Go to `http://themes.wordpress.net/`, pick a theme you like, and download it.

2. Once it's downloaded, unpack the zip file to `C:\Program Files\xampp\htdocs\wordpress\wp-content\themes\` (or `/Applications/MAMP/htdocs/wordpress/wp-content/themes` on your Mac). The theme information will all be inside a single folder, which should be at the root of the Themes folder.

3. On the WordPress Dashboard, navigate to the Presentation screen and you will see the new theme as an option.

4. Click the image of the new theme to activate it and then follow the View site link at the top of the Dashboard. You will see that your blog looks completely different.

Summary

In this chapter we got you ready to roll with your own web site. You have a local server running that can be your training ground for the real site, and you have WordPress installed, which allows you to start writing your different pages and posts.

We also explained what to expect of the Web as it stands right now and how to get the most fun out of participating in it. We covered some of the dangers to avoid and listed some of the annoyances you will have to brace yourself against.

You already should have gotten a slight insight into the amazing amount of free stuff available on the Web (in this case, plug-ins and themes for WordPress). In the next chapter we'll tell you a lot more about this. Are you ready to learn about more things to take on, or do you want to play around with WordPress to get yourself acquainted with it first? It is your choice.

3

4 SPOILED FOR CHOICE—WHAT THE WEB OFFERS YOU

By Chris Heilmann and Norm Francis

We live in exciting times for web development. Although it was hard in the past to get content or links from and to your web site, it is becoming increasingly easy to set up a web site with lots of information and to connect to other sites.

This is partly because a lot of mistakes—like trying to protect and keep all your information to yourself or even charge for content that is not even up-to-date—have been made and a lot of companies paid the price when the dot.com bubble burst.

Right now, the Web is experiencing a renaissance, and new offers attract venture capital and new business plans turn into successful companies. The practical upshot for you is that the Web is full of free stuff you can use on your own sites. In this chapter you'll see examples of what you can find where, and in the next few chapters you'll learn how to use this information and data in your own site.

RSS feeds/REST APIs

The Web is experiencing a shift right now. Initially participating on the Web meant having a site and providing a way to communicate with you—either in the form of an email link (and expecting visitors to be on a computer where they can use an email client) or with a web form. When a lot of people (too many to be exact) realized that there is a lot of money to be made on the Web by selling things and allowing people to order through e-commerce systems, it became even more important to communicate with your customers. "Build it and they will come" didn't work any longer as there were far too many competitors doing the same thing. A new way to bind customers and communicate new offers to them had to be found—and was discovered in the form of newsletters. These meant a lot of maintenance, though, as you had to protect your customers' emails from spammers (which didn't work all the time, sadly enough) and keep up with subscriptions and, of course, develop and maintain the newsletter.

This maintenance overhead called for a different method for distributing and syndicating content—something that would allow the maintainer to concentrate on the content and leave it up to the subscribers to decide when and how they wanted to read it. This is where RSS as a syndication format and REST APIs as a request format came into play.

RSS feeds

A really simple way out of the subscriber maintenance dilemma are RSS feeds, and one of the first high-profile web sites to offer them was the BBC. You can see all their RSS offers at http://news.bbc.co.uk/1/hi/help/rss/default.stm, as shown in Figure 4-1.

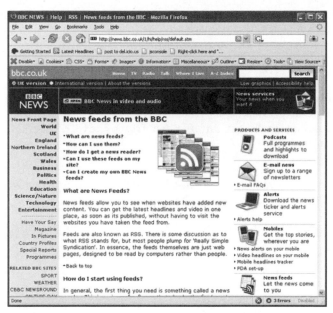

Figure 4-1. The BBC's RSS offer web site, showing all the content available as feeds

RSS stands for "Really Simple Syndication" and is basically what it says on the can. Instead of sending out a newsletter every time you update the web site, you update a small file in XML format on the server, and instead of signing in for a newsletter, the visitors check this file periodically to get updates. In addition, affiliates and friends of yours can display the information from your RSS feed (which is normally a list of headlines with a summary, linked to the full article or product page on your server) on their sites. Figure 4-2 shows the difference between the communication models of RSS and newsletters.

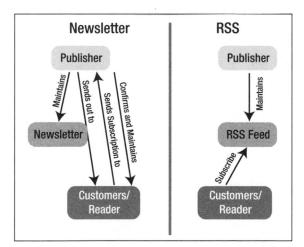

Figure 4-2. Newsletters mean you need to reestablish the connection to subscribers every time you want to send an update; subscribers do that on their own account when you use RSS.

The RSS format, defined at http://blogs.law.harvard.edu/tech/rss, is extremely easy. In its purest form, it is an XML document with the following elements:

```
<?xml version="1.0"?>
<rss version="2.0">
  <channel>
    <title>My RSS feed</title>
    <link>http://www.mywebsite.com/</link>
    <description>Newest information from my site.</description>
  </channel>
</rss>
```

This is the main shell of your information; it tells an RSS reader program what your RSS is about, what its name is, and which web site it came from.

Each entry you want to offer in RSS has to reside in an item element inside this shell:

```
<?xml version="1.0"?>
<rss version="2.0">
  <channel>
    <title>My RSS feed</title>
    <link>http://www.mywebsite.com/</link>
    <description>Newest information from my site.</description>
      <item>
        <title>My First Item</title>
        <link>http://www.mywebsite.com/?item=1</link>
        <description>I just found out a great thing about something...➡
        </description>
      </item>
      <item>
        <title>My Second Item</title>
        <link>http://www.mywebsite.com/?item=2</link>
        <description>I just found out a great thing about something➡
          else... </description>
      </item>
  </channel>
</rss>
```

Information provided as RSS is called a feed, and by using an RSS feed reader or an RSS feed service, visitors can subscribe to this information and be notified about new items when they check your feed. This normally happens automatically when they open their feed reader software. Figure 4-3 shows some readers and services and their display of RSS information.

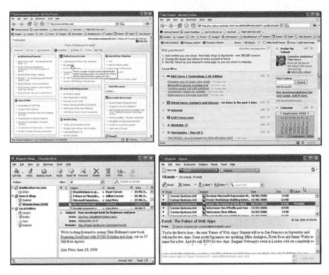

Figure 4-3. Various RSS display formats. From top to bottom: Netvibes.com, Mozilla Thunderbird, My Yahoo!, and Opera's built-in RSS reader

You might not want to offer an RSS feed of your data, but if you do, most blogging systems, including WordPress, will do this automatically for you. What you can do, however, is benefit from the wealth of data already available on the Web in RSS format. With a few lines of code (or using a WordPress plug-in called inlineRSS, available at http://www.iconophobia. com/wordpress/?page_id=55), you can offer your visitors all kinds of information:

- Entertainment news: http://rss.news.yahoo.com/rss/entertainment
- Weather information: http://xml.weather.yahoo.com/ forecastrss?p=USNY0996&u=f (in this case, New York)
- Jokes: http://yahooligans.yahoo.com/content/jokes/jotd_rss
- Cute photos of animals: http://mfrost.typepad.com/cute_overload/rss.xml
- Music: http://radio.weblogs.com/0141318/categories/electronica/rss.xml (Electronica, in this case)
- Events: http://upcoming.org/syndicate/v2/metro/49 (in this case, London)
- Movies: http://www.youtube.com/rss/tag/star+wars.rss
- And lots more...

You'll learn more about how to do this in the next chapter.

REST APIs

Lately a lot of companies went even further with the idea of offering their data to the world, and to provide developers with a way to tap into their systems to retrieve product data in various formats, RSS being the most common one. These offers are called **application programming interfaces (APIs)**, and they allow you to retrieve exactly the data you want by calling methods and resources from the system of the company offering the API.

In most cases this is achieved via a method called REST (Representational State Transfer), for which Wikipedia offers a detailed explanation (http://en.wikipedia.org/wiki/Representational_State_Transfer). REST allows you to reach the data you want to get to via a URL. You could say any web site is a REST API. You go to (they're fictional—don't try to find these examples) http://www.example.com/ and you get to the index document of that web site. You go to http://www.example.com/wombats/ and you get information about wombats. If you wanted to find information about dingos, http://www.example.com/dingos/ might be a good step. REST APIs work the same way, but offer more customization options. In most cases you point to an API URL and provide parameters to define what kind of information you need.

If you want to find jobs via Yahoo!'s HotJobs, for example, you can do this by calling the following URL:

http://hotjobs.yahoo.com/rss/version/*country*/*state*/*city*/*category*/*keywords*

The last five words—*country*, *state*, *city*, *category*, and *keywords*—are placeholders that should be replaced either by a real value or a hyphen. For example:

- http://hotjobs.yahoo.com/rss/0/USA/-/-/-/design finds design jobs in the whole of the United States and returns an RSS feed.
- http://hotjobs.yahoo.com/rss/0/USA/CA/Los+Angeles/-/- finds jobs in Los Angeles.
- http://hotjobs.yahoo.com/rss/0/USA/CA/San+Jose/NEW/- finds new media jobs in San Jose.

> *These addresses (URLs) could be a bit confusing to look at. The reason is that they are not only an address but also a request to the HotJobs API. We'll come back to the HotJobs API and URL structure in more detail in the next chapter.*

You can find a vast array of APIs at http://www.programmableweb.com, shown in Figure 4-4, and you'll learn more about using them in the next chapter.

Figure 4-4. Programmableweb.com is always up-to-date about APIs you can use to add content to your web sites.

CSS templates

CSS (Cascading Style Sheets) is the layout system of the Web. This technology takes the content of a web page and layers visual information over the top. With one CSS file on your web site, you can control almost every aspect of the way a browser renders the page to your visitors, including layout, text spacing, colors, images, and typography.

Although CSS was created with simplicity in mind, using fairly easily understandable rules for controlling the design of elements, it can still take a while to master its intricacies. Whether it be the bugs and subtle differences between web browsers, or some of the advanced concepts, CSS is a skill that is quick to learn but can take a long time to master.

CSS first became viable on the Web at the start of this century. Prior to this, most web pages were laid out using a combination of tables and spacing images, while fonts and colors were controlled using inline declarations.

If you were to read some older books on web development—and by older, this can mean as recently published as 2003—they will be full of tips on how to pad out areas of pages with "spacer GIFs" and how to specify a page heading using a <font> tag.

These ways of designing web pages still work, but they have a significant downside—each web page has to contain all of the design information. This makes it nontrivial to update the design across an entire site. By keeping the styling information separate from the individual pages (in a separate CSS file), the look of an entire site can be changed at once without altering your actual content pages.

Luckily, unless you are determined to style your web site in your own unique way, several options are available to you to make your site look better without having to learn CSS.

CSS page layouts

As the CSS revolution got under way, the basic layout structure of a site was still a skill to learn. Consequently, if you use a search engine to track down some prepackaged layouts, you will mostly find the most basic of templates.

For example, one of the most common questions asked when CSS was first being used was how to create a three-column layout. The first few of the CSS layout reference sites answered this question, and so still rank highest in Google for the search term "css layouts."

Here are some of the most popular layout references:

- The Layout Reservoir (Figure 4-5): http://www.bluerobot.com/web/layouts/
- CSS layout techniques: http://www.glish.com/css/
- Little Boxes: http://www.thenoodleincident.com/tutorials/box_lesson/boxes.html
- Sample CSS page layouts: http://www.maxdesign.com.au/presentation/page_layouts/

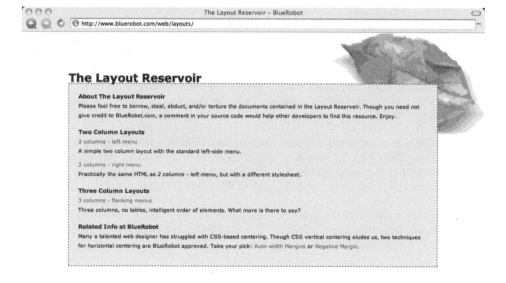

Figure 4-5. The original CSS templates, from BlueRobot's Layout Reservoir

For even more complex layouts, there is Yahoo!'s "CSS Grids" system (Figure 4-6), which can be found at `http://developer.yahoo.com/yui/grids/`. Created from the Yahoo! design pattern library, it encompasses seven basic grid components, which can then be combined into over 100 different layouts.

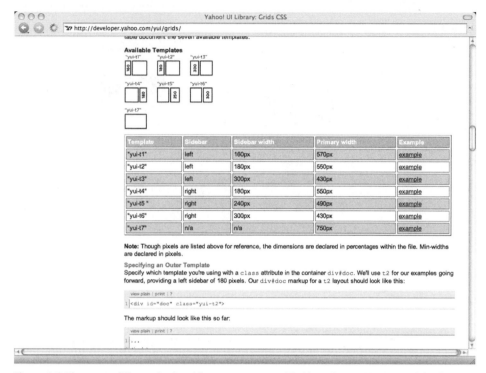

Figure 4-6. The seven different basic grid components provided by Yahoo!'s CSS Page Grids. These combine to form over 100 different layout options.

Reproduced with permission of Yahoo! Inc. © 2007 by Yahoo! Inc. YAHOO! and the YAHOO! logo are trademarks of Yahoo! Inc.

These are still very valid resources for anyone wanting to study CSS and learn how to construct complex layouts. However, if all you want is to style your site quickly, they are somewhat lacking. All of these layouts are simply frameworks, providing the scaffolding upon which the rest of a page's design rests.

WordPress themes

WordPress, like CSS itself, separates the content of your site from the presentation. As we briefly mentioned in Chapter 3, you can choose from over 800 designs made available by other members of the WordPress community. Using the search options on the main page, `http://themes.wordpress.net/` (Figure 4-7), you can find themes based on your choice of options, such as the number of columns, the main color scheme, whether they have fixed or fluid widths, and whether they use images in the design.

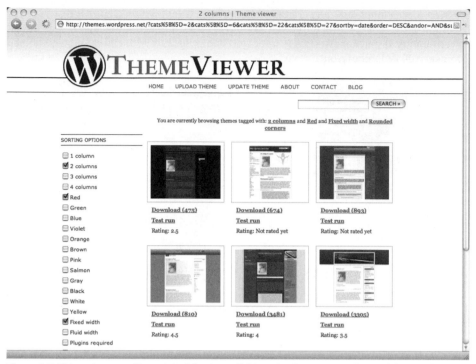

Figure 4-7. This web page offers a lot of freely available styles for your WordPress-driven web site.

For each theme you think you will like from the image thumbnails, you can click the "Test run" link to see a preview of the theme in use on a sample WordPress page. Once you have found the one you want to use, download the zip file, then extract it to c:\Program Files\xampp\htdocs\wordpress\wp-content\themes\ (or /Applications/MAMP/htdocs/ wordpress/wp-content/themes on your Mac).

> Some WordPress themes require more that just the basic installation instructions provided here in order to work. You should pay attention to any extra instructions provided with the theme you choose.

Within the WordPress administrative interface located at http://localhost/wordpress/ wp-admin/ (or http://localhost:8888/wordpress/wp-admin/ on your Mac), you can use the Presentation section to preview the themes you have installed and to select a different theme. Click the preview image of the theme you want to use to activate it, then view your site again to see that new design in action on your content.

If you would like to create your own style, you can also create your own theme for WordPress, and even upload it to the theme library to share it with the rest of the world. You can find more information on this in the WordPress Codex at http://codex. wordpress.org/Theme_Development, and we will cover more advanced CSS techniques in Chapter 8.

JavaScript libraries

JavaScript is a great technology that makes web surfing a lot more dynamic and interesting. JavaScript enables interaction beyond the clicking of links and sending of form data. Furthermore, it allows for changes to the web page after it has been downloaded from the server. This means that you can interact with an HTML document without having to wait for the whole page to reload, or you can even interact with it while it is still being loaded (enabling this option is an advanced JavaScript skill, though).

You can create effects and functionality with JavaScript that are executed by the browser on the visitor's computer. While this is great—the visitor gets a much quicker and richer web site experience and your server gets fewer hits and less traffic and is not strained with computations necessary for each visitor—it also brings problems with it. Writing JavaScript solutions for the Web means working in a demanding and confusing development environment:

- You have no way of knowing what the visitor on the other side is capable of—she might not be able to use a mouse, she may be sight-impaired, or she may have an old, unreliable mouse or keyboard.

- You don't know how fast the connection of the visitor is, or how busy her computer is with other calculations—which can slow down your JavaScript effects.

- While JavaScript is largely supported and turned on by default, browsers implement it differently and in an inconsistent fashion.

- Each new generation or even make of browsers attempts to fix bugs of the one before it (or the others), but is also likely to introduce new problems.

All of this makes writing JavaScript a skill that is not that easy to master, which is why a lot of developers who know their scripting in and out come up with solutions and collect them in so-called JavaScript libraries. Figure 4-8 shows how that works.

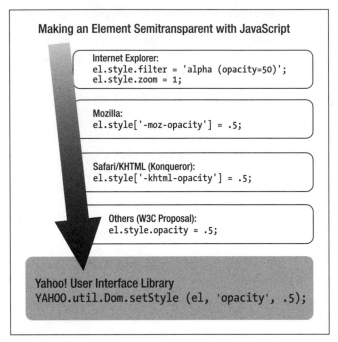

4

Figure 4-8. Working around browser inconsistencies by using JavaScript libraries

There are different kinds of JavaScript libraries. They all have something in common: they work around the browser and implementation issues by providing shortcuts that work. The following is pseudo-code but should give you an insight as to how helpful these shortcuts are. Without using a JavaScript library, you'd need to code something like this:

```
function withoutLibrary(arguments) {
  element = 'myElement';
  if( testForElement() === true ) {
    if (conditionForBrowserGroupA) {
      doBrowserGroupAimplementation();
      doThingsToStopBrowserGroupA();
    } else if (conditionForBrowserGroupB) {
      doBrowserGroupBimplementation();
      doThingsToStopBrowserGroupB();
    } else {
      fixThingForReallyOddBrowsers();
    }
  }
}
doBrowserGroupAImplementation(){
  convertDataForThisGroup();
  workAroundIssues();
}
```

```
doBrowserGroupBImplementation(){
  convertDataForThisGroup();
  workAroundIssues();
}
doThingsToStopBrowserGroupA() {
  specificCode();
}
doThingsToStopBrowserGroupB(
  specificCode();
)
fixThingForReallyOddBrowsers() {
  fixAndHacks()
}
```

Using a JavaScript library, the code can be shortened to something like

```
// versus
libraryName.doThings(element);
```

The library takes over the job for you and converts the instruction into this shortened form, which also means you don't have to know all the various issues browsers have with a certain code example.

Another thing most libraries do for you is collate common tasks into functions. These could be simple things like changing the look and feel of an element, testing an entered value, or telling you the position of an element. They could also be complex things like full-blown dynamic navigations, simulated browser windows, controls that are normally not available in browsers (like sliders or sortable tables), or ways to connect to the server and retrieve data without leaving the page (commonly known as Ajax, which is explained in the next chapter). Figure 4-9 shows some page controls that are easy to achieve with library code but that would be a nightmare to implement on your own.

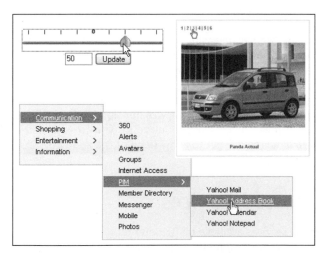

Figure 4-9. Page widgets created by libraries: sliders, menus, and image displays

Some libraries have even higher aspirations and change the syntax of the language itself to make code shorter and easier to grasp. Others try to make JavaScript look and work the same as other programming languages such as Java, Ruby, or Python.

This can be deceiving and cause unwanted results. For example, a lot of libraries offer you a function to retrieve elements in the page by CSS selectors. While browsers have built-in CSS parsers that can handle this task quickly and without much computation overhead, a JavaScript solution will have to convert the library code to standard JavaScript code, and then compare each and every element in the page with the criteria to match the CSS selector rules. Depending on the size of your page and the complexity of your selector, this process could be very slow and use a lot of memory—both things that can make your page look sloppy and hard to use. Imagine a CSS selector like #nav ul li.mainitems a. A function to return all the links to you needs to

- Get the element with the ID nav
- Get each of the ul items in this element
- Get all the li items in each of the uls
- Test if the className attribute of these lis contains mainitems
- Get all the A elements inside these matched lis and put them in a collection
- Return the collection

For each ul and li inside the element with the ID nav, the script has to go through nested loops and compare with the className attribute, which means reading from the browser.

Libraries make our life a lot easier, but they are no replacement for at least a basic knowledge of what you do and what the side effects of using a certain solution are. Libraries that promise to solve all problems for you are most likely advertising themselves too much—in the end, you want to know what you do, no matter how easy it seems to just rely on what you are given. Therefore, it is a good idea to pick a library that is well supported by the initial makers, that is backed up by a community that can give you support if you need it, and has a proven track record to work across different browsers and operating systems.

JavaScript libraries are the new big thing for anyone who is into development of this language and wants to give something to the world. The number of libraries out there is simply staggering, and if you care to follow the JavaScript geared blogs and publications there'll be a new library that is a lot cooler and easier and quicker announced every few days. In the end, a lot of those will cease to be supported by their developers, or the novelty wears off quite quickly. Right now, the JavaScript Library playing field is the Wild, Wild West and it wouldn't make much sense to introduce you to each and every one of the characters involved in it. You will get to know some of the good guys in Chapter 9.

"Web 2.0" hosted services

There are also many services available on the Internet that will take away all of the heavy lifting of hosting your created content and information. Many of these services are known by the term "Web 2.0," because they embody and demonstrate a new type of service operating on the Internet now—one where the user of the service starts to take an active and front-and-center role in the creation of the site. Examples include the following:

- http://www.flickr.com/: Yahoo!'s flickr service (Figure 4-10) is much more than just a photo-sharing site, precisely because of the sense of fun and play that comes with the sharing of photos in groups, and all of the toys that have been built on the site using its API.

- http://www.youtube.com/: Google's YouTube is much more than just a video-sharing site. The sense of community and of conversations taking place raises it up above other video sites, as does the ease with which people can share videos.

- http://upcoming.org/: Yahoo!'s Upcoming site allows people to share the events they're going to attend with their friends.

- http://del.icio.us/ and http://ma.gnolia.com/: Both allow users to bookmark, tag, and comment on other web pages.

- http://digg.com/ and http://reddit.com/: Both allow users to indicate stories and web pages that they have found useful, enabling these sites to become an aggregate of people's attention on the Web right now.

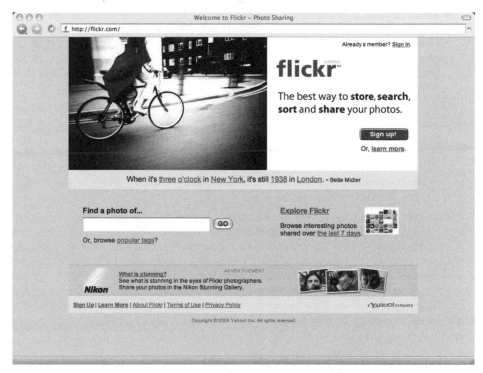

Figure 4-10. Flickr, one of the most popular Web 2.0 sites, allows people not only to store their photos online but to share and remix them in numerous ways.

These sites all have one thing in common—they put the users of the site in the driving seat. They provide nothing other than organization, cataloging, and data access through the site and RSS and API feeds. They are not afraid to share the data of the site with other web sites as well, allowing anyone to remix this content with other content to create further sites (colloquially called "mashups").

It is these Web 2.0 sites that you will be using throughout this book to provide your own site with rich media content.

The social Web

The ability to extract information from the Web 2.0 sites listed previously is not the only reason for their success. Community is probably the most important factor. These sites allow individuals not only to store their own data but also to connect with others.

There are many reasons for sharing information with others, even beyond just sharing photos and videos with friends and recommending sites you think they might be interested in. What is known as "social software"—software that attempts to codify human behavior into an automated computer system—gives an individual three real bonuses:

- **Personal benefit**: Anything that you put into the system is for your own benefit. In the case of Flickr, you have somewhere to store and share your photographs with people. This gives you a backup, in case anything ever happens to your computer and your copies of the photographs you've taken. It also means you no longer have to think about how to arrange and show your photos on a web site—Flickr provides all this.

- **Connection with others**: By sharing information in these systems, you can connect with other people who like the same things and feel the same way. Your goal may be simply to stay in contact with people you already know. In the case of Flickr, you can create a circle of friends and acquaintances with whom to share your photos. But you can go further and enter your photos into groups all while having fun and connecting with random strangers from around the world who also like to take photos of ATM machines, for example.

- **Create aggregate value**: Any system with enough users starts to create a new level of collective wisdom, thus combining the admittedly selfish actions of individuals into a whole. Again, using Flickr as an example, there are now millions of photos that people have taken that can be plotted against a map; searched against by title, description, or keyword; and shared with the world. Many photos on Flickr are licensed for people to reuse. Pretty soon (if it isn't already!) Flickr will become the biggest resource for stock photography on any subject. And it's all available to you, the end user, for free, because many millions of other individuals wanted to share their photos.

By taking part in these systems, you will be giving to the world your experience and expertise in whatever field you are in.

That could sound quite intimidating to you. But you shouldn't let it worry you. Unless people already know you, they are highly unlikely to sit there stalking you across the Internet.

And the benefits for you personally will far outweigh any public embarrassment from people discovering that you secretly like Care Bears.

By using these software systems, you can easily store and manage all sorts of information that you need to store and manage. By using del.icio.us, you can keep your bookmarks in a central location so that wherever you are you can find "that page with the video where that dog does the funny thing." If you're at a friend's house, it doesn't matter that you don't have a laptop. Your bookmarks are on the Web already, and you can look your bookmark up and share it. The same is true for your photos with Flickr, and for the music gigs you're going to next month with Upcoming, and so on. You would use this software because it makes your life and your web site easier to manage and control. The fact that you're also helping the entire human race create a whole greater than the sum of its parts is irrelevant to you and what you want to get out of storing your bookmarks in the system—unless you're a natural philanthropist.

4

What's in it for me?

As previously mentioned, you can use Flickr to store, arrange, manage, and catalog all of your photos. You can create sets of photos under one theme, and each photo can be in multiple sets. You can add titles and descriptions to help you remember, or to explain to others, what was going on. You can annotate your photos, putting notes over sections of the photo (for example, to name the individuals in the picture or to describe the different parts of an object), add keywords (which Flickr and many other Web 2.0 sites call tags) to help you find related pictures that either you, or anyone else, has taken. You can also take part in a community of millions of photographers, from people just taking quick snaps with a cell phone to professional photographers. You can get advice, take part in games and competitions, or just spend hours finding new and exciting photos.

You can use YouTube to store your personal video clips and experiments. As in the case of Flickr, you can add all sorts of titles, descriptions, and keywords. You can create playlists of videos to share with other people, find other videos in the same vein, take part in groups, and give feedback to other amateur video makers. Or if you want, you can find an endless array of videos of people falling over and running into things.

The bookmarking sites del.icio.us and ma.gnolia will store your bookmarks so you can find them again later. You can add your own title, description, and keywords (this is a common theme, you'll agree). You can search for other interesting sites and pages on any topic you care to mention, or find out what's the most popular at the moment either across the entire site or in only one focused area.

The "attention" sites Digg and reddit will allow you to keep a record of stories you have found interesting and to find new ones in any given area, or just across the Web in general. On the surface, this would seem to be similar to bookmarking, but there are two main differences. First, these sites consider pages across a much shorter time span, so they are more like "late-breaking news" compared to the "reference library" of del.icio.us and ma.gnolia. And second, in the case of reddit, they allegedly will learn your preferences to deliver news that is more tailored to your needs.

Upcoming allows you to keep track of the events in your area. You can mark if you plan to attend them, to get reminders in your calendar, or to alert others as to where you are going to be; you can watch events to receive notifications of changes even if you're not sure if you're going. You can find new events in your area, or tell the world about the event you are organizing or a gig you've heard of that you think others might like, even if you're not going or involved yourself.

Sites like these become successful partly because of the aggregate value they bring to groups and the world as a whole. But mostly, they solve a problem that individuals have (they "scratch an itch")—and they do it well.

Summary

In this chapter you learned about the services and facilities that are available on the Web to make your online life easier—from feeds to templates and libraries to services.

You now have a list of sites you can use to find prepackaged CSS and JavaScript that you can use to add style and interactivity to your site.

Also, you learned about the social Web 2.0 sites that you can use to store and catalog your online life. You can follow the example of these sites to add extra content and media to your own site to lift it up from a simple blog to become a reflection of you and your life.

5 RETRIEVING AND DISPLAYING CONTENT WITH REST AND AJAX

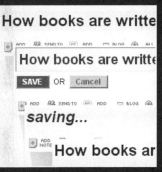

By Chris Heilmann and Norm Francis

This chapter is a bit of a breakout of the overall WordPress-driven development approach. It will also be a lot more technical than the previous chapters. It is, however, important to understand the concepts in this chapter to ensure that your final web site works nicely for a wide range of visitors and that you know what you are doing when you use an out-of-the-box Ajax solution.

> *The code examples in this chapter are available on the friends of ED web site (www.friendsofed.com). Please download them, create a new folder in the htdocs folder of your local server called ajax, and unpack the zip with all the code there.* **Do not type in the code examples** *here or copy and paste them from the PDF (in case you got the e-book). The code examples in this chapter have been cut down to show only the part explained and* **will not work on their own**. *Get the code examples and try them out on your local server instead.*

Don't worry if you don't understand the inner workings of all the examples in this chapter. We are not trying to turn you into an Ajax developer. Our aim is to give you an insight into how to plan an Ajax script and explain what an Ajax solution is. We also want to raise awareness that some Ajax solutions out there might look simple but have some complex inner workings whereas others oversimplify things. It is easy to rely on a one-line-of-code solution but it's hard to fix when something goes wrong.

To get you started, we will delve into explaining REST and what it means for you, describe the why and how of Ajax, and round off the chapter with some coding exercises demonstrating how you can write your own Ajax solutions using the Yahoo! User Interface Library.

What is REST?

Wikipedia (http://en.wikipedia.org/wiki/Representational_State_Transfer) provides a verbose explanation of REST (Representational State Transfer). In effect, it means that you point your browser or application to a certain location on the Internet or any other network and retrieve the information provided for you there. The URL (Uniform Resource Locator) shows the path the application should go to find that information. This sounds complex, but it becomes a lot easier when you realize that you are already using REST.

> *In effect, surfing the Web is using REST. When you enter a URL like* http://en.wikipedia.org/, *you tell your browser to find the server that is connected to the address* en.wikipedia.org *and retrieve the default document this server provides. If you want a wiki entry on Wikipedia about the red panda (otherwise known as the fire fox), you can go to* http://en.wikipedia.org/wiki/Red_Panda, *and if you want to know about the otter, you go to* http://en.wikipedia.org/wiki/Otter.

In other words, the location of the document on the Web (the URL you enter) allows you to define the content that gets returned to you. A site maintainer could, for example, make it easy for you to link to articles on his page by storing all his articles in a folder called articles, and creating subfolders with the name of the article and an index file. That way, you can easily remember the URL of different articles without having to go back to the index page. The term *hackable URL* has become common for this kind of technique. The more common use of REST is in connection with application programming interfaces (APIs). When an API supports REST, it is called RESTful, and it means that you can define information returned to you via the URL. A real-world example is Yahoo! HotJobs, which offers a RESTful RSS interface.

> *Just to recap, as we covered RSS before: RSS stands for Really Simple Syndication and is basically what it says on the can. RSS is an XML format that allows you to get information from other web sites without visiting them. You simply request (subscribe to) the RSS feed in an RSS reader like Netvibes (http://netvibes.com) or Google Reader (http://www.google.com/reader/view/), or by using applications like Yahoo! Mail (http://mail.yahoo.com) and Mozilla Thunderbird (http://www.mozilla.com/en-US/thunderbird/). Offering an RSS feed means that visitors will be notified when you make a change to your site (which means much less work than creating a newsletter, maintaining subscriptions, and sending the letter out to subscribers), and using an RSS reader means you don't have to surf to a lot of pages every morning to find out if they changed. You can learn more about RSS at http://en.wikipedia.org/wiki/RSS_%28file_format%29.*

To retrieve targeted RSS data from Yahoo! HotJobs, use the following URL:

```
http://hotjobs.yahoo.com/rss/v/c/s/city/category/keywords
```

The different parts of the URL allow you to drill down to the information you want:

- *v* is the version of the API—right now this is 0.
- *c* is the country you want to search in—for example, USA for the United States, GBR for Great Britain, or DEU for Germany.
- *s* is the US two-character state code—for example, AZ for Arizona or CA for California.
- *city* is the name of the city. If the city has spaces in its name, use the plus character instead—for example, San+Francisco.
- *category* is the job category—for example, CUS for Customer Service or NEW for Internet/new media.
- *keywords* is what you want to search for (separated by a + sign).

If you want to omit any of these, simply replace them with a hyphen (-). If you wanted to get an RSS feed of the latest new media jobs in San Francisco, all you'd need to enter in your browser (or, even better, RSS reader) is

```
http://hotjobs.yahoo.com/rss/0/USA/CA/San+Francisco/NEW/
```

If you want to filter this rather long list down to only jobs for designers, you can add a keyword:

```
http://hotjobs.yahoo.com/rss/0/USA/CA/San+Francisco/NEW/designer
```

If you want to search for the same jobs in London, you change the URL to

```
http://hotjobs.yahoo.com/rss/0/GBR/-/London/NEW/designer
```

All the options of the HotJobs interface are available at `http://developer.yahoo.com/hotjobs/`. You will find the list of country codes there as well (`http://developer.yahoo.com/hotjobs/#param`). Other RESTful interfaces also allow you to define the amount of returned data. The interfaces require you to get an application developer ID, though. One example is the Yahoo! Web Search API. The main URL of this RESTful API is

```
http://search.yahooapis.com/WebSearchService/V1/webSearch
```

Instead of appending your request parameters to the URL separated by slashes, you need to provide a parameter string to the URL. Parameter strings start with a question mark and continue with name and value pairs separated by equal signs. In between each name and value pair and the next one, you need an ampersand (&). The web search API needs two parameters to work: a developer ID and a query. If you want to search for lunch on Yahoo! and get the data returned as XML you can use

```
http://search.yahooapis.com/WebSearchService/V1/webSearch?➡
appid=YahooDemo&query=lunch
```

The YahooDemo ID used in this parameter string is a developer ID that works for providing examples, but it is a lot better to get your own ID if you want to use the API in your own products. You can define more parameters, such as the number of results and the region. Suppose you want the first five results in the UK for the query "lunch"—simply add the results parameter:

```
http://search.yahooapis.com/WebSearchService/V1/webSearch?➡
appid=YahooDemo&query=lunch&region=uk&results=5
```

Other RESTful APIs work more or less the same; you use the URL to tell the API what to give back to you and in which format. It is a quick and easy way to retrieve exactly what you need without having to know where the data is located in the system you are retrieving it from. The ability to define how much data you want returned also makes it easy for you to create responsive applications—no big data chunks have to be downloaded and processed.

What is Ajax?

Ajax is a term coined by Jesse James Garrett in his essay "Ajax: A New Approach to Web Applications" (`http://www.adaptivepath.com/publications/essays/archives/000385.php`) in February 2005. It stands for "Asynchronous JavaScript and XML." The essay describes a development plan for web applications that uses XML and JavaScript to create an asynchronous experience for the end user.

This means that the normal browsing experience of clicking a link, loading a page, clicking another link, loading the page, filling out a form, and, yes, loading the page again is replaced by a process that changes only the part of the document that is affected by the change you made.

> *This was not necessarily breaking news to those who developed web applications in the past (Microsoft's Outlook web interface had something similar in 1997), but the essay and the examples that followed it made it obvious that the market is ready for this kind of technology. Browsers have finally begun supporting this technology without making you hack around with frames or invisible images (we won't go into detail about these older solutions because there is nothing to gain from them these days).*

One very obvious example where Ajax makes it a lot easier to fulfill a certain task is the photo-hosting site flickr (http://www.flickr.com). After you have uploaded images, you can change the heading above the image simply by clicking it. The heading will change to an editable field with a save button, and you can change the text immediately. Once you click the save button, the data is transmitted to the server, and you can still interact with the rest of the interface. When the server has stored the data, the editable field turns back into normal text. Figure 5-1 shows the whole process from start to finish.

Figure 5-1. Changing an image heading in Flickr is as easy as clicking the text, changing it, and clicking a save button. The interface stays as it is and you don't need to reload the whole document.

Another interface element of Flickr that uses the same principles is photo tagging. Flickr—much like other so-called Web 2.0 applications (see Chapter 4)—takes searching to a new dimension by allowing you to add memorable and relevant terms to the photo that are not part of the name or the description. This meta-information (information that is not the content but enhances it) is called tags, and allows you and others to easily find your photos.

As the quality of search results stands and falls with the quality of the tags, Flickr wanted to make sure it is as easy as possible for users of the system to add or delete them. The interface here is again Ajax driven: you add your tags, you hit the save button, the data is sent to the server, and only the list of tags is refreshed when the data is successfully stored. Figure 5-2 shows the process of adding tags to a photo.

Figure 5-2. Adding tags to a photo in Flickr works in the background; all you need to do is add your tags and click an add button, and they will appear below the other tags.

A bit of theory about Ajax

The concept of Ajax is properly explained in Jesse James Garrett's essay, but just to recap, here's the theoretical model of it.

The classic model of interaction with the Web is that your browser requests information from the server and the server responds to this request and sends back a brand-new HTML document every time you request a change. Figure 5-3 shows how that looks as a schema.

Ajax, on the other hand, adds an extra layer to the whole concept—a layer that runs on your computer and requests data only when and if it is needed. The user interface gets loaded once, and only changes in the sections you request to get changed. Figure 5-4 shows this idea as a schema.

All in all, this interaction model results in an asynchronous interface, which means that information can flow between the server and your browser without a complete refresh of the interface. This allows for less information going back and forth between the server and the visitor's browser, and consequently results in more responsive interfaces.

At the heart of this technology is a JavaScript object called XMLHttpRequest, which has different methods that allow you—as the name says—to send an HTTP request to the server and retrieve XML from it. You can start a request with XMLHttpRequest.open(), send it to the server with XMLHttpRequest.send(), and abort it with XMLHttpRequest.abort(). During the sending and retrieving of data, you can check the status of the connection, and once the request is successfully finished, you can retrieve the data via XMLHttpRequest.responseXML as XML data or via XMLHttpRequest.responseText as text data.

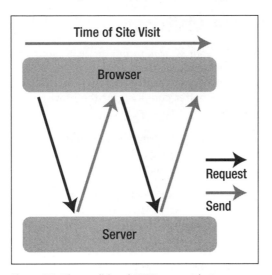

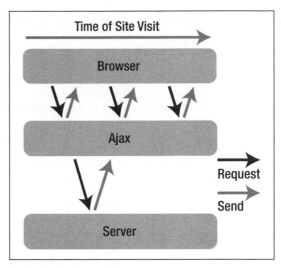

Figure 5-3. The traditional HTTP request between a browser and a server

Figure 5-4. Ajax sits in between the server and the browser and retrieves data from the server only when it is needed.

In Ajax's initial form, you retrieved XML data from the server, which is still a very common way of interacting with the back end. For example, a server-side script pulls information from a database and assembles an XML string to your needs. You retrieve this XML document via Ajax, convert it to HTML (which is a special form of XML), and display it in the browser. Now, some years later, Ajax solutions increasingly use other forms of data as XML tends to result in large documents (which means the applications are slower as transmission takes too long). More and more solutions also skip the XML conversion part and retrieve HTML directly from the back end.

What Ajax is not

Ajax is about moving server-side logic one level up and thus making it possible to create interfaces that are less obstructing than traditional interfaces. In order for an application to be Ajax, it needs to use JavaScript and load XML asynchronously from the server. Anything else is not Ajax. As Ajax is still a rather hot topic, you will find a lot of web sites, blog posts, code examples, and articles claiming to be Ajax, but don't believe the hype. Interface tricks like mirroring images, rounded corners on the fly, or drop shadows are not Ajax. Neither is showing and hiding interface elements that are already in the document with JavaScript and CSS Ajax. If there is no interaction between browser and server via JavaScript—or in simpler terms if nothing gets loaded and displayed in the same document when you click a link or a form element—it is not Ajax.

This is all very exciting, but what can Ajax do for you as a newcomer to the world of web development?

How to use Ajax to help your visitors

Ajax-driven web sites can make it a lot easier for your visitors to interact with your site. One thing you should know about people on the Web is that they are always busy. They are annoyed that their computer, their Internet connection, or their browser is too slow. It is amazing how quick the new fast connection, the better computer, or the browser with all the new features appears slow and inadequate.

Years of advertising of the Web as the new media and the Information Superhighway have left us subconsciously brainwashed that we will miss something if it doesn't happen immediately. Any time waiting is time wasted as we could miss something important.

Although this is not really true (as some things are worth waiting for), it is a good idea to plan for this mind-set. Ajax-driven web sites are not necessarily faster, but they give visitors that impression. It is reassuring that you can load content on the fly and still interact with the rest of the page.

Here are some examples of what Ajax-driven applications and web sites can do for you:

- Web-based applications like email clients or word processing tools can automatically save your document in a certain interval (such as every two minutes). If you accidentally close the application or get disconnected (this still happens, especially with flaky wireless connections), you haven't lost all the text you entered.

- Applications can load content on demand. For example, web-based email clients can load the headers of your emails while you scroll through your inbox. Non-Ajax webmail clients needed to either load a massive chunk of data eating into the available RAM of your computer or make you load the header information for 10, 20, or 50 emails at a time waiting for the whole page to load and appear in between.

- Traditional "let's get a coffee as this will take a while" tasks like uploading files can now run in parallel. You start uploading a massive file and begin typing the rest of the data you want to send in a form. The file is uploaded in the background and you will be notified once it is done. That way, you spend a lot less time filling in a form.

- With the ability to load several feeds of information at once, you can cut down the time spent on your daily information gathering immensely. Feed aggregators like Netvibes (shown in Figure 5-5) make it easy to get updates from dozens of web sites. You can start reading the first incoming updates while the rest are still loading in the background.

- It is possible with Ajax to speed up information gathering—for example, by offering close matches of a search while you are typing something in the search field, or immediately checking if a username has already been chosen by somebody else. In short, you get guidance not to do the wrong thing while you are still interacting with a form. Without Ajax, this meant a lot of frustrating reloads of the same form.

- Ajax allows for something called *edit in place*, which means that you can click a page element, it turns into an editable area, you type in your content, and it gets stored when you press Enter (see our previously mentioned flickr example). Before Ajax you either reloaded the whole document or you got a pop-up window to enter the information.

More of these use cases and good uses of Ajax are collected on so-called Ajax pattern sites like http://www.ajaxpatterns.org. *Instead of technical solutions, these sites talk about good solutions to recurring problems. The idea is copied from design patterns that offer solutions for web design and user interface problems. One example is the Yahoo! User Interface Design Pattern Library at* http://developer.yahoo.com/ypatterns/. *Even if you don't know how to technically solve a certain problem, you can provide feedback and help on these sites. It is all about how to make things easier for end users of applications.*

Figure 5-5. Feed aggregator sites like netvibes.com allow you to get information from dozens of web sites simultaneously and read updates from one while the others are still loading in the background.

Ajax solutions for your visitors

While most of these patterns apply to Ajax applications like intranets, large complex forms, or email clients, there are some that you can think about using for your web site.

One such pattern involves extending links with dynamic data when the user clicks them rather than sending them to another web page. The most bulletproof way of embedding data from other servers is to do it on the server side. However, the initial loading and rendering time of your web site is very important, as web surfers simply don't like to wait. If you pull your del.icio.us links, Flickr photos for a certain post, or links of other blogs dealing with the same matter on the server via PHP, all of these requests and the resulting data add to the overall page loading time and page weight (the file size of the document that gets sent to the visitor's browser).

Instead, you could wait until the visitor wants to see this information and then send the requests to retrieve this information via Ajax. Figure 5-6 shows how a solution like this may look to the visitor; we will get to create this example later in this chapter.

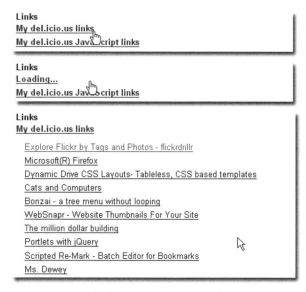

Figure 5-6. Instead of sending your visitors to del.icio.us to see your bookmarks, you can pull them into your site via Ajax.

Another solution might be a suggest-as-you-type search for your web site. This is a search form field that offers the user possible solutions to their search while they are typing. Figure 5-7 shows an implementation on my blog that uses the out-of-the-box AutoComplete widget of the Yahoo! User Interface Library available at http://developer. yahoo.com/yui/autocomplete/.

Figure 5-7. Using a suggest-as-you-type interface with Ajax offers users possible results for searches while they type them. This cuts down immensely on the time the user needs to find what they came for.

The value for the visitor should be obvious: instead of typing a search query, submitting the form, finding the right solution in a search results list, and following that link to reach their target, they can immediately choose the option offered and go directly to the page. Instead of waiting for three page loads and having to find a certain result in a list, visitors immediately get what they came for.

The problems with Ajax

Ajax is not without its problems, though, and it is important to know what can go wrong when you use it. Forewarned is forearmed.

JavaScript dependency

The most obvious and also easy-to-tackle problem with Ajax is that it depends on JavaScript, which might not be available. The workaround is simply not to rely on JavaScript but rather enhance the HTML elements and functionality that is already given. Our upcoming example offering the del.icio.us links does exactly that. The HTML involved is the following simple HTML link (codepo8 is my del.icio.us ID; you'd have to replace it with yours):

```
<a href="http://del.icio.us/codepo8" class="deliciouslink">
Check out my my del.icio.us bookmarks</a>
```

Visitors who have JavaScript disabled and search engines will simply follow the link and get to the del.icio.us page. Users with JavaScript enabled will, however, not have to go there but get the information directly on the same page.

> *You can never expect the user agent (normally a browser) to have JavaScript enabled, so simply don't rely on it. If you have functionality like links that only work when JavaScript is enabled, then use JavaScript itself to create those links (if JavaScript is not available, the links will not be created and you will not be offering false hopes). This concept is called unobtrusive JavaScript and you can read up on it at* http://onlinetools. org/articles/unobtrusivejavascript.

Slow and unreliable connections

Nowadays, you can get affordable Internet connections in the Western world at speeds that were mere science fiction some years ago, so it is hard to imagine that not everybody has a steady and fast connection to the Internet. However, there are people out there who still have very slow or flaky connections, and even our high-tech environments (wireless networks in particular) can let us down from time to time. It is also a misconception that your web site will be able to get the whole bandwidth of a fast connection, as people do tend to download things in the background and max out their connections. This is another psychological aspect of web surfing. Although we generally don't pay by the minute any longer for Internet access (unless you are in a hotel or an airport lobby that still follows these antiquated billing principles—no, we are not bitter about this right now), we still have a nagging thought in the back of our heads that only a maxed-out connection is worth the money we pay.

In short, connections may fail or time out or just get very, very slow. On a traditional web site, the browser will tell you that and show the timeout screen instead of loading the document. With Ajax, however, you start several connections in parallel and when one of them fails the browser won't automatically tell you about it.

The trick is to start a timer when you request a document asynchronously. When a certain amount of time has passed without any data coming in, this timer aborts the connection attempt and shows a message that the resource could not be loaded. You can also give the user an option to retry.

Making the visitor aware of what is going on

Another problem of Ajax applications is that users will not necessarily realize what is going on when they click a link and the page does not change. Years of surfing the Web have formed a certain expectation in web users and Ajax applications—albeit more responsive and intuitive—break this convention. Therefore, it is very important to give the visitor a visual clue that they initiated a data request. There are several ways to achieve this:

- You can show a loading animation or message at a predefined location. Google Mail does that by showing a loading message in the top-right corner of the screen.

- You can show a small loading animation next to the link that was clicked.

- You can change the text content of the interface element that the visitor activated, such as a link or a button.

- You can change the text and make the element inactive—this makes a lot of sense when you submit forms since you don't want the visitor to submit them twice.

None of these are hard to achieve but all have a great impact on the usability of your application.

Security restrictions

One of the biggest thorns in the side of aspiring Ajax developers is that with the commonly accepted way of retrieving data—the XMLHttpRequest object—it is impossible to retrieve data from locations outside the current domain. This means an Ajax script running on the server connected to the domain http://www.example.com can retrieve http://www.example.com/data.xml and http://www.example.com/otherdata/data.xml but won't be allowed to retrieve http://www.otherexample.com/data.xml. The reason is security. Browser vendors didn't want to allow scripts retrieving information from other servers, as that would mean you could read out information about your computer and send that to a different server or include code from another server without you knowing it.

The workaround is to use a proxy script, which is a server-side script to get the information and pass it on to JavaScript. Another solution is using hidden frames, which has other security, usability, and accessibility issues. Or you can use a data format called JSON (JavaScript Object Notation), which allows you to retrieve data. We will look into this and the proxy option later in the code example.

Changing surfing behavior patterns

When you create an Ajax-driven web site you are making it easier for users, but you also mess with their expectations. Badly designed web sites make it hard for visitors to find their way around. Every time they end up on a wrong page there is a helper they can use to get back on track: the browser's back button. Every time visitors go to a new document by following a link, the browser adds this document to its history and they can go back to it by pressing the back button.

With Ajax, however, the document does not change—only part of it does. This is breaking the expected functionality of the back button. There are several hacks to get around the problem. In essence, you add an IFRAME to the document and change its location every time you click a link in your Ajax page. That way, the browser adds this change to the history and the back button works again. There is a good explanation and solution for the problem available in an article by Mike Stenhouse at http://www.contentwithstyle.co.uk/Articles/38/fixing-the-back-button-and-enabling-bookmarking-for-ajax-apps and a ready-to-use library at http://www.unfocus.com/Projects/HistoryKeeper/.

5

Assistive technology

Another issue is dealing with users of assistive technology like screen readers. These are programs that run on top of browsers and read out the content of the document to the user. While this is a feasible approach for static documents, not all screen readers inform the user when content on a page has reloaded (they can notify that a page has loaded).

A technical workaround is to change the text of the element that the user triggered to initiate the loading of the content (for example, a link changing from "my links" to "loading" and "ready" once the content was loaded) and to reset the focus of the document with JavaScript once the new content has been loaded.

An easier workaround is not to rely on JavaScript and Ajax and offer a server-side alternative that links to the same content as an option at the beginning of the document.

Some simple Ajax examples

All right, let's plunge in. From now on you will be confronted with code. We start with a simple Ajax example that works without a server-side component. We then explain why you will need a server-side component, and finally we show an example that uses JSON to retrieve data without a server-side component.

We will use the Yahoo! User Interface Library available at `http://developer.yahoo.com/yui/` for these examples. This is not the smallest or easiest library to use but it has several benefits:

- It is tested across browsers and platforms and will be upgraded every time a new browser is released that gets a lot of users.
- It is backed up by Yahoo! and thus tested on very large-scale sites with millions of users.
- It comes with full documentation and examples.
- It is backed up by a large community who are happy to help you when you get stuck.

Displaying lyrics via Ajax

The first example we'll tackle is a page that displays lyrics of songs. We'll create an index page linked to several pages with lyrics, and load the lyrics into the page when and if JavaScript and Ajax is available. Without JavaScript, the visitor will simply get to the lyrics page and will have to follow a link to return to the index. Figure 5-8 shows the different user experiences in the Ajax version.

Figure 5-8. The Ajax example indicates that content is being loaded by changing the text of the link and either loads the content or gives out error messages explaining to the visitor what went wrong.

The example shown in Figure 5-8 is a file called `lyricsindex.html` in the code pack you should have downloaded and unpacked to your local server. Open it by entering `http://localhost/ajax/lyricsindex.html` in your browser with your server running and you should be able to see the effect for yourself.

The important parts of the HTML document are basically two IDs we define. One for the navigation, which is an unordered list:

```
<ul id="lyricsnav">
  <li><a href="lyrics-everybody-knows.html">Everybody Knows</a></li>
  <li><a href="sync.php">This will time out</a></li>
  <li><a href="lyrics-viva-las-vegas.html">Viva Las Vegas</a></li>
```

```
<li><a href="lyrics-pepper.html">Pepper</a></li>
<li><a href="notthere.html">This will not be found</a></li>
<li><a href="lyrics-lust-for-life.html">Lust for Life</a></li>
<li><a href="lyrics-we-care-a-lot.html">We Care A Lot</a></li>
<li><a href="http://www.yahoo.co.uk">Yahoo</a></li>
</ul>
```

and another one, which will be the container for the content we load via Ajax:

```
<div class="yui-b">
<h1>Lyrics</h1>
<p>Please select from the lyrics menu which lyrics you'd like➡
to read.</p>
<div id="lyricscontainer"></div>
</div>
```

For the function we are about to develop, we need three parts of the Yahoo! User Interface Library:

- The YAHOO main object, which makes sure that the functions developed and the library itself works nicely together with other functions without interfering with them

- The event object, which helps you to react to things that happen to the document, like it's finished loading or a visitor is activating a link

- The connection object, which allows you to connect to the server and load other documents

We include these as their minified versions in the head of the document:

```
<script src="yahoo-min.js" type="text/javascript"></script>
<script src="event-min.js" type="text/javascript"></script>
<script src="connection-min.js" type="text/javascript"></script>
```

> All the Yahoo! User Interface Library components come in three versions: the standard version, which contains comments and all the code in a readable fashion; a debug version that reports a lot of messages to the output console; and a minified version that has no comments, is not really human readable, but is the smallest file. When in doubt, use the minified version.

Once we have all this set up, we can start our function. The comments included should give you an idea of what is happening. This is not a book about JavaScript, so we won't go into details. This is just for you to understand what is needed to create a good Ajax solution.

This function allows for several of the issues described earlier. When a file cannot be found, the visitors get an error message; when the file takes too long to load, visitors are asked to try again; and when the visitors click a link, the text of the link is turned into a loading message and back into the original link text when the document is successfully loaded.

```
// This function will be called every time the user clicks on the
// navigation list
YAHOO.example.lyricsajax = function(e){

  // Get the element that was clicked on by using the getTarget()
  // method of the event utility
  var t = YAHOO.util.Event.getTarget(e);

  // ensure that the element is a link by comparing its node name
  if(t.nodeName.toLowerCase() === 'a'){

    // This function is called when the file was successfully loaded
    function success(obj) {
      // reset the link text back to the original text
      t.innerHTML = currentText;
      // get the text content of the file that was loaded
      var d = obj.responseText;
      // remove all the whitespace to turn it into one line
      d = d.replace(/\n|\r/g,'');
      // remove everything before and including the starting tag of➡
      // the content DIV
      d = d.replace(/.*<div id="lyricscontainer">/,'');
      // remove the rest of the document after the lyrics
      d = d.replace(/<\/div>.*/,'');
      // insert the lyrics content into the document
      document.getElementById('lyricscontainer').innerHTML = d;
    }

    // This function is called when there was an error
    function failure(obj) {
      // reset the link text back to the original text
      t.innerHTML = currentText;

      // if the connection timed out, tell the visitor that
      if(obj.status === -1){
        var error = '<h2>There was an error</h2>';
        error += '<p>The connection timed out. You can try to ';
        error += '<a href="' + t.href + '">load the document➡
again</a>.</p>';

      // if the document couldn't be found, tell the visitor that
      }else if(obj.status === 404){
        var error = '<h2>There was an error</h2>';
        error+= '<p>The document was not found.</p>';
        document.getElementById('lyricscontainer').innerHTML = error;
```

```
          // report other errors, too
        } else {
          var error = '<h2>There was an error</h2><p>' +➡
obj.statusText + ' </p>';
        }

        // display the error message inside the lyrics container
        document.getElementById('lyricscontainer').innerHTML = error;
      }

      // Define the handlers for the connection.
      //    - success defines the function that is called when the
      //      document was loaded
      //    - failure defines the function that is called when
      //      there was a problem
      //    - timeout defines the amount of time in milliseconds
      //      to wait before the connection is considered timed out.
      var handlers={
        success: success,
        failure: failure,
        timeout: 2000
      }

      // get the url to load from the link's HREF attribute
      var url = t.href;

      // define a new asynchronous request loading the
      // URL using the parameters defined in handlers
      var cObj = YAHOO.util.Connect.asyncRequest('GET', url, handlers);

      // store the link text in a variable called currentText
      var currentText = t.innerHTML;

      // turn the link text into a loading message
      t.innerHTML = 'loading...';

      // don't follow the link when the visitor clicks it by using the
      // preventDefault method of the event utility
      YAHOO.util.Event.preventDefault(e);
    }
  }

// When the element with the ID lyricsnav is available, attach
// an event listener that calls the function
// YAHOO.example.lyricsajax when the user clicks the
// element
YAHOO.util.Event.addListener('lyricsnav', 'click',➡
YAHOO.example.lyricsajax);
```

Now, this takes care of loading content from the same server, but when you try to load content from a third-party location it will not work.

Using a server-side proxy script

The last link in the lyrics example links to the UK Yahoo! homepage. If you click it you will be taken to the web site. However, this is not by design but because of an error (the idea is that all content should be displayed on this page without leaving it, remember?). If you look at the JavaScript error console, you will see the following error in Firefox:

Error: [Exception... "'Permission denied to call method XMLHttpRequest.open' when calling method: [nsIDOMEventListener::handleEvent]" nsresult: "0x8057001e (NS_ERROR_XPC_JS_THREW_STRING)" location: "<unknown>" data: no]

This not-very-readable error message means that there was an event (which is the click on the link) that tried to call the XMLHttpRequest.open method and didn't get permission to do so. The reason—that the URL to open is outside the current domain—is not given, though.

The way around this issue is to use a server-side script that pulls the data from the other server. If you check the example called proxyexample.html on your local server, you will see that you can pull information from a third-party service—in this case del.icio.us—when you use a server-side script as a proxy. The server-side script is called get.php and uses the PHP extension CURL to retrieve the data from the other server:

```php
<?php
// set the correct header to return a real XML document
header("Content-Type:text/xml");

// retrieve the URL that was sent by the paramater with the same name
$url = $_GET['url'];

// get the document and print it out
$feed = getResource($url);
echo $feed;

// this function CURL to read $url from a different server
// and return it
function getResource($url){
  $ch = curl_init();
  curl_setopt($ch, CURLOPT_URL, $url);
  curl_setopt($ch, CURLOPT_RETURNTRANSFER, 1);
  $result = curl_exec($ch);
  curl_close($ch);
  return $result;
}
?>
```

5

If, for example, you enter http://localhost/ajax/get.php?url=http://del.icio.us/rss/codepo8 in your browser, you will get an XML file, although you called up the get.php document.

All we need to do to allow Ajax to retrieve third-party content is to loop our request through this server-side component. The following script generates the functionality shown earlier in Figure 5-7.

The HTML component of the script is rather easy; we offer two links that point to our bookmarks at del.icio.us. One time we point to all the bookmarks, and the second time we want to show only links with the tag JavaScript:

```
<p><a href="http://del.icio.us/codepo8"
        class="delicious">My del.icio.us links</a></p>
<p><a href="http://del.icio.us/codepo8/JavaScript"
        class="delicious">My del.icio.us JavaScript links</a></p>
```

For visitors without JavaScript, these links simply lead to the appropriate pages on del.icio.us, but for those with JavaScript enabled, we want to hijack this functionality, load the link data via Ajax, and display it directly on the page.

To retrieve link data from del.icio.us as an RSS feed, all you need to do is to add rss between the domain and the link, in this case http://del.icio.us/rss/codepo8 and http://del.icio.us/rss/codepo8/JavaScript.

We'll use the classes applied to the links as a means to define which links need to get the functionality applied to them. For this, we need another part of the Yahoo! User Interface Library, namely the Dom utility. This means the head section gets another SCRIPT element including this library component:

```
<!DOCTYPE HTML PUBLIC "-//W3C//DTD HTML 4.01//EN"➥
"http://www.w3.org/TR/html4/strict.dtd">
<html>
<head>
  <title>Proxy example</title>
  <link rel="stylesheet" type="text/css" href="reset-min.css">
  <link rel="stylesheet" type="text/css" href="fonts-min.css">
  <link rel="stylesheet" type="text/css" href="grids-min.css">
  <script src="yahoo-min.js" type="text/javascript"></script>
  <script src="event-min.js" type="text/javascript"></script>
  <script src="dom-min.js" type="text/javascript"></script>
  <script src="connection-min.js" type="text/javascript"></script>
  <script src="proxyajax.js"></script>
</head>
```

Once this is included, we can create our script to change each link with the class delicious into a trigger to load and display the link data. As the returned data is in XML, we'll have to convert this into HTML by means of DOM methods.

```
YAHOO.example.proxyajax={

  // the initialization function
  init:function(){

    // get all links with the class "delicious"
    var links = YAHOO.util.Dom.getElementsByClassName('delicious','a');

    // fire the "get" method when the user clicks them
    YAHOO.util.Event.addListener(links,'click',➡
YAHOO.example.proxyajax.get);
  },

  // the get method that retrieves the information
  get:function(e){

    // if the data has not been loaded yet ...
    if(this.hasloaded===undefined){

      // get the href attribute, which is the URL we will load
      var url = this.getAttribute('href');

      // store the original link in a variable
      var origin = this;
      // store the original link text in a variable
      var text = this.innerHTML;
      // display a loading message
      this.innerHTML = 'Loading...';

      // To turn a normal del.icio.us URL into a feed, just add RSS
      var feedurl = url.replace(/\.us/,'.us/rss');

      // the function to call when the loading was successful
      //  the paramater o is the data retrieved from the feed as XML
      function delicioussuccess(o) {

        // reset the text of the link
        origin.innerHTML = text;

        // set a flag that the content was already loaded
        origin.hasloaded = true;

        // get the root element of the XML feed
        var root = o.responseXML.documentElement;

        // get all the "item" elements in the feed
        var items = root.getElementsByTagName('item');
```

5

```
          // loop over all items, retrieve the link data and add it
          // to a string
          var output = '';
          for(var i=0, j=items.length; i<j; i++){
            var title = items[i].getElementsByTagName('title')[0]➡
           .firstChild.nodeValue;
            var url = items[i].getElementsByTagName('link')[0]➡
           .firstChild.nodeValue;
            output+='<li><a href="' + url + '">' + title + '</a></li>'
          }

          // create a new list element and give it the CSS class➡
          // linkslist
          var list = document.createElement('ul');
          list.className = 'linkslist';

          // insert the list after the link parent (which is the➡
          // paragraph it resides in)
          origin.parentNode.parentNode.insertBefore(list,➡
          origin.parentNode.nextSibling);

          // and add all the links as its content
          list.innerHTML = output;
        }

        // if there was any communication error, just redirect
        // the browser
        function deliciousfailure(o){
          window.location = url;
        }

        // the handlers for the connection
        var delicioushandlers={
          success: delicioussuccess,
          failure: deliciousfailure
        }

        // send the URL to the server side script as an asynchronous
        // request
        var cObj = YAHOO.util.Connect.asyncRequest('GET',➡
'get.php?url='+feedurl, delicioushandlers);

      // if there is already a list of links, just toggle their display
      } else {
        var list = this.parentNode.nextSibling;
        list.style.display = list.style.display === 'none' ?➡
        'block' : 'none';
      }
```

```
            // don't follow the clicked link
            YAHOO.util.Event.preventDefault(e);
        }
    }

    // When the window has finished loading, call the init method
    YAHOO.util.Event.addListener(window,'load',➥
    YAHOO.example.proxyajax.init);
```

Using a server-side proxy script is the safest option to make sure you can read information from a third-party server. However, you can also open your server to attacks from malicious hackers with a script like this. In this case they could check your source code and find out that the PHP script that pulls in the data is called get.php and try to use this to read other files from your server. The PHP proxy component of your script must therefore check that only URLs outside your server or inside a certain folder are available. Make sure that any Ajax solution you use out-of-the-box allows you to do that; otherwise, your server may be vulnerable to hackers just because you wanted to load something with Ajax. You can test that by opening get.php on your server and sending a local file name as a parameter, such as get.php?url=index.html.

Retrieving del.icio.us links with JSON

When all you want to do is display your del.icio.us links, you can also do that without having to resort to a server-side proxy. The del.icio.us maintainers listened to Douglas Crockford, who discovered the JavaScript Object Notation (JSON; http://www.json.org) and offer JSON as an optional output format. If you enter, say, http://del.icio.us/feeds/json/codepo8 in your browser, you will get the following code:

```
    if(typeof(Delicious) == 'undefined') Delicious = {};
    Delicious.posts = [
      {
        "u":"http://icant.co.uk/sandbox/Flickrdrillr",
        "d":"Explore Flickr by Tags and Photos - Flickrdrillr",
        "t":["Flickr","json","photos"]
      },
      {
        "u":"http://www.msfirefox.com/",
        "d":"Microsoft(R) Firefox",
        "t":["firefox","microsoft"]
      },
      {
        "u":"http://www.dynamicdrive.com/style/layouts/",
        "d":"Dynamic Drive CSS Layouts- Tableless, CSS based templates",
        "t":["webdesign","css","layout","templates"]
      }
    ]
```

5

This is only an example and we cut it down to three links. By the time you read this, the content will have changed as the URL always gives you the ten latest links on my del.icio.us page. This construct is generated for you by the people working for del.icio.us. First it tests if an object called Delicious exists and, if it doesn't, it creates a new one. Then it defines the property posts as an array of objects containing link data. Each object has three properties: u, which contains the URL of the link; d, which is the description; and t, which is an array of all the tags associated with this link entry.

Nevertheless, this rather cryptic and braces-heavy syntax has a great advantage over the XML you normally get returned from del.icio.us: it is already JavaScript and you don't need to convert it to something JavaScript understands before converting it again to something a browser can display (HTML). The lack of tags also makes sure that the file you get sent is a lot smaller, which means that it can be retrieved a lot faster than the XML version.

There is an explanation and a demo script illustrating how to use JSON to show your latest links on the del.icio.us help page at http://del.icio.us/help/json/posts, but this explanation lacks information on how you can make it even easier to use: the feed allows for another parameter called callback, which allows you to define a function name that will be wrapped around the JSON object. For example, the URL http://del.icio.us/feeds/json/codepo8?callback=myfunc results in

```
myfunc(
  [
    {
      "u":"http://icant.co.uk/sandbox/Flickrdrillr",
      "d":"Explore Flickr by Tags and Photos - Flickrdrillr",
      "t":["Flickr","json","photos"]
    },
    {
      "u":"http://www.msfirefox.com/",
      "d":"Microsoft(R) Firefox",
      "t":["firefox","microsoft"]
    },
    {
      "u":"http://www.dynamicdrive.com/style/layouts/",
      "d":"Dynamic Drive CSS Layouts- Tableless, CSS based templates",
      "t":["webdesign","css","layout","templates"]
    }
  ]
)
```

Why is that better? It allows you to define a function with the same name that gets the whole data set as a parameter. All you then have to do is loop through each of the items in that data and retrieve the information you need. If you open the example simpleJSON.html, you will get our latest ten links inside a document, and all that was needed was to put the following into the document body:

```
<script type="text/javascript">
function myfunc(o) {
  var out = '<ul>';
  for (var item in o) {
    out += '<li><a href="' + o[item].u + '">' + o[item].d +➥
    '</a></li>';
  }
  out += '</ul>';
  document.write(out);
}
</script>
<script type="text/javascript" src="http://del.icio.us/feeds/json/➥
codepo8?callback=myfunc"></script>
```

Notice that we don't use the "tags" data to keep the display short and sweet. The SCRIPT
tag that gets the JSON object does not have to be in the document. You could just as easily create it on the fly, as we've done in the following script, which does exactly the same
as the proxy example but does not need any server component. You can try out the script
by opening the file called examplejson.html.

```
YAHOO.example.jsonajax={

  // the initialization function
  init:function(){

    // get all links with the class "delicious"
    var links = YAHOO.util.Dom.getElementsByClassName('delicious','a');

    // fire the "get" method when the user clicks them
    YAHOO.util.Event.addListener(links,'click',➥
    YAHOO.example.jsonajax.get);
  },

  // the get method that retrieves the information
  get:function(e){

    // if the data was not loaded already
    if(this.hasloaded===undefined){

      // get the link's href attribute, store the link data in
      // properties and change the text to "loading"
      var url = this.getAttribute('href');
      YAHOO.example.jsonajax.origin = this;
      YAHOO.example.jsonajax.text = this.innerHTML;
      this.innerHTML = 'Loading...';
```

```
                    // In order to turn a normal del.icio.us URL into a JSON
                    // feed, just add feeds/json/
                    var feedurl = url.replace(/\.us/,'.us/feeds/json/');
                    // and add the callback function name as a parameter
                    feedurl += '?callback=YAHOO.example.jsonajax.datafound';
                    // create a new script element, with the URL as the src attribute
                    var s = document.createElement('script');
                    s.src = feedurl;
                    // and apply it to the body
                    document.body.appendChild(s);

                   // if there is already a list of links, just toggle their display
                   } else {
                     var list = this.parentNode.nextSibling;
                     list.style.display = list.style.display === 'none' ?➡
                     'block' : 'none';
                   }

                   // don't follow the clicked link
                   YAHOO.util.Event.preventDefault(e);
                },

            // when the generated script element has retrieved the JSON data,
            // it will call this method
            datafound:function(o){
              // assemble the list items from the JSON data
              var out='';
              for (var item in o) {
                out+='<li><a href="'+o[item].u+'">'+o[item].d+'</a></li>';
              }

              // change the link back to the original text
              YAHOO.example.jsonajax.origin.innerHTML =➡
              YAHOO.example.jsonajax.text;

              // create a new output list, set the hasloaded
              // property and add the list
              // to the document after the link
              var list = document.createElement('ul');
              list.className = 'linkslist';
              YAHOO.example.jsonajax.origin.hasloaded = true;
              var parent = YAHOO.example.jsonajax.origin.parentNode;
              parent.parentNode.insertBefore(list, parent.nextSibling);
              list.innerHTML = out;
            }
        }
```

```
// When the window has finished loading, call the init method
YAHOO.util.Event.addListener(window,'load',➡
YAHOO.example.jsonajax.init);
```

Using JSON makes for much faster and shorter scripts, and if you get the chance to use it as a data format, go for it. The option to use it in a dynamically created SCRIPT tag has several benefits:

- You can use it without having to resort to a server-side proxy script; indeed, you don't even need a server as you don't need to use HTTP.

- Results will be cached, which means the next time you request the same data it won't have to load from the server (if you want to avoid this, add a random number as a last parameter).

- You won't need to convert the data to anything else before writing it out: JSON is already JavaScript.

Summary

In this chapter we took an in-depth look at using Ajax. We didn't dwell too much on the technicalities of XMLHttpRequest, but concentrated on what Ajax is, how to implement it (using the Yahoo! User Interface Library), and what interfaces to use with Ajax.

We looked at RESTful APIs and showed you how to retrieve data from them, how to create an Ajax-driven web site that degrades gracefully, and how to address the problems with Ajax.

We investigated the various approaches to work around the security issues of Ajax, such as a server-side proxy script or an alternative to Ajax: using dynamic SCRIPT tags for JSON APIs.

We hope that after this chapter you are able to differentiate between good and bad Ajax solutions and can successfully avoid the bad ones. Ajax is a great methodology and it's powerful if applied correctly. It can also make a web site appear fancy but be totally inaccessible at the same time.

By Chris Heilmann and Norm Francis

It is often said that on the Web "content is king." The text in web pages is what gives sites good or bad rankings in search engines; allows people to find what they are looking for; and explains, demonstrates, and elucidates.

But there is another well-known saying: "A picture is worth a thousand words." Sometimes just having endless streams of prose is not enough, and you can illustrate your point with, well, with an illustration. Or a picture, a video, a map, music... the list goes on. Multimedia in web sites also makes them more attractive to visitors and more usable—sometimes a simple map can explain how places in the world relate to each other more easily than can text or images.

So in this chapter you'll learn some easy ways to embed different types of media within your site.

Images with Flickr

While there are many web sites on the Internet that will allow you to store and share your photographs and other images, Yahoo!'s Flickr (http://www.flickr.com—see Figure 6-1) is one that is very popular with computing professionals and bloggers. One of the biggest differences is that Flickr does far, far more than just allow you to upload and share your images. For starters, you can organize your images into albums (called sets on Flickr), but unlike many other sites, you can put the same image into more than one set without having to upload it again.

Figure 6-1. An example photo shared on Flickr.com

However, Flickr's unique strength is that of community. Anyone on Flickr can comment on your photos (as long as you don't make them private). Flickr also has groups, which allow many different people to share images with a common theme. Some people use groups to collect photos of events, such as weddings and conferences; some use groups to play games—such as "Guess Where London" (found at http://www.flickr.com/groups/guesswherelondon/), in which players have to figure out where in London a photograph was taken. It is this sense of play with your friends that elevates Flickr above other sites that are "just" about sharing photos.

Then there are the wonderful games and applications that are built on top of Flickr, such as "fd's Flickr Toys" at http://bighugelabs.com/flickr/. Here you can find many different photo-manipulation toys, such as "CD Cover Maker" to make your own CDs, "Warholizer" to create a pop-art version of a picture, "Magazine Cover" to put yourself on the racks of your newsstand, and "Hockneyizer" to create a montage from a set of Polaroids that just happens to look like your photo (as demonstrated in Figure 6-2!). Or the Color Picker at http://www.krazydad.com/colrpickr/ (see Figure 6-3), which helps you to browse Flickr images based on the main color of the image. And there are many more examples—you can find a list of the most popular at http://www.flickr.com/services/.

6

Figure 6-2. A "Hockneyized" version of a photo from Flickr

Figure 6-3. The Flickr Color Picker will find photos on Flickr that match the color you select from the wheel.

All of these add-ons to Flickr are made possible by its rich API, which also benefits you by hooking your images into your web site. Let's try that now.

Inserting Flickr images into your posts

Before you go any further, you will have to sign up to Flickr. If you already have a Yahoo! ID (if you use Yahoo!'s Mail or Instant Messenger, for example), you can just use that. Otherwise, you will have to create a new one. You can sign in and sign up by visiting http://www.flickr.com/.

Once you are signed in to Flickr, you will need to upload some photos so that you can experiment putting them into your web site. Visit http://www.flickr.com/photos/upload/ to upload them manually, or you can download some software to help automate this process from http://www.flickr.com/tools/ (Uploadr comes highly recommended, and is available for Mac and Windows, and users of the iPhoto or Aperture software on the Mac can find plug-ins on this page that make it a breeze to upload photos directly from your photo library).

Now, before you can use your Flickr images in your site, you will need at least one WordPress plug-in. You can use the WordPress Flickr Post Bar plug-in from http://tantannoodles. com/toolkit/wp-flickr-post-bar/. Grab the zip file from there and extract it to your WordPress plugins directory. Then open up WordPress in your browser and click the Plugins tab (or go directly to http://localhost:8888/wordpress/wp-admin/plugins.php). Under plugins you will now see a new entry for WP Flickr Post Bar. You should click Activate for that plug-in, then click the configure link in its description (see Figure 6-4.)

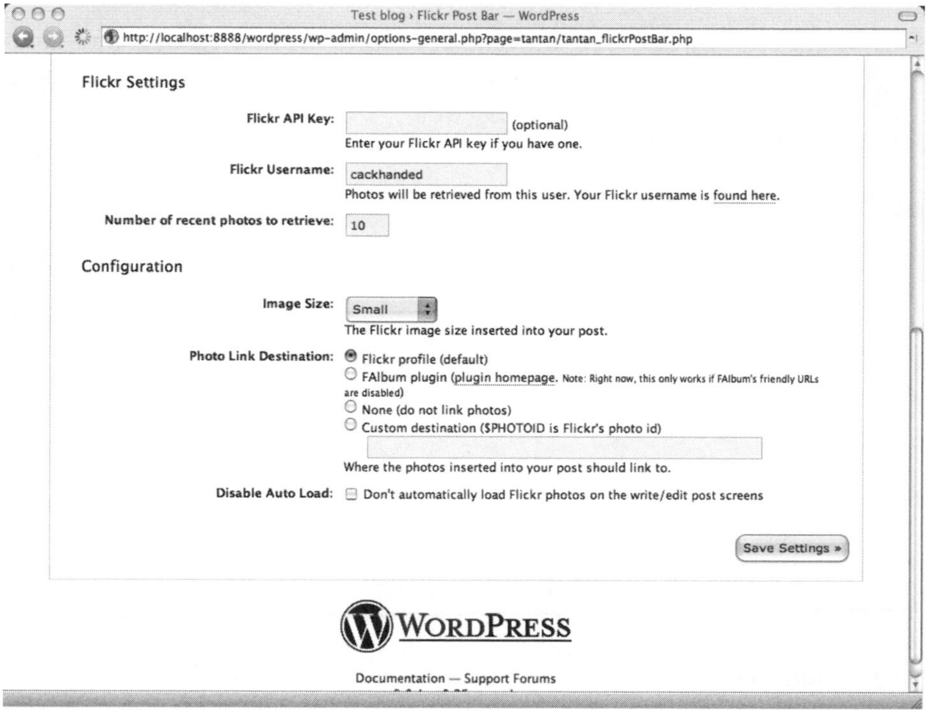

Figure 6-4. Configuring the "WP Flickr Post Bar" plug-in

The only thing that has to be entered here is your Flickr username. This may or may not be the same as your Yahoo! ID as Flickr allows you to create a different username for use on Flickr. You can change this within Flickr at http://flickr.com/account/prefs/ screenname/. You can also change things such as how many photos are retrieved by the plug-in when you compose a new post (use a smaller number if you are on dial-up or another slow Internet connection), the size of the photo to include in your post (most people use small—or medium if the photo is the only thing in the post), and where photos will go to when viewers click on them.

Now, whenever you go to write a new post, you will see the most recent photos from your Flickr account under the main text area (as seen in Figure 6-5), and you only need click on the photo you want to add it to your post. You can enter a tag to find matching photos if you want to find one that isn't in the most recent list. Easy.

127

Figure 6-5. The most recent photos from your Flickr account now appear when you write posts.

Show your most recent Flickr images

As an alternative to having to create a post to show off your images on Flickr, you can instead show a selection of all of your most recent images in the sidebar of your site. Go to http://eightface.com/wordpress/flickrrss/, download the zip file, and extract it to your plugins directory. Within the WordPress admin interface, select the Plugins tab and activate the flickrRSS plug-in. Then under the Options tab, choose flickrRSS to alter its settings (see Figure 6-6).

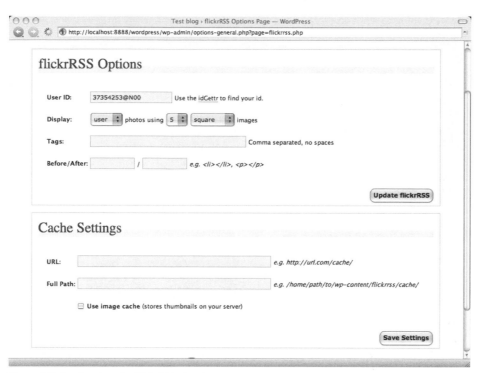

Figure 6-6. Configuring the flickrRSS plug-in

As with WP Flickr Post Bar, you need to tell this plug-in who you are on Flickr, but it wants this information in a more programmer-friendly way—the actual ID used by Flickr internally. You won't know what that is, so it's fortunate that this page contains a link to a site you can use to look it up. Click the idGettr link and enter the URL of your Flickr photos, and it will look up your ID. Copy and paste that into the flickrRSS configuration.

The other options are similar again—you can change how many photos to display (by default this is set to just 1, so you should change it to something more like 5) and of what size; and choose any tags you wish to use to find photos within your collection. You can also change the HTML that surrounds each image, which we'll look at in a minute. The last two options control keeping copies of the images from Flickr on your site. Although some people think this is a good idea, it's not necessary. Yahoo! has much more bandwidth than you, and will normally serve up the images much faster.

The next thing to do is to edit the file sidebar.php in your themes directory and add the following:

```
<h2>Recent flickr photos </h2>
<li>
  <?php get_flickrRSS(); ?>
</li>
```

Now reload your site. You should see your most recent photo(s) in the sidebar. But they're just smooshed together. So, go back to the options page for the plug-in, and in the Before/After options add <li> for before and </li> for after. Next, in the sidebar.php file, change <?php get_flickrRSS(); ?> to <ul><?php get_flickrRSS(); ?></ul>. Then, save and reload your site. Now they will be slightly better formatted, as seen in Figure 6-7.

Figure 6-7. Flickr images integrated into the sidebar

A gallery powered by Flickr

The last way we'll discuss here to display Flickr images in your site is a comprehensive plug-in called Flickr Photo Album (see Figure 6-8), which will take all of the sets (albums) you have created using Flickr and display them on your site instead. This is a very involved plug-in with a fair amount of configuration, but the end result is worth it if you want to have your images displayed on your own site rather than sending your visitors off to Flickr to see more.

Figure 6-8. Photo galleries on your own site, created, organized, and distributed entirely by Flickr

Start by downloading the plug-in at http://tantannoodles.com/toolkit/photo-album/ and unzipping it into your plugins directory. Then open the WordPress admin interface, bring up the Plugins tab, activate the Flickr Photo Album plug-in, and click configure.

This plug-in wants to use the Flickr API quite heavily, so you have to apply for a key in order to use it. Go to http://www.flickr.com/services/api/keys/apply/ to apply for a key. Fill in your name, email, and a brief description of what the key is to be used for. Once the key is granted (this happens immediately under normal circumstances), you can view the details at http://www.flickr.com/services/api/keys/.

Click Edit key details and change the authentication type (toward the bottom of the page) to desktop application. Save the changes, and then copy the API key and shared secret value into the configuration page of the Flickr Photo Album plug-in. This page should then reload, bringing in all sets you have created in Flickr. If you have several, this can take some time, so be patient.

Once they have all loaded, you can control where the galleries appear on your site, whether or not each group appears in your gallery, and more.

> At the very least you should select the option to hide photos you have marked private— because the images are being fetched from Flickr by the plug-in as if it were you, it has the ability to see your private photos. If you have marked them as private on Flickr, the chances are you would like them to remain private elsewhere as well.

Inserting videos with YouTube

YouTube (see Figure 6-9) is a prime example of social networking on the Internet. YouTube, on the face of it, is simple sharing of video clips online. But by enabling more community-like features, it encourages people to sign up, reply to videos with videos of their own, start conversations, and more. Due to this encouragement, YouTube quickly forged its place as the default location for video storage and sharing on the Web.

If you have video you wish to share on your site, it couldn't be easier. By signing up to YouTube, you can upload short (10 minutes or less) video clips from your computer or cell phone. Putting this video onto your site is also incredibly easy.

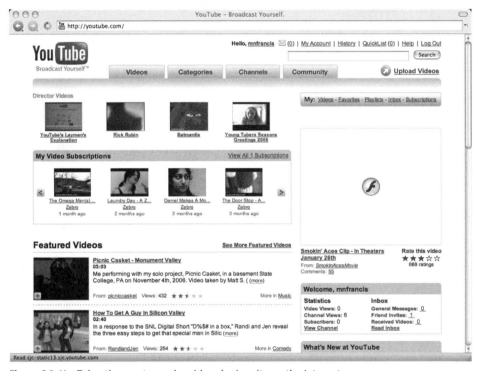

Figure 6-9. YouTube, the most popular video sharing site on the Internet

Visit http://www.robertbuzink.nl/journal/2006/11/23/youtube-brackets-wordpress-plugin/, download the YouTube Brackets plug-in, and extract the file to your plugins directory. There is no configuration for this plug-in. Simply navigate YouTube to the video you wish to share, and then copy the URL from your browser's location bar.

Create a new post within WordPress, and in the main text area type [youtube=, paste in the URL, and then add], like so:

```
[youtube=http://www.youtube.com/watch?v=D4l8n6c-TMs]
```

> *Make sure that there is no space between the brackets, the* youtube=, *and the URL; otherwise, this will appear as text in your post rather than the video appearing.*

Publish the post and then check your site (see Figure 6-10)—you should see the preview image of your video (this allows your visitors to choose whether or not to see the video—very important for users on dial-up or with very slow Internet connections).

Figure 6-10. A new post with a YouTube video attached

Adding music and podcasts with Odeo

Odeo (http://odeo.com/) is an audio-sharing site, which allows you to record, edit, and publish MP3 (the most common audio format) files. If your computer has a microphone attached, you can record audio directly to Odeo via their Studio (http://studio.odeo.com/create/studio—see Figure 6-11) without needing any software other than your web browser.

Figure 6-11. Odeo Studio allows you to record your own podcasts directly to their site without needing any other software.

Odeo also tracks how many times audio is listened to via the web site and, if you were to publish a podcast, how many subscribers (people wanting to be notified automatically when you publish new audio) you have.

Like YouTube, audio from Odeo is very simple to integrate into your site. First, download the Odeo plug-in from http://patrick.bloggles.info/2006/09/30/odeo-plugin/, unzip the file into your plugins directory, and activate it from the WordPress interface.

Create a new post within WordPress, and in the main text area type [odeo=, paste in the URL, and then add], like so:

```
[odeo= http://odeo.com/audio/2005850/view]
```

> *Again, make sure that there is no space between the brackets, the* odeo=, *and the URL; otherwise, this will appear as text in your post rather than the audio appearing.*

Publish the post, then check your site. You will have an audio player appearing in the post, as shown in Figure 6-12. The audio will not automatically play until the visitor to your site clicks the play button; only then will the audio start streaming so that they can hear it (as with YouTube, this is very important for users on dial-up or with very slow Internet connections).

Figure 6-12. A new post with audio from Odeo attached

Adding maps with Google Maps

When Google released their Maps product, they changed the way web sites were developed. Granted, other solutions that also offered very responsive interfaces were created beforehand, but backup by a major web company has made the idea of using a map that can be dragged around and loads the map data on demand mainstream-compatible. In its wake, other rich user interfaces have become more fashionable.

This section has several code examples in it. You will find these examples in the accompanying code download zip file for this book at http://www.friendsofed.com. *Don't get discouraged if some of the examples appear too advanced for you; there is no dark magic to adding maps to your page, and you don't need to know all that is shown here—we just added it to give you a slight glimpse under the hood of Google Maps.*

Google Maps has made it much easier to find places on the Web than its predecessors. Before Google Maps, having a map on a web site meant reloading the whole document every time visitors clicked a directional arrow (or zoom control) to move around the map. Google Maps simply replaces the map section and leaves the rest of the page as it was.

Furthermore, it allows visitors to drag the map around to navigate rather than just clicking arrows to move around. The other new feature Google Maps provides is the ability to swap plain maps and satellite photos, which has resulted in a lot of people spending hours trying to find oddly shaped buildings or their own house online. Figure 6-13 shows the different views of Google Maps in comparison.

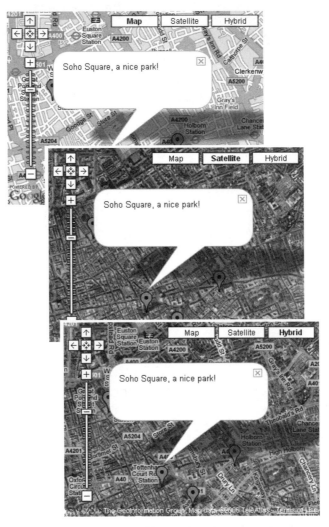

Figure 6-13. Google maps in different views: from top to bottom—as a map, as a satellite photograph, and as a hybrid view showing street names and other data on top of the photograph

Maps are a great visual aid to show people where to find you. A single map—even a static one—can bring people to you a lot quicker than long-winded explanations. Be aware, though, that not every one of your visitors will be able to use or see the map, so don't rely on it as the only means of describing where you can be found.

Before Google Maps, adding a map to your web site was a pain, and meant you had to spend a lot of money on royalties and in most cases had to link to a third-party server in a frame. Google Maps and its competitors make it easy to tell visitors where you are or where your next gig or exhibition is. As this chapter is about Google Maps, we won't go into more details about the competitors, but keeping your eyes open for other options like Yahoo! Maps (http://developer.yahoo.com/maps/) is always a good idea.

Start by getting your Google developer key

To use Google Maps, you need to sign up for a free developer key on the homepage: http://www.google.com/apis/maps/.

Make sure you read the terms and conditions and see what to avoid. There is not much you can do wrong, but as Google Maps is a free service, make sure you don't violate those terms and conditions.

Your key is connected to your domain and can only be used on that server. Keep that in mind when you're trying to test maps based on Google Maps on your local server. You'll find some code examples later in this chapter that use a key that works with a localhost; be sure to change this key to your real one when you upload the map documents to your server.

The lazy option: let others do the tricky work for you

The good news for you is that maps have fascinated developers ever since companies started making them available for the world to use. If you take a look at http://www.programmableweb.com (where developers can find APIs to play with and upload information about the mashups they've created with them), you will most certainly find mapping to be one of the most used tags and map APIs counting among the largest amount of mashups.

At the time we're writing this, Google Maps scores in the top position with 539 mashups, followed by Amazon's product search (an API you can make money with) and Yahoo! Maps. The popularity and creativity of mapping mashups is simply fascinating, and if you are interested check out all the things people come up with at http://www.programmableweb.com/api/GoogleMaps/mashups.

If you want to find out more about Google Maps, along with tips, tricks, and tools to automatically generate maps, go to "Google Maps Mania" at http://googlemapsmania.blogspot.com/.

The Online Map Maker

One amazingly easy tool listed at Google Maps Mania is the Map Maker by Richard Stephenson. The Map Maker can be found at http://mapmaker.donkeymagic.co.uk/ (shown in Figure 6-14) and allows you to create a map in a matter of minutes. The Map Maker even creates the code for you; all you need to do is save it as a file on your server.

6

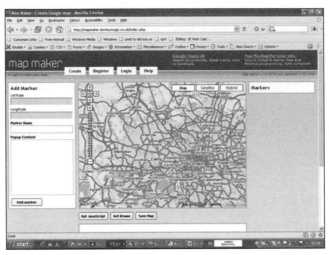

Figure 6-14. The Map Maker by Richard Stephenson makes creating your own map easy.

All you need to do to create some code you can save on your own server is to

1. Navigate to the location you want to show.
2. Add a marker by clicking on the location.
3. Enter a name for the marker and the content to show in the marker info bubble (you can use any HTML).
4. Click Get JavaScript and copy and paste the resulting HTML and JavaScript code in your editor.
5. Change the developer key to your own key.
6. Save the document and transfer it to your server.

You can add as many markers as you want to with the Map Maker, and if you sign up you can also store the final map. This allows you to make changes to the map at a later stage, and it also allows you to create a map that is hosted on the Map Maker server to include in your site by using an IFrame.

The GEOPress WordPress plug-in

If you are using WordPress more or less exclusively, then there is just no way around the GEOPress plug-in available at http://www.georss.org/trac/trac.cgi/wiki/GeoPress. Ravi Dronamraju, Mikel Maron, and Andrew Turner have done a tremendous job making it as easy as possible to add maps to your WordPress posts.

All you need to do is to download the plug-in, copy it to your plugins directory, and activate it. Once it's activated you'll see that the main WordPress menu now has an extra item called GeoPress, which you'll use to add your developer key to make the plug-in work. You will also find documentation explaining how to use the plug-in and a map to set your default locations.

Once activated, the plug-in extends the original blog post entry form with fields and a map to connect the blog post with a certain location on the planet. Once you've chosen the location, you can add the term INSERT_MAP into the post and this is where the map will appear. Figure 6-15 shows what that may look like.

Figure 6-15. The GEOPress plug-in makes it really easy to connect a blog post with a location and show a map in the post.

The DIY option: using the Google API

As handy as the Map Maker, the WordPress plug-in, and similar solutions by other developers are, they are normally limited to the most basic functionality of Google Maps. If you want to use maps more efficiently you'd need to use the API and write some JavaScript yourself. This goes beyond the normal scope of a blog or even a simple web site, but it may help you find any issues with the "out-of-the-box" solutions.

Displaying a map with a marker

Let's start simple: if you want to add a map with a marker to a document, all you need to do is add an element to host the map and call some of the API methods.

The first step, however, is to get information about which map you want to show and where to set the marker. The information you need is the latitude and the longitude coordinate of the address you want to show.

The easy option is to use the Map Maker and double-click where you want the map to center and then set a marker. You will then get both values displayed in the appropriate form fields, and you can simply copy and paste them as shown in Figure 6-16.

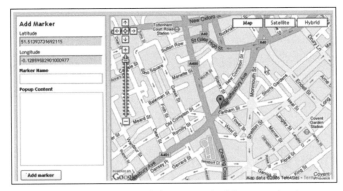

Figure 6-16. Navigating around the map and adding a marker in Map Maker gives you the latitude and longitude values of the location you want to show.

Another simple solution is to enter the postal code or other information in Google Maps and click the Link to this page link, as shown in Figure 6-17.

Google Maps will change the browser URL to something like this:

```
http://maps.google.com/maps?f=q&hl=en&q=WC2H+8AD&ie=UTF8& ➥
z=16&ll=51.514859,-0.128381&spn=0.004967,0.021629&om=1&iwloc=A
```

The important bits of data to extract from this are the z value, which is the current zoom level of the map, and the ll value, which represents the latitude and longitude. This way of retrieving the data is more versatile but also less precise than using the official postal code to get access to latitude and longitude conversion tables (which cost money), so don't get confused when your end result varies a bit from the map you see in Google Maps.

Figure 6-17. Activating the Link to this page link in Google Maps gives you all the information you need to replicate the current map in the resulting URL.

With this information at hand, adding a Google map to an HTML document is as easy as including the Maps API and writing a few lines of JavaScript:

```
<!DOCTYPE HTML PUBLIC "-//W3C//DTD HTML 4.01//EN" ➥
"http://www.w3.org/TR/html4/strict.dtd">
<html dir="ltr" lang="en">
<head>
  <meta http-equiv="Content-Type" content="text/html; charset=utf-8">
  <title>A Google MAp with a Marker</title>
  <style type="text/css">
    *{
      margin:0;
      padding:0;
    }
    body{
      font-family:arial,sans-serif;
    }
    #map{
      width:400px;
      height:300px;
    }
  </style>
```

```
    <script src="http://maps.google.com/maps?file=api&amp;v=2&amp;➡
key=[YOUR KEY]" type="text/javascript"></script>
    <script type="text/javascript">
      function addMap() {
        if (GBrowserIsCompatible()) {
          var map = new GMap2(document.getElementById("map"));
          map.addControl(new GSmallMapControl());
          map.addControl(new GMapTypeControl());
          map.addControl(new GScaleControl());
          var point=new GLatLng(51.51393731692115,-0.12859582901000977);
          map.setCenter(point,16);
          var marker = new GMarker(point);
          map.addOverlay(marker);
          GEvent.addListener(marker, 'click', function(){
            map.openInfoWindowHtml(point, 'This is where I work');
          });
        }
      }
      window.onload = addMap;
      window.onunload = GUnload;
    </script>
  </head>
  <body>
    <div id="map"></div>
  </body>
</html>
```

Notice that you need to set a width and height to the map element in CSS to make it display as a map. Let's go through the code bit by bit to see what is happening:

```
    <script src="http://maps.google.com/maps?file=api&amp;v=2&amp;key=➡
ABQIAAAAijZqBZczrowoXZC1tt9iRT2yXp_ZAY8_ufC3CFXhHIE1Nvw➡
kxQQBCaF1R_k1GBJV5uDLhAKaTePyQ" type="text/javascript">➡
    </script>
```

This line of code retrieves the Maps API from the Google server and makes it available to you. The key used here is one that works on your local server.

```
    <script type="text/javascript">
      function addMap() {
        if (GBrowserIsCompatible()) {
```

The addMap() function starts with an if condition that tests whether the browser is capable of supporting Google Maps.

```
var map = new GMap2(document.getElementById("map"));
map.addControl(new GSmallMapControl());
map.addControl(new GMapTypeControl());
map.addControl(new GScaleControl());
```

You then define a new map by calling the GMap2() method of the Maps API and tell it which page element to turn into a map. In this case, this is the <div> with the id map. You add several controls to the map to allow the visitor to navigate around it.

```
var point = new GLatLng( 51.51393731692115,➡
    -0.12859582901000977 );
map.setCenter(point,16);
```

You then define a new point on the map with the latitude and longitude coordinates you retrieved from Google Maps. You define this point as the center of the map by using the setCenter() directive and set the zoom level as a second parameter. This takes care of the map—it would already display. However, you also want to have a marker in the center.

```
var marker = new GMarker(point);
map.addOverlay(marker);
GEvent.addListener(marker, 'click', function(){
  map.openInfoWindowHtml(point, 'This is where I work');
});
```

You define a new marker with the point as its location on the map and add it to the map with the addOverlay() directive. You then add something called a *listener*, which is an instruction to tell the map what to do if the user reacts with the marker. In this case you call a new function when the marker is clicked that shows an information window above the point that states "This is where I work."

```
      }
    }
    window.onload = addMap;
    window.onunload = GUnload;
  </script>
```

You tell the browser to execute the function addMap() when the window has finished loading and to call GUnload() when the window gets closed. The latter is necessary to allow Google Maps to clean up after itself, as maps are a rather complex interface and can cause some browsers to use up a lot of memory and slow down the computer.

If all went well, you will see the same map as shown in Figure 6-18.

6

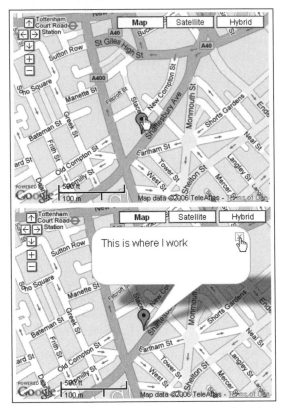

Figure 6-18. A Google map showing a message when the visitor clicks a marker

A more accessible alternative

This is pretty cool, but the problem is that you expect JavaScript to be available to convey information on how to contact you. This is not the safest of options, and it also has the problem that search engines won't find that information.

The easiest workaround is to add information inside the <div> with the id map that gets replaced once the real map can be applied. However, because you want to display something inside the marker pop-up, wouldn't it make more sense to reuse data that is already in the document?

If you use microformats to define an address as an hCard, you have an optional format called geo that defines where this address is located on the planet as latitude and longitude. The final address with microformats information could, for example, look like this:

```
<div id="address" class="vcard">
  <span class="given-name">Christian</span>
  <span class="family-name">Heilmann</span>
```

```
    <div class="organization-name">Yahoo! UK Ltd</div>
    <div class="street-address">125 Shaftesbury Avenue</div>
    <div class="locality">London</div>
    <div class="postal-code">WC2H 8AD</div>
    <span class="geo">
      <span class="latitude">51.513577</span>,
      <span class="longitude">-0.12866</span>
    </span>
  </div>
```

> If you haven't heard anything about microformats yet, go to http://www.
> microformats.org to learn what benefits this very easy technique can provide
> you with. There is also a great no-nonsense introduction to microformats
> available at http://www.digital-web.com/articles/microformats_primer/.
> In essence, microformats mean that by adding some simple HTML classes
> you can make your web site indexable by other technology and people can,
> for example, add your contact data to their email clients without having to
> copy and paste the information.

6

Together with some clever JavaScript, you can reuse this information to replace the
address with a map showing the rest of the information in a marker pop-up.

```javascript
function addMap() {
  if (GBrowserIsCompatible()) {
    var ad = document.getElementById('address');
    var store = ad.innerHTML;
    var mapContainer = document.createElement('div');
    mapContainer.id = 'map';
    ad.parentNode.insertBefore(mapContainer,ad);
    var map = new GMap2(mapContainer);
    map.addControl(new GSmallMapControl());
    map.addControl(new GMapTypeControl());
    map.addControl(new GScaleControl());
    var elms = ad.getElementsByTagName('*');
    for( var i=0; i<elms.length; i++){
      if(elms[i].className == 'latitude'){
        var lat = elms[i].firstChild.nodeValue;
      }
      if(elms[i].className == 'longitude'){
        var lon = elms[i].firstChild.nodeValue;
      }
    }
    var point = new GLatLng(lat, lon);
    map.setCenter(point, 16);
    var marker = new GMarker(point);
```

```
      map.addOverlay(marker);
      GEvent.addListener(marker, 'click', function(){
        map.openInfoWindowHtml(point,store);
      });
      ad.style.display='none';
    }
  }
  window.onload=addMap;
  window.onunload=GUnload;
```

The changes in code are marked in bold. They don't really have much to do with the Maps API, and here is a quick explanation of what the code does in addition to the earlier example:

1. You tell the browser to take the element with the id address, read its contents, and keep a copy of it in the variable store.

2. You create a new <div> element, give it the id map, and add it to the document before the address.

3. You then add the map, like before.

4. You go through all of the elements contained in the address element and test whether they have a class name of latitude or longitude. If either is the case, you store that data in the appropriate variable.

5. You define the map center, add a marker, and show the content of the address element you kept in the first step when the visitor clicks the marker.

6. You then hide the address by setting its style display to none.

Figure 6-19 shows how this example looks with JavaScript available and without it. Notice that the geo data was hidden with CSS as it does not make sense to a human visitor.

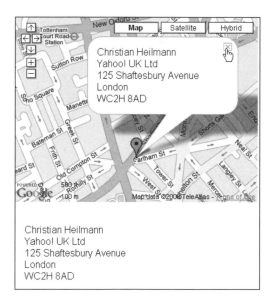

Figure 6-19. By reusing real document content, you can keep the address accessible to all and turn it into a map only when the browser allows it.

Using XML for marker data

Adding each marker by hand can become rather tedious and make the code very verbose. Therefore, if you have a lot of markers to add to a certain map, it might be a good idea to have the marker and HTML data someplace other than the JavaScript. This also makes maintenance a lot easier. To this end, the Google Maps API provides a special method that allows you to keep all the data in an external XML file.

You can, for example, use the latitude and longitude values as attributes and the HTML content of the pop-up as a child element:

```xml
<?xml version="1.0" encoding="utf-8"?>
<markers>
  <marker lat="51.513469937485795" lng="-0.1279306411743164"➥
label="Work">
    <infowindow><![CDATA[
      The <a href="http://uk.yahoo.com">Yahoo!</a> office.
    ]]></infowindow>
  </marker>
  <marker lat="51.5212945726301" lng="-0.1391315460205078"➥
label="Computer Fair">
    <infowindow><![CDATA[
      Every Saturday there's a computer fair here,<br />
      where you can buy all kind of stuff very cheap.
    ]]></infowindow>
  </marker>
  <marker lat="51.516808256819814" lng="-0.12235164642333984"➥
label="Pancake House">
    <infowindow><![CDATA[
      My old Dutch, a pancake house!
    ]]></infowindow>
  </marker>
  <marker lat="51.50965060011969" lng="-0.12599945068359375"➥
label="Mousetrap">
    <infowindow><![CDATA[
      This is where Agatha Christie's "The Mouse Trap"<br />
      is being performed, now for 53 years in a row!
    ]]></infowindow>
  </marker>
  <marker lat="51.509249951770364" lng="-0.13338088989257812"➥
label="Wagamama">
    <infowindow><![CDATA[
      Wagamama, a good and cheap Japanese restaurant.
    ]]></infowindow>
  </marker>
```

6

```
    <marker lat="51.51508571459469" lng="-0.13200759887695312"➡
label="Soho Square">
   <infowindow><![CDATA[
     Soho Square, a nice park!
   ]]></infowindow>
 </marker>
</markers>
```

The JavaScript to pull in this data—saved as locationdata.xml—is a bit more complex, but let's quickly go through it. You start with a reusable addLoadEvent() function. This function allows you to make the browser call several functions when the window has loaded. In this case, you call a function called loadMap() and another one called addPoints().

```
var map;
function addLoadEvent(func) {
  var oldonload = window.onload;
  if (typeof window.onload != 'function'){
    window.onload = func
  } else {
    window.onload = function() {
      oldonload();
      func();
    }
  }
}
addLoadEvent(loadMap);
addLoadEvent(addPoints);
```

The loadMap() function does nothing new; all it does is create a new map and center it at a certain position.

```
function loadMap() {
  map = new GMap2(document.getElementById("map"));
  map.addControl(new GLargeMapControl());
  map.addControl(new GMapTypeControl());
  map.setCenter(new GLatLng( 51.51508571459469,➡
-0.13200759887695312), 14);
  map.setMapType(G_MAP_TYPE);
}
```

The addPoints() function is a bit trickier. First, it initiates a new XML request—a function the Google Maps API gives you. It loads the file locationdata.xml and fires off a new function when the file was loaded successfully (which means that its readyState property is 4).

```
        function addPoints() {
          var request = GXmlHttp.create();
          request.open("GET", "locationdata.xml", true);
          request.onreadystatechange = function() {
            if (request.readyState == 4) {
```

You then take the XML data that was loaded, retrieve all <marker> elements, and loop over them.

```
            var xmlDoc = request.responseXML;
            var markers = xmlDoc.documentElement.getElementsByTagName(➥
        "marker");
            for (var i = 0; i < markers.length; i++) {
```

You read the lat and lng properties, which are strings of characters, and turn them into numbers using parseFloat(). You retrieve the information window HTML by using the gXML.value() method of the Google Maps API.

```
              var lat = parseFloat(markers[i].getAttribute("lat"));
              var lng = parseFloat(markers[i].getAttribute("lng"));
              var html = GXml.value(markers[i].getElementsByTagName(➥
        "infowindow")[0]);
```

You create a new map point with that data, and call the createMarker() function with the point and the HTML as parameters. This function returns a new marker object that you can add to the map as an overlay—much as we did in the earlier examples. All you need to do then is send the request to get the XML data.

```
              var point = new GLatLng(lat,lng);
              var marker = createMarker(point, html);
              map.addOverlay(marker);
            }
          }
        }
        request.send(null);
      }
```

The createMarker() function creates a new marker, adds a listener to show the HTML when the visitor clicks the marker, and sends it back to the initial function.

```
        function createMarker(point,html) {
          var marker = new GMarker(point);
          GEvent.addListener(marker, "click", function() {
            marker.openInfoWindowHtml(html);
          });
          return marker;
        }
```

6

Together with the XML data earlier, this function generates a map with a lot of markers with different information attached to them, as shown in Figure 6-20.

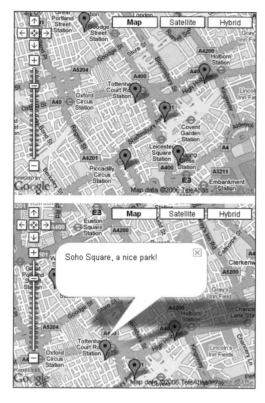

Figure 6-20. A map with a lot of markers retrieved from an XML document

There is a lot more to Google Maps than we've covered here, but with the API constantly changing and getting extended, your best bet is to keep up to date with the URLs provided in the beginning of this chapter and use the tools described here.

> *Maps are great, but it is also easy to get too excited about them. Not all your blog posts need geolocations, and on slow connections, maps can be more of an annoyance than a great feature.*

Summary

In this chapter we showed you how to easily add various types of media to your site to liven it up and to help your visitors better understand the context of the page. Rich media sites can require your visitors to have good Internet connections (or a lot of patience), so you need to be careful and avoid overdoing things. Nevertheless, keep in mind that your site will be more memorable to people if you make effective use of multimedia.

7 PROMOTING YOUR CONTENT

By Chris Heilmann and Norm Francis

Now that your site is ready to rock and roll, it is about time to get known and allow people to find you. There are several good practices to help you make sure search engines find your site, but there is no silver bullet.

Search engine optimization (SEO) is a vast field and also a large industry. Search engines battle spammers and SEO experts that try to play the systems daily, and it is rather amazing to what level of detail people go to promote web content.

SEO is a full-time job and you have to keep up with a lot of changes and be quick on your toes to avoid tricks that were amazing a month ago but might get you banned from search engine indexing now. If you are thinking about SEO for your sites, make sure you scrutinize the companies that offer to promote your site for you—the number of black sheep among the SEO crowd is staggering and some quick-win solutions can bite you back some months down the line.

The ideas expressed in this chapter are basic tips and tricks to make your site indexable and search engine friendly. They will not result in immediate results, such as having a top spot on Google, but in time they will drive people to your site. As an example of how effective they are, you can enter "unobtrusive" or "ugly yellow form fields" in Google and find two of Chris's posts on the top spot—the latter being a real shock when he discovered that it ranked that high since he didn't promote it at all.

Basic SEO for your site

There are many aspects of web development that affect search engines, and they change constantly. However, there are some aspects that have always made it easier for your site to get recognized and indexed by search engines:

- A meaningful page title with relevant keywords
- Relevant textual content in the document as early as possible
- A good page structure including weighed headings (h1 to h6, with h1 being the main document title—not the sitewide branding)
- Alternative text for images and other media (sound, video, Flash movies)
- New content added to the site all the time
- A page description in a meta-tag (this is not relevant for search engines themselves any longer, but it will be displayed after your link in some search engine results)
- Links from other sites pointing to this page and links from this page linking to other sites

The first six points are technical and content changes that are completely under your control. The last one, however, needs a bit of work. More on that in the rest of the chapter, but for now let's concentrate on some quick examples for page titles and headings.

Your page title is probably the most important part of the document in terms of SEO. It also is very important for visitors—it is not only shown on their browser window but also becomes the title of a bookmark when they add your site to their browser or their favorite social bookmarking tool.

Say you have a band and you want to write about a concert you gave. At the spur of the moment you might be inclined to go for something like

We so rocked the house last Saturday!

This might be true but doesn't help anyone who is not in the know about your latest movements and what you do. However, a page title that tells the where, when, and what allows search engines to bring this information to people. Here's an example:

"The Good Guys" rocked the Marquis in Camden Town, London on 26 April 2000

In there you have the name of your band (The Good Guys), the name of a club (Marquis), a location (Camden Town, London), and the date it happened, which is less ambiguous than last Saturday!.

There is a better way of advertising events on the Web and we will come back to that toward the end of the chapter. For now just remember that all of these pieces of information are likely to be searched for on the Web, and your site might show up on the result pages of these searches because you gave this information in the page title.

The same applies to headings of your document and alternative text of images. When writing longer passages it is very tempting to separate text with headings that are connected to the immediate content around them. A heading like "But what if that is not possible?" may be a nice poetic device when you write a book or a print article, but for the Web other rules apply that affect both SEO and accessibility:

- **Headings should make sense out of context and should be properly nested**: This means you start with an h1 (and use only one for the document), go to an h2, h3, h4, back to another h3, and so on. Don't start with an h5 and return to an h1.

- **Links should make sense out of context**: Assistive technology such as screen readers and search engines read links independently of the text. Therefore, you should avoid using "click here" links, as there is no "here" for a blind visitor or a search engine. Instead use keywords in the links pointing to third-party and internal sites. Instead of a To see photos of us rocking click here, it is better to use something like Stephen shot lots of photos of the Marquis gig and we rocked.

- **Alternative text of images should explain what the purpose of the image is, not how it looks**: The biggest problem with alternative text on images (added via the alt attribute) is that Internet Explorer shows them as tooltips when you hover your mouse over the image. This continuously leads designers to add information to an image with the alt attribute rather than provide a replacement for it. The alternative text of a man playing guitar should not be something like this guy rocks but something like Stephen Fields playing a guitar solo.

These are just some simple tricks, and there is a lot more you could do. The practical upshot of sticking to these guidelines is that you do something both for the accessibility of your site and for SEO. This also means that search engine maintainers are not likely to punish you for trying to play the engine, which can easily happen with other SEO tricks you find on the Web.

7

Blog search engines and aggregators

In the world of blogging—and as we use WordPress here we do actually blog—things work a bit differently than on the rest of the Web. Sure, Google indexes and brings up search results from blogs, but whether that makes sense or not is disputed. Not everybody wants information from personal blogs, and a lot of these cluttering the search results pages can be annoying. Therefore, a lot of blogs will automatically add an attribute to all links called `rel="nofollow"`, which tells search engines that they shouldn't take these links in.

So how do blog posts become famous and get around? For this, you have blog search engines or aggregators such as `http://www.technorati.com` or `http://www.bloglines.com`. These are not normal search engines insofar as they don't randomly send search spider programs out to index the Web but instead wait until you tell them to recognize your blog and inform them every time there is an update.

If you sign up for Technorati at `http://www.technorati.com/signup/`, for example, you have an option stating, "I have a blog and would like to claim it now," which allows you to enter information about your blog, what you are likely to talk about, and who you are.

Automatically telling blog search engines about updates

Once claimed, you can tell the blog search engines every time you enter a new post by pinging them. Technorati's ping page can be found at `http://www.technorati.com/ping`, which is great, but going there every time you update your site can become quite annoying, which is why there is a way to automate the process.

If you go to your WordPress installation admin tool and select Options and then Writing, you'll find a text box at the bottom of the form (shown in Figure 7-1) that allows you to enter URLs of automatic pinging services. You can find a comprehensive list of available services on the WordPress codex page at `http://codex.wordpress.org/Update_Services`.

Figure 7-1. WordPress allows you to automatically tell blog search engines that you have updated your content.

While most blog search engines have their own ping service, it might be a lot easier to use one of the services that automatically notify a lot of other sites. Probably the most known

is Ping-o-Matic at http://pingomatic.com/ but a lot more are listed at http://www.
quickonlinetips.com/archives/2005/09/one-click-multiple-blog-services-pinging.
Figure 7-2 shows you the options Ping-o-Matic offers for notifying services about your
blog updates.

Figure 7-2. Services such as pingomatic.com make it easy to tell a lot
of blog search engines about updates in one single ping.

Tagging—the other way to get found

Currently most widely known in the world of blogging, tagging is another way to promote
content or make it easy to find again. Originally bloggers started adding arbitrary keywords
to their blog posts in order to tell people what the blog post was about without actually
having to use these words in the text and rely on a search engine to find them. Adding a
rel attribute of tag to any link element makes these keywords a tag. Blog search engines
list your post entry when users look for the same tag—for example:

```
<a href="http://technorati.com/tag/unobtrusive" ➥
rel="tag">unobtrusive</a>,
<a href="http://technorati.com/tag/ebooks" rel="tag">ebooks</a>
```

When you set up WordPress, the categories you define are converted into tags, but you
may want to add extra tags to certain blog posts. To do that you can simply add the rel
attribute yourself, but it is a lot easier with the SimpleTags WordPress plug-in available at
http://www.broobles.com/scripts/simpletags/.

157

Once you have the plug-in installed, you can add tags inside brackets to any blog post and they will be converted to tags linking to the Technorati tag search facility. Figure 7-3 shows how this looks on our blog.

Figure 7-3. Adding extra tags linking to Technorati is easy with the SimpleTags plug-in for WordPress.

The great thing about tags in comparison to normal search-and-find scenarios is that humans and not machines define what is searchable and what to look for. It is a much more accurate way of finding and offering information on the Web than any automated search tool.

Improving the page search

Once you have readers and visitors on your site, it would be good to keep them there. The most important factor when considering this is to allow them to find other relevant and interesting content on your site. Luckily enough, WordPress helps you there with built-in search functionality that allows your readers to find out more. However, the search is not clever; it only indexes the blog posts, while some of the better information may be in pages you developed or even in comments readers wrote on your site.

There is a workaround for that in the form of a plug-in called Search Reloaded by Denis de Bernardy available at http://www.semiologic.com/software/search-reloaded/. Once installed, this plug-in will extend the page search to find everything inside WordPress, customizable in a panel in your admin options and shown in Figure 7-4.

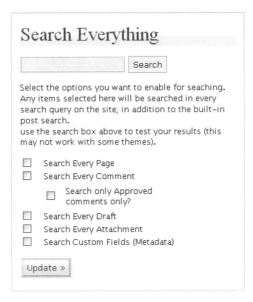

Figure 7-4. The Search Reloaded plug-in allows you to determine what should be indexed by the WordPress search.

This, however, checks only what is inside WordPress, and it could be that you have a lot more files on your server that you might want to enable your visitors to search for.

Adding a web search option with Yahoo!

The good news about adding a web search to your site is that if you look at the developer section of Yahoo! at http://developer.yahoo.com you'll find that almost any of the searches possible on their site are also available as an API to build your own search tools, as shown in Figure 7-5.

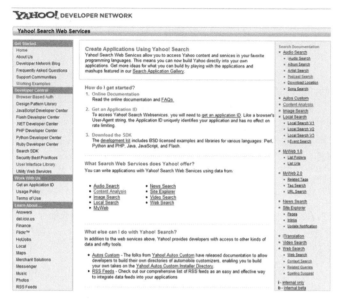

Figure 7-5. Yahoo! offers almost all of their search options as APIs to use on your own pages.

Reproduced with permission of Yahoo! Inc. © 2007 by Yahoo! Inc. YAHOO! and the YAHOO! logo are trademarks of Yahoo! Inc.

The number of offers on the page is amazing and new options are added constantly. You could use any of these APIs and build your own search functionality as explained in Chapter 5, but as you might have guessed, someone already has done this work for you.

The Yahoo! Search plug-in, available at http://www.robinsonhouse.com/2005/09/22/wordpress-yahoo-search-plugin/ allows you to add a search bar that returns web search results from Yahoo! inside your WordPress blog. After installing the plug-in, you have an extra section in the options menu called Yahoo! Search that allows you to define the web location you want to display search results for, how many results per page, which data format, and which language. You can also add your own developer ID as shown in Chapter 5. Notice that by default the plug-in will show results from the blog location, but you can actually show results from any web site out there.

In order to make the search form show up, simply add one line of code to the template where you want it to appear:

```php
<?php yahooSearchForm(); ?>
```

You can edit the template inside the editor of WordPress by choosing Presentation and opening the current template in the Theme editor. For example, if you want the search form to appear below the content, select the Main Index Template from the menu on the right and add it before the navigation DIV. This would show a search form below the main content that will display search results when the visitor searched for something inside your page, as shown in Figure 7-6.

Figure 7-6. The Yahoo! Search plug-in allows you to show web search results inside your page.

Reproduced with permission of Yahoo! Inc. © 2007 by Yahoo! Inc. YAHOO! and the YAHOO! logo are trademarks of Yahoo! Inc.

Many more search APIs are available, and there are plug-ins for almost any of the searches Yahoo! offers, including Flickr, del.icio.us, HotJobs, video, and audio. Third-party search results tend to be a bit older, though, as search engines need time to index, archive, and analyze your blog before they show your content. The WordPress internal search, however, is instantaneous.

Cross-linking with the attention services

Optimizing the content of your HTML, using proper headers and titles, is one way to get search engines to sit up and pay attention. However, the number and quality of links is one of the most important factors in the way the search engines calculate how relevant and authoritative a page is. As the title and headers are the most important parts of the page, so the hyperlink is the most important part of the entire Web.

The revolution in search that was pioneered by Google in the late 1990s and early 2000s was based on the concept that the relationships expressed between sites was more important than the content of the site itself—that as more sites linked to a specific page or site, that site was deemed to be more valid and more relevant.

For your site this means that cooperating with systems that will promote links both to and from your site will increase the perceived relevancy of your site. The more inbound links from trusted sources you have, the better.

Sites that are used to bookmark or otherwise register people's attention on the Web—such as Yahoo!'s del.icio.us and the independent sites such as Digg, reddit, and ma.gnolia—can be valuable resources of links. Furthermore, by participating in these systems, you ensure that your content can also easily be found by the users of these systems as well as by search engines.

Showing your attention

Inbound links are all well and good for you, but part of participating in these attention systems is also the outbound links, the things you think are important. It is worth being an active contributor more than a passive consumer, especially if you want to be noticed. So we'll integrate the pages on the Web that you think are important with the other content of your site.

Open your web browser, go to `http://del.icio.us/`, and click the register link to create an account (see Figure 7-7).

> *Although the del.icio.us registration page asks for more information, all you actually need to provide is a username, a password, and the text in the image to verify that you are a human rather than a spam program.*

Figure 7-7. The homepage of the social bookmarking site del.icio.us

After this, you will be prompted to install a toolbar or "bookmarklet" in order to make adding new bookmarks to del.icio.us easier—the actual suggestion will differ depending on the browser you use.

From now on, when you find a page on the Internet interesting, you should hit the button you were provided with to tag or post the page to your set of bookmarks on del.icio.us. This will bring up a page on the del.icio.us site for you to enter more information about what you are bookmarking, either for later reference or simply to help you find it again.

For every page you bookmark, you can enter a short description of the page, a longer set of notes about the page, and a set of tags. Tags are merely keywords that describe the page and help you to look up the page again later. Tags also help other people find pages you have bookmarked on the same subjects as they are interested in. As an example, any-one paying attention to the tag wikipedia to find new and interesting pages on Wikipedia will find the bookmark added in Figure 7-8 about the game Rock, Paper, Scissors. The rea-son is that we added wikipedia as a tag.

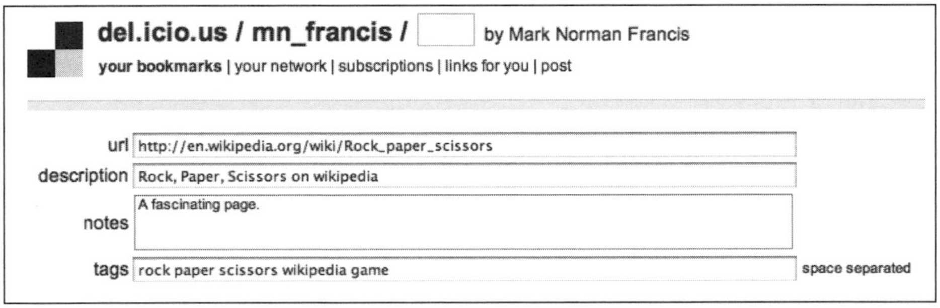

Figure 7-8. Entering a new bookmark in del.icio.us—in this case a page from Wikipedia

Now that you have bookmarked a few sites or pages that you find interesting with del.icio.us, you can integrate these bookmarks as links into your site. There are several plug-ins for WordPress that will fetch bookmarks and display them, but we will use one called Delicious Cached++—the advantage of this is that it keeps a copy of your links within your WordPress, which reduces the load on del.icio.us itself (and means you can pat yourself on the back for not wasting Internet bandwidth).

Fetch the zip file using the download link on http://weblog.jcraveiro.com/projectos/delicious-cached-pp/. Extract the one PHP file and copy it to the plugins directory C:\...\wp-content\plugins (or /Applications/MAMP/htdocs/wordpress/wp-content/plugins on the Mac). Then open the plugins page of the WordPress interface at http://localhost/wordpress/wp-admin/plugins.php (or http://localhost:8888/wordpress/wp-admin/plugins.php on the Mac). If everything has worked correctly, you should see a listing for Delicious Cached++. Click the activate link on that row.

Now edit the file sidebar.php in the wp-content/themes/default directory (if you are not using the default theme, you can temporarily change back to it for this section—visit http://localhost/worldpress/wp-admin/themes.php, or http://localhost:8888/wordpress/wp-admin/themse.php on the Mac).

7

In the file, find these few lines:

```
<li><h2>Categories</h2>
  <ul>
    <?php wp_list_cats('sort_column=name&optioncount=1& ➥
hierarchical=0'); ?>
  </ul>
</li>
```

Add the following directly after it:

```
<li><h2>Recent del.icio.us links</h2>
  <ul>
    <?php delicious_pp('XXX'); ?>
  </ul>
</li>
```

but substitute your del.icio.us account username for the XXX. Reload your site and you should now see a new list of links in your most recently added bookmarks.

If you wish to include more information, or alter the way links are presented, you can. For example, changing the delicious_pp('XXX'); call to

```
<?php delicious_pp( 'XXX', 3, 1, 5 ); ?>
```

will alter the output to use only the most recent three bookmarks, include the description after the link, and reveal up to five of the tags you used with the bookmark.

The full list of options you can give the delicious plug-in are

- 'mn_francis': The del.icio.us user ID your bookmarks are stored under. This must be surrounded with single or double quotes, as shown (in fact, all but the numerical properties need to be surrounded by quotes).
- 10: The number of bookmarks to show.
- 0: Do not display the notes associated with the bookmark, or use 1 to show them.
- 5: The number of tags to display with each bookmark.
- 'link:': The text to show before each item.
- 'added by me': The text to show after each item.
- 'more:': The text to show before the notes.
- '(description)': The text to show after the notes.
- 'Tags:': The text to show before any tags.
- ',': The text to place between tags.
- '.': The text to place after the tags.

You can use as many or as few of the extra options as you like, but the only required option is the user ID. If you use more than one option, you must separate them with commas. You cannot skip options (you can't use the option to control the number of tags shown without also using the number of bookmarks and the 0 or 1 setting to decide whether or not to display the notes). The results of using the plug-in are shown in Figure 7-9.

Figure 7-9. Integrating some del.icio.us links into the right-hand column of the default WordPress theme

Encouraging others to bookmark you

It is quite simple to encourage others to bookmark your posts on del.icio.us. Within the wp-content/themes/default directory, edit the file single.php. Find line 18, which should contain

```
<?php link_pages('<p><strong>Pages:</strong> ', '</p>', 'number'); ?>
```

On the next line after this, add the following code:

```
<p> Post to: <a href="http://del.icio.us/post?url=<?php
the_permalink(); ➥
 ?>&title=
<?php the_title() ?>">del.icio.us</a>. </p>
```

Then go to any individual post on your WordPress site. You should see Post to: del.icio.us. after the text of the post.

This allows any visitor to your site (or you, for that matter) to easily bookmark an individual post within del.icio.us. It also serves as a mental trigger for the action of bookmarking and could help you receive more bookmarks than you might get otherwise.

Alternatives to del.icio.us

We have covered how to integrate your del.icio.us bookmarks into your site. There are many, many alternative bookmarking sites on the Internet, all with varying feature sets. Two of the more popular ones are Digg and ma.gnolia.

If you would like to encourage the users of digg.com, you can download and install the DiggClick plug-in from http://opensolaris.biz/archives/diggclick/. When installed and activated, this plug-in will place a suitably styled button at the start of each post that will say how many *diggs* (times read/recommended by Digg users) the post has received, and allows anyone reading the article to "digg" it themselves.

If you would prefer to use the ma.gnolia.com bookmarking service, you can download and install a plug-in from http://www.barryprice.co.uk/archives/2006/08/17/magnolia-wordpress-plugin-12/—which behaves in a similar fashion to the del.icio.us plug-in mentioned earlier.

> *While it is possible to include 5, 10, 15, or more* bookmark this in… *links or buttons on your articles, it is probably going to alienate more readers than it serves. It is best to stick to just one or two bookmarking services, and ones that you personally also use.*

Promoting your events with Upcoming.org

Upcoming.org is a social events calendar site (as shown in Figure 7-10.) Anyone can enter details of an event they know about or are attending, and this makes it easy for people to find out what their friends are planning to do in the future. It is also a great resource for finding music gigs, techy events, and other get-togethers in your area.

> *Signing up on Upcoming is more restrictive than del.icio.us, in that you must have a valid email address—a confirmation email is sent to it that activates your upcoming account.*

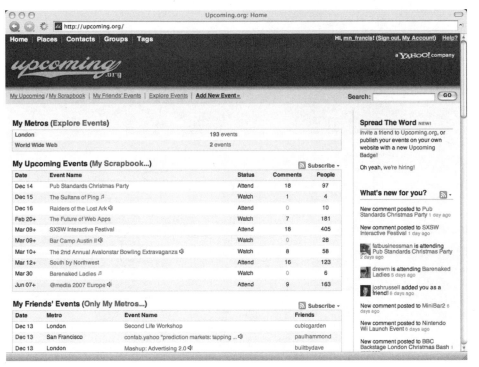

Figure 7-10. Upcoming.org, the social events calendar on the Web

By finding the area you live in (called a metro in Upcoming), you can browse for events that you might want to go to. After finding some, and indicating your intention using either the I'm attending or I'm watching button on the event's page, or by creating some new events of your own, you can then extract your personal list of events.

Upcoming makes this quite easy by providing a badge that you can add to your web site. Visit http://upcoming.org/badge/ in your browser after signing into Upcoming. This will walk you through how you want to present your badge and the level of detail you want in it. At the end, you will be presented with some code to copy and paste into your site.

Edit the file sidebar.php in C:\...\wp-content\themes\classic (or /Applications/ MAMP/htdocs/wordpress/wp-content/themes/classic on the Mac) and find line 41, which should contain the code

```
<?php wp_list_pages('title_li=<h2>Pages</h2>' ); ?>
```

Directly after this paste in the text from Upcoming, save the file, and reload your site. You should see your list of events, as shown in Figure 7-11.

Figure 7-11. Upcoming.org events integrated into your example WordPress site

The advantage, however, of using Upcoming over simply creating a post in your site (as was illustrated at the start of the chapter) is twofold. Existing users of Upcoming are much more likely to find your events within Upcoming itself than they are to find it via your site or a web search. Also, Upcoming, by its very nature, encourages word of mouth for future events. Once someone starts using it and tells their friends, and those friends tell their friends... quickly a sizable network of people is created. Just one of them adding your event to their future schedule will let that entire network know about your event.

Summary

In this chapter you were introduced to the benefits of optimizing your site for search engines, and we gave some pointers on how to do this quite effectively. You also learned how to utilize at least one of the social attention applications on the Web to promote your content to a much wider audience than might otherwise find your site. And finally, you saw how easy it is to let people in your area know about any forthcoming events you might be hosting or attending.

8 LAYOUT AND NAVIGATION

By Chris Heilmann

In this chapter we're going to take a closer look at layout and navigation issues of web sites. The purpose is to make you aware of problems you should avoid and show you how to make it as easy as possible for visitors to find out more once they arrive at your site. We'll look at various types of menus and layouts and discuss their pros and cons. First, however, let's explain what web navigation is and how people can find you online.

Navigation is not a matter of technology

It is amazing how alien the concept of web site navigation is to many people. A lot of web sites out there are loosely put together by links all over the page pointing here and there. A big danger sign is if you find yourself adding a link that points to the page you came from, which is something that should almost never be necessary. You will also find that the navigation changes from page to page, making it hard to understand where to go next. If you are struggling with the idea of web site navigation and you are a bit confused about the technicalities of it, stop and shut down the computer for a moment.

Go to a big shopping center and try to find your way around. You will see that in well-designed centers you know where you will end up before stepping on an escalator. At the end of it you'll find information sheets or posters telling you where to go next. You will also be able to find ATMs, checkouts, and information booths wherever you are. In addition, you'll most likely be able to find the next restroom or food court quite quickly.

Designers of shopping malls have discovered that if you give people information about where they are and what options are available to them and also offer ways to make the stay as enjoyable as possible, visitors will stay longer, spend more money, and go home with an enjoyable experience in the back of their minds. The next time these people go shopping, this lingering memory will resurface and drive them to come back. This is exactly the same experience and memory you want to give a visitor of your site when they visit it for the first time. We'll come back to this in a second, but first let's remind ourselves how people end up on your site to begin with.

How do visitors get to your site?

The first misconception a lot of new web contributors have is to overemphasize the need for a homepage. Homepages are necessary, but they assume that this is the first encounter visitors have with your site. People arrive on homepages in several ways:

- By typing in your URL because they found it in some magazine or ad, or heard it from other media like radio or podcasts
- By clicking a link on a partner site or someone linking directly to your homepage
- Via a search engine result page that listed your homepage as a first result

It is, however, more likely that the homepage is not the first point of entry for visitors, for several reasons:

- Content pages are more likely to be focused, with a page title, a main heading, and copy dealing with the same subject. Search engines love that and are prone to listing these higher in the results list.

- The same applies to other people linking to you. Unless you are already established as a source of good material for either a particular subject or in general, you will find others linking to different content pages and not the homepage.

- As search engines list content pages higher up than the homepage, these are also more likely to be forwarded by people who researched a certain subject that led to them.

- It is much easier to send people directly to the content page than to explain your navigation (go to the homepage, click "archives," enter "October 2000," and so on is not likely to be fun to explain to someone).

The bare necessities of a good site menu

Because you cannot know the entry point of your visitors (or you lose a lot of potential visitors if you force them to go via the homepage), you need to cater to visitors arriving at any place in your site. There are some simple rules any menu system should follow to be usable and accessible regardless of how fancy it turns out to be in the end:

- At any point in time the visitor should know where in the page hierarchy they are and what is available in the immediate surroundings.

- The menu should be obvious to the visitor in the first few milliseconds they see the page. In order for a visitor to feel at ease with your site, it is crucial to distinguish between the page content and the connection to all the other things you have to offer.

- The current page should never link to itself—why should it? (One exception is if the link is a permutation of the current page, like a print version or a permanent link for a blog entry, but neither should be part of a menu.)

- There should be a way to get back to the homepage, one level up in the hierarchy, or to use a search (more on that later).

- The menu entry of the current page or, if you are on a page deeper in the hierarchy, the entry and its parent section should look different than the rest of the menu. Visitors should be able to quickly identify which part of the site they are in.

In addition to these basic principles for the site menu, there are other ways of giving visitors a helping hand when they arrive on one of the pages of your site.

What can you do to help visitors find content in your site?

There are many ways to promote and allow people to find out more about the content of your site. The main menu with submenus is the lifeline of your web site. Using it should allow visitors to get anywhere in your site. This does not mean that you need to offer all options in a single menu; that could become overwhelming and counterproductive. It means that before you even start thinking about what kind of navigation you want to offer, you should think about how to sort and collate all the information you want to convey.

The skill set to be able to find common terms to collate information and sort it in a logical manner is called *information architecture*, and it happens on both the page and the site level. If you visit a web site like the Yahoo! homepage or Amazon and you wonder why some material is shown in a certain way on the screen and which content is available only by drilling down into certain sections, you might not at first realize it but a lot of research and testing went into those, and there are reasons for the placement of everything on the page.

A big part of being able to offer information that can be easily found and used is connected with psychology and heuristic information about how humans use web sites. This is called usability—the science that analyzes and defines how we use things. This could be an ATM, a coffee maker, or a web site—in the end, the human factor plays a very important part in how successful any product will be.

Some visitors will not use your menu at all but will immediately seek a search option to find what they are looking for. This is why sites should always offer a site search, even when you just start out with 10 pages—it is amazing how fast your site can grow. Almost every large search engine out there offers you ways to implement their search forms catered to your look and feel in your site, and blog systems such as WordPress have a built-in search. We already talked about this in Chapter 7.

When your main menu is not detailed enough—for example, when a visitor is looking for a specific piece of information located several levels down—there are fallback mechanisms.

Fallback mechanism 1: the site map

One rather important fallback mechanism is a site map linked from the footer or the header of the document that should be on every page of the site. This shows all the pages in a hierarchy and allows visitors to go directly to the page they are looking for without having to drill down through each of the levels. These very link-heavy pages are not likely to be indexed by search engines any longer (as spammers created similar pages—so-called link farms—by the truckload to promote their products), but they are still an amazingly handy tool for visitors since they can find a link deep inside your hierarchy without the visitor having to click through the parent pages. Furthermore, a site map gives an overview of all the options you offer the visitor, and it may allow people to find sections they wouldn't have found using the site menu.

Fallback mechanism 2: the FAQ page

A section with frequently asked questions or short FAQs is another helpful part of a web site, especially when you provide a lot of content and you discover people sending you emails asking where they can find a certain piece of information.

Collect these questions and offer them your answers in an FAQ section and you might get fewer people asking you these things. Additionally, you can offer a section of the FAQ on a contact page. There are out-of-the-box FAQ systems available on the Web, such as phpMyFAQ (http://www.phpmyfaq.de/), which is a free open source solution (shown in Figure 8-1) or the commercial Kayako SupportSuite (http://www.kayako.com/).

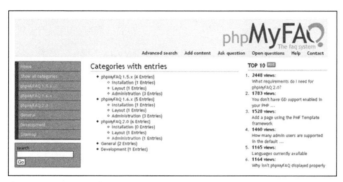

Figure 8-1. Automatic FAQ systems harvest frequently asked questions and offer them as alternatives to emailing you. This can help a visitor immediately and save them from awaiting your answer and can also cut down on your email inbox size.

Site internal linking

It is also a good idea to make visitors aware of what other content you offer by showing promotions of other content or contextual links. These are links you may have encountered on news sites.

Offering chronological navigation

One system of finding content is searching by chronological order. The WordPress engineers have thought of that for you; there is an archive of all blog posts that can be navigated either by month or directly via a calendar. Furthermore, each blog post provides links to the previous and next posts. Figure 8-2 shows what these might look like.

Figure 8-2. WordPress automatically creates an archive page with all the posts available by month, or you can choose the date from a calendar. Each blog post also offers links to the previous and next posts.

The archive option is not that useful unless visitors are looking for seasonal information (was there a Christmas special on this site?) or they know the time frame they are looking for. Archives also make sense in web sites that are chronological by nature and that feature daily information that does not have any relationship to other posts. Examples would be picture- or joke-of-the-day sites or a daily web comic.

The previous and next post links make more sense as they can lead the visitor to stay on the site and read on—if the link text is sufficiently interesting. This leads to another way to keep visitors on your site: pointing out content that is of similar interest as the stuff they just read.

Offering similar content pages via categories

Blog systems such as WordPress allow you to promote similar content with a list of categories. You can add or remove categories and associate blog posts with them, and the system will automatically offer links to the current categories and an overview of them all in most templates. Figure 8-3 shows the various interfaces of WordPress in terms of categorization.

Figure 8-3. WordPress allows you to define categories and associate blog posts with them, and offers a list of all the categories as a menu. This allows visitors to quickly find similar content.

Categories allow visitors to quickly narrow down the information so that they can see only what they are interested in. The flipside is that you need to make sure you don't offer too many categories; a list that is too long is hard to take in. This is why bloggers came up with another technique to allow visitors to find information quickly: tags.

Tags—the less rigid category option

Tags are a wonderful idea insofar as they are quite anarchic in structure. You can associate any tag with any piece of information if you consider it worthwhile to make it a keyword to find that information again. When confronted with tagging as an idea, many editors and professional web copywriters start analyzing the text and take out keywords to turn into tags. That is only half of what tags are about. Tags should be an aid for you and other people to find this information and can therefore be keywords that are not in the text.

Tags are also very personal and rely on the way of thinking of the person tagging this piece of information. It is pretty interesting to see how different people tag the same information in completely different ways. If you take social software products such as Flickr or del.icio.us and see what tags people add to one of your URLs or photos, it can be rather insightful and show you a completely different angle to how you thought people find your content. In return this will also allow you to promote other material that satisfies this new search angle.

> *One of the authors has written an experimental application that allows you to navigate Flickr content by tag and see how tags change when you go from one to the other. It is called flickrdrillr and is available for playing with tags at* http://icant.co.uk/sandbox/flickrdrillr/. *The application uses some of the APIs mentioned in this book and shows how easy it is to create something engaging by using them in conjunction with a bit of scripting and HTML.*

Tags are marked up in HTML with an attribute called rel, which takes the tag as a value and allows blog search engines such as http://www.technorati.com to find them and offer your content for this specific tag.

By default, WordPress turns every one of your categories into tags, but you might not want to add that many categories. To avoid setting up a lot of categories, get the extension SimpleTags at http://www.broobles.com/scripts/simpletags/, which allows you to add any tag to a post or page by enclosing a comma-separated list inside [tags][/tags] constructs.

In essence, SimpleTags allows you to add tags that help visitors find your content without having to add a category in WordPress. Categories should only be used when you have several posts on the topic and you want visitors to be able to see all of them at once. For a one-off tagging of a post, it is much cleaner to use the plug-in since your category list is easier to take in when it doesn't have a lot of entries. Once you've installed the extension, you can, for example, tag content with "music," "live," and "rock" simply by adding [tags]music,live,rock[/tags] anywhere inside the text of the post. Figure 8-4 shows what that can look like.

Figure 8-4. SimpleTags is a plug-in for WordPress that allows you to tag blog posts without having to add another category.

Pagination

When the page you want to display is a result set (for example, a search result or when the visitor browses a catalog or thumbnail gallery), then there is another type of navigation: a pagination menu. Pagination menus show you on which page of how many you are and allow you to go to either the next or previous page, but also jump several pages ahead and go to the first or last page in the whole set. Depending on how large the set you browse is, you might also get a menu that has several of the in-between steps omitted and allows you to enter a page number to go to. Figure 8-5 shows several examples of pagination menus.

Figure 8-5. Examples of pagination menus on Flickr

Lately you might have encountered a different kind of pagination that is related to a page rather than the site. These solutions are meant to make the best use of the screen space available while offering a lot of information. You'll find, for example, news excerpts on Yahoo! News changing every few seconds, but they also allow you to navigate through them. Figure 8-6 shows this kind of menu.

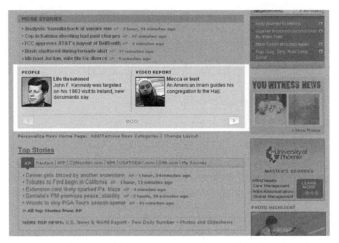

Figure 8-6. Yahoo! News has a menu that shows a lot of content in a small space. You can either wait a few seconds for the two news items to change or click the arrow buttons. The dots in between the arrows indicate how many items there are in total and which ones you are seeing at the moment. You can also click the dots to go directly to that set of news items.

Reproduced with permission of Yahoo! Inc. © 2007 by Yahoo! Inc. YAHOO! and the YAHOO! logo are trademarks of Yahoo! Inc.

These are rather high-tech examples of page-internal navigation, but there are some more basic ones we should take a look at.

Page-internal navigation

Although it is important to allow visitors to find their way around the site, it might also be necessary to offer a menu for the current page. This is only needed when you are dealing with large documents such as scientific papers or legalese terms and conditions.

The first trick of page-internal navigation is to use semantically sensible HTML for different parts of the document. We've already covered this in Chapter 2, but it might be interesting to remind ourselves that using the different heading elements (h1 to h6) gives a document structure and will enable visitors with assistive technology (such as a screen reader) to easily jump to the section they want rather than having to read through the whole document to get there.

Browsers don't automatically offer this functionality, which is why you need to write your own in HTML. The classic example of scientific texts published on the Internet is to use proper heading elements but also offer a table of contents menu linked to these headings.

You can link from one part of the document to the destination (the anchor) by using the # sign in the href attribute followed by the name or ID attribute of the element you want to link to.

Here's a simple HTML example:

```
<!DOCTYPE HTML PUBLIC "-//W3C//DTD HTML 4.01//EN"➥
"http://www.w3.org/TR/html4/strict.dtd">
<html dir="ltr" lang="en">
<head>
  <meta http-equiv="Content-Type" content="text/html; charset=utf-8">
  <title>Table of contents example</title>
  </head>
<body>
<h1>How to build a network of contacts</h1>
<h2><a name="toc">Table of Contents</a></h2>
<ul id="toc">
  <li><a href="#ways">Ways to contact other people on➥
the Web</a>
    <ul>
      <li><a href="#email">Email/Mailinglists</a></li>
      <li><a href="#forums">Forums</a></li>
      <li><a href="#irc">IRC</a></li>
      <li><a href="#im">Instant Messaging</a></li>
    </ul>
  </li>
  <li><a href="#social">Social Software</a>
    <ul>
      <li><a href="#delicious">del.icio.us</a></li>
      <li><a href="#flickr">flickr</a></li>
    </ul>
  </li>
</ul>

</ul>

<h2><a name="ways" id="ways">Ways to contact other people on the➥
Web</a></h2>
<!-- content here -->
<p><a href="#toc">Back to table of contents</a></p>

<h3><a name="email" id="email">Email/Mailinglists</a></h3>
<!-- content here -->
<p><a href="#toc">Back to table of contents</a></p>

<h3><a name="forums" id="forums">Forums</a></h3>
<!-- content here -->
<p><a href="#toc">Back to table of contents</a></p>
```

```
<h3><a name="irc" id="irc">IRC</a></h3>
<!-- content here -->
<p><a href="#toc">Back to table of contents</a></p>

<h3><a name="im" id="im">Instant Messaging</a></h3>
<!-- content here -->
<p><a href="#toc">Back to table of contents</a></p>

<h2><a name="social" id="social">Social Software</a></h2>
<!-- content here -->
<p><a href="#toc">Back to table of contents</a></p>

<h3><a name="delicious" id="delicious">del.icio.us</a></h3>
<!-- content here -->
<p><a href="#toc">Back to table of contents</a></p>

<h3><a name="flickr" id="flickr">flickr</a></h3>
<!-- content here -->
<p><a href="#toc">Back to table of contents</a></p>

</body>
</html>
```

> *You might wonder why we use both* name *and* id *with the same value on each of the links. Technically it is possible to only use* id. *The* name *attribute is only there to provide support for browsers and assistive technology that is older.* id *as the destination definition was, for example, not supported in Netscape 4 or older versions of Window Eyes (a screen reader).*

When a visitor clicks any of the links in the table of contents, the browser will send them immediately to the heading associated with this link, allowing them to reach where they want to go faster. Activating the "back to table of contents" links will return them to the table of contents.

> *Internet Explorer 6 has a rather curious bug: in any browser, keyboard users can jump to the correct section of the text when they activate the link pointing to it and press the Enter key. However, when they press the Tab key to get to the next link or form field following the target, IE will send the user to the link following the one they initially activated. The workaround—as odd as it may sound—is to set a width to the target in CSS. More detailed information about the bug and the workarounds is available at* http://juicystudio.com/article/ie-keyboard-navigation.php.

This technique is also important in terms of accessibility of your web page. If you have a lot of repetitive links that are not related to the current page (such as the main menu) but appear before the main content, a sight-impaired visitor will have to hear all of them before they reach the main content. A visitor who is dependent on a keyboard has the same problem because they'd have to press Tab (or the A key in Opera) to jump from link to link to reach the main content.

The workaround consists of *skip links* that are located before a menu in the document to allow the visitor to bypass the menu and go directly to the main content of the page. An HTML example could be

```
<!DOCTYPE HTML PUBLIC "-//W3C//DTD HTML 4.01//EN"➡
"http://www.w3.org/TR/html4/strict.dtd">
<html dir="ltr" lang="en">
<head>
  <meta http-equiv="Content-Type" content="text/html; charset=utf-8">
  <title>Skip Link Example</title>
  </head>
<body>
<p><a href="#content">Skip to content</a></p>

<ul id="nav">
  <li><a href="ways.html">Ways to contact other people on the Web</a>
    <ul>
      <li><a href="email.html">Email/Mailinglists</a></li>
      <li><a href="forums.html">Forums</a></li>
      <li><a href="irc.html">IRC</a></li>
      <li><a href="im.html">Instant Messaging</a></li>
    </ul>
  </li>
  <li><a href="social.html">Social Software</a>
    <ul>
      <li><a href="delicious.html">del.icio.us</a></li>
      <li><a href="flickr.html">flickr</a></li>
    </ul>
  </li>
</ul>
<div id="content">
  <!-- Main Content -->
</div>
</body>
</html>
```

Figure 8-7 shows how that looks on a blog (after we added some CSS for styling).

8

Figure 8-7. Skip links are an aid for people who either cannot see or are dependent on using a keyboard to navigate a site. Make sure you keep them visible to cater to the latter.

Different menu formats for different needs

We're now going to look at different formats of menus and look at their pros and cons in addition to where it makes sense to use them. Instead of looking at implementations, we'll use the different widgets of the Yahoo! UI Library (YUI) to show the types of menus and allow you to create them immediately.

Hierarchical and tree menus

Both of these are probably the most common forms of menu on the Web. The static version shows all the menu items of the first level and the ones below the current one. In a static version this menu offers only what is necessary to get around the site. An example can be found at `http://beginningjavascript.com/Chapter8/navigation/`. Dynamic versions of this kind of menu offer all the menu items, and you can expand and collapse different sections to reach deeper. This is how Windows Explorer works when you navigate around your hard drive. In the example page we mentioned earlier, you can choose to "switch to advanced navigation" to see the effect. A different and more versatile out-of-the-box solution for this kind of menu is the YUI TreeView widget (`http://developer.yahoo.com/yui/treeview/`), shown in Figure 8-8 in several designs.

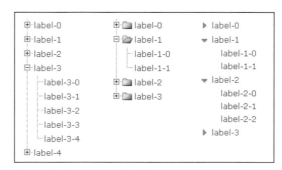

Figure 8-8. A tree menu in different styles

Dynamic tree menus like the ones shown here allow the visitor to drill down to the page they want to access without having to load all the pages in the hierarchy above that one. The problem is that you show and hide the other links with JavaScript and CSS, and not all visitors will have that functionality available to them. These visitors will have to deal with all the links on every page. This adds to the overall page weight and makes it hard to find your way around. If you have a menu with 15 items with 10 nested items each, that's a total of 150 links. If the user has JavaScript disabled, this means that he has loaded 140 links without really needing them. The YUI TreeView widget also allows you to load the link information on demand and only when it is needed.

There are not many pages where it doesn't make sense to use a tree-style menu. It is a simple concept to grasp and also mirrors the site hierarchy, giving the visitor an easy option to go up one level.

Drop-down, pull-down, or fly-out menus

These kinds of menus (all three names are quite common and describe the same type) were all the rage when browsers first began to support JavaScript and we were able to show and hide page elements consistently across browsers. A drop-down menu is what you see in applications in the menu bar or, in the case of Windows, as the main operating system menu.

Figure 8-9 shows two examples of the YUI Menu widget (http://developer.yahoo.com/yui/menu/) with open sublevels.

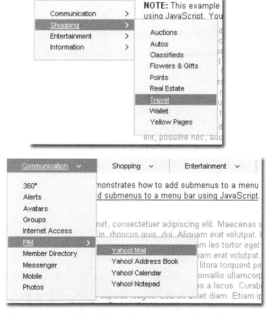

Figure 8-9. Multilevel drop-down menus show the hierarchy of your site and provide a familiar experience for the user because most applications use the same kind of menu to show options.

While it is easy to simulate a menu like this, there is a real science to making it right. If you look at the Start menu of Windows, for example, you'll see that simply showing and hiding the menu levels below the current one is not enough. An accessible multilevel drop-down menu needs to do much more:

- You should be able to navigate the menu with a keyboard using the cursor keys and not have to tab from link to link and hit Enter to show the menu items under the current one.

- Elements below the current one should not disappear immediately but after a short delay to allow for user errors. You cannot expect every user to be able to use the mouse with precision. A slight delay allows for more erratic and diagonal rather than only horizontal and vertical mouse movement.

- Before the menu under the current item is shown, you need to check that there is enough screen space for it to show up without causing scrollbars. If there is not enough space to the left or bottom, the menu should show up to the right or above the current one.

There are probably hundreds of DHTML drop-down menus available on the Web. Most of those don't offer these options but are developed to make it easy for the site maintainer rather than the end user. Don't fall into this trap. Drop-down menus are considered a shortcut and increase usability. They shouldn't become a barrier. The YUI Menu widget and several others such as the commercial Ultimate Dropdown Menu (http://www.udm4.com/) have been developed and tested with the above-mentioned features in mind.

Tabs

Tabs are a great way of showing the visitor which elements are available and which one of them is currently active. They allow you to offer a lot of information without overwhelming the visitor. In application design you will find tabs in preference and option menus where it is important that you know what you are changing at the moment. In web design you will find tabs a lot on e-commerce sites, allowing the maintainers to show off the variety of the available stock without taking away the focus on the section the visitor chose to see.

Figure 8-10 shows the YUI TabView widget (http://developer.yahoo.com/yui/tabview/), which turns a rather simple HTML construct into a tabbed interface.

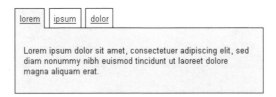

Figure 8-10. A simple HTML construct turned into a tabbed interface with the YUI TabView widget

The HTML necessary to create these tabs with the YUI TabView widget is amazingly close to the earlier example of the table of contents. Pending some extra DIVs with classes necessary for the script to work, all you need to do is to create a menu list linked to different content parts with anchors. The component not only comes with the script to create the tab functionality but also includes a basic style sheet that creates the tabular look and feel. This is not an easy CSS to create but it saves you a lot of time fixing bugs for different browsers. The complete HTML document with all includes looks like this:

```
<!DOCTYPE HTML PUBLIC "-//W3C//DTD HTML 4.01//EN"➥
"http://www.w3.org/TR/html4/strict.dtd">
<html dir="ltr" lang="en">
<head>
  <meta http-equiv="Content-Type" content="text/html; charset=utf-8">
  <title>TabView Example</title>
  <link rel="stylesheet" type="text/css" href="css/example.css">
  <link rel="stylesheet" type="text/css"➥
href="../../build/tabview/assets/tabview.css">
  <link rel="stylesheet" type="text/css"➥
href="../../build/tabview/assets/border_tabs.css">
    <script type="text/javascript" src="../../build/yahoo/yahoo.js">➥
</script>
    <script type="text/javascript" src="../../build/event/event.js">➥
</script>
    <script type="text/javascript" src="../../build/dom/dom.js"></script>
    <script type="text/javascript"
src="../../build/tabview/tabview.js">➥
</script>
  <style type="text/css">
    #demo { width:30em; }
    #demo .yui-content { padding:1em;} /* pad content container */
    #demo.yui-navset-top p.back{display:none;}  /* hide back to menu➥
links */
  </style>
  <script type="text/javascript">
     // create a new tab menu from the HTML construct with the ID demo
    YAHOO.example.init = function() {
        var tabView = new YAHOO.widget.TabView('demo');
    };
    YAHOO.example.init();
  </script>
</head>
<body>
<div id="doc">
  <div id="demo" class="yui-navset">
    <ul class="yui-nav">
      <li class="selected"><a href="#email"><em>Email/Mailinglists➥
</em></a></li>
```

```
                   <li><a href="#forums"><em>Forums</em></a></li>
                   <li><a href="#irc"><em>IRC</em></a></li>
                   <li><a href="#im"><em>Instant Messaging</em></a></li>
                 </ul>
                 <div class="yui-content">
                   <div id="email">
                     <h3>Email/Mailinglists</h3>
                     <p>Lorem ipsum dolor sit amet, consectetuer adipiscing elit</p>
                     <p class="back"><a href="#demo">Back to menu</a></p>
                   </div>
                   <div id="forums">
                     <h3><a name="forums" id="forums">Forums</a></h3>
                     <p>Lorem ipsum dolor sit amet, consectetuer adipiscing elit</p>
                     <p class="back"><a href="#demo">Back to menu</a></p>
                   </div>
                   <div id="irc">
                     <h3><a name="irc" id="irc">IRC</a></h3>
                     <p>Lorem ipsum dolor sit amet, consectetuer adipiscing elit</p>
                     <p class="back"><a href="#demo">Back to menu</a></p>
                   </div>
                   <div id="im">
                     <h3><a name="im" id="im">Instant Messaging</a></h3>
                     <p>Lorem ipsum dolor sit amet, consectetuer adipiscing elit</p>
                     <p class="back"><a href="#demo">Back to menu</a></p>
                   </div>
                 </div>
               </div>
             </div>
           </body>
         </html>
```

You can predefine different tabs as the originally selected ones by moving the "selected" class to a different list item. There are literally dozens of predefined styles and options for the tabs available as examples at http://developer.yahoo.com/yui/examples/ tabview/index.html.

Tabs are a very usable interface but have the problem that they work reliably on only one level. There are web sites that show multilevel tabbed interfaces and try to keep them usable and easy to understand by relying on color schemes, but it never works out. For starters, your visitors could be color-blind and in general it is hard to distinguish different elements when too many colors are involved.

The other problem with tabs is that the horizontal space on the screen is always limited and can shrink rapidly once you have to add more options or translate them into other languages. Languages such as German or Finnish tend to have much longer words than English and no abbreviations for them.

You don't encounter such problems just with tabs (a too-narrow left-hand navigation will have the same problems), but this is a general issue to consider when you plan your site. Web sites are not fixed constructs—they need to change to accommodate the circumstances. This is actually one of the biggest opportunities web development gives you—you can quickly change a whole layout without having to spend extra time and money. Once a print design is fixed, it's hard to get all the magazines back and change it—on the Web you have the power to do so any time.

The organic growth of a web site and how to cater for it

Here's something most web designers/developers learn early in their career: a web site is never finished. If you already expect the site structure and size to change, you'll save yourself a lot of trouble and frustration.

Do not waste your time building a menu that has a fixed size and caters only to a certain amount of menu entries. Instead, make sure that you can add or delete items, replace link texts with other terms, and extend items with other entries in the hierarchy below them.

Imagine your site structure as a family: you start with a small number of siblings, but there may be more in the future. The other siblings in themselves might bear children and those again grandchildren. Sometimes somebody dies and it may happen that for a short time one grandchild has to stay with their aunt or grandmother. This is not really good and disturbs the overall harmony of the family, and therefore should be the exception to the rule, but it is wise to cater for the possibility.

8

In other words: a good web site has a menu that can be easily changed, extended, and even renamed. You can achieve that in one of two ways:

- Use real HTML text links as the menu and give it a logical semantic structure (normally an unordered list). This means that you can easily change the text when you need it and translate it into other languages should you want to offer a multilingual site in the future, while visitors can easily resize the menu to their needs (not everybody can see as well as you might). In this day and age, you can use CSS to make a text menu look as fancy as a graphical one. Figures 8-11 and 8-12 show two web sites that can help you achieve that.

- Use server-side includes and a server-side language to maintain the menus. This is also what content-management systems or blogging systems such as WordPress do for you.

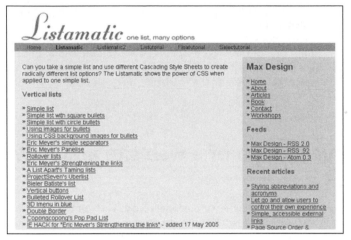

Figure 8-11. Listamatic (http://css.maxdesign.com.au/listamatic/) is an amazing showcase site about what you can do with a simple unordered HTML list. You can choose from dozens of premade CSS solutions to make the menu look pretty.

Figure 8-12. WellStyled (http://www.wellstyled.com/) offers many articles and tutorials on CSS, including a trick for using background images to make a menu look like a graphical menu without having to wait for all image states to download.

Link and menu accessibility

With the menu being the main tool to find your way around a web site, it is very important to keep it accessible to all visitors regardless of ability or technical setup. If you want to delve deeper into this matter, check out the free version of Joe Clark's web accessibility book available at http://joeclark.org/book/sashay/serialization/, especially the chapters "Text and Links" and "Navigation."

Here's a short version of the things you need to be aware of when it comes to links and menus in terms of accessibility:

- Assistive technology can pull out all the links on a page, regardless of location, and present them in a list to allow the visitor to jump directly to them without having to read or hear the rest of the content. This means

  - Links will be available outside of their context and should therefore always make sense on their own. For example, instead of "<u>Click here</u> to see videos of our latest concert" it is better to use "Check out the <u>videos of our latest concert</u>".

  - No matter what clever CSS or scripting tricks you use to hide menu items, some visitors will get all the links you have in your document. This may be overwhelming depending how many links you offer. Hiding things visually does not remove them from the document, and you are effectively offering a site map on each page as the menu.

  - Make sure that you tell the visitors in the link text if you offer links to file formats other than HTML (for example, a link to a PDF or text file). One reason is that not everybody will be able to see (or experience) the other format in their browser and instead will get prompted to download it. This is not only an accessibility barrier but also a worry for the virus-afraid out on the Web. Another reason to do this is that the link might be offered outside the current context and the extra information will get lost if it is not part of the link text. As an example, "<u>Download and print the flyer to get $4 off our next concert (PDF, 1.2MB)</u>" makes a lot more sense than "<u>Download and print the flyer to get $4 off our next concert</u> (PDF, 1.2MB)". Some assistive technology like screen readers allows users to only get a list of all the links in a document as a navigational shortcut. In this scenario the former link tells them that this is a PDF whereas the latter example might lead visitors to click the link although they might not be able to access PDF documents.

- It is quite difficult to make menus with images accessible. Alternative text for each item is a must, but that only helps a sight-impaired visitor. Visitors with slight vision impairment can benefit a lot more from a menu that is text on top of background images. While newer browsers like Opera 9 and IE 7 allow visitors to zoom the whole screen (including form elements and images) to their needs, older browsers only allow changing the size of the text. The other benefits of HTML text mentioned earlier also make it a tough decision to go with a graphical menu. Of course, it is up to you.

- Always make sure that your menu is available at least in the most basic form necessary to navigate the page without extra technologies such as scripting, Java, or Flash. Each of these can and will be turned off by visitors or their computer administrators.

8

- Ensure that any dynamic menu is capable of reacting to various input devices. Try your menu with a keyboard and see how much of a hassle it is to find your way around. Also use an older mouse or a trackpad, or try to navigate the menu in less-than-perfect surroundings (for example, on a bus or a train) to see how problematic your menu would be for an elderly or disabled visitor who cannot use the mouse in a highly coordinated fashion.

- Many accessibility publications advocate using access keys (defined with the accesskey attribute) to allow for keyboard access to several parts of the page. Don't bother with those—they have proven to be ineffective and in some cases even harmful to disabled visitors. If you want to know much more about this problem, check out the articles "Using Accesskeys—Is It Worth It?" (http://www.wats.ca/show.php?contentid=32) and "Accesskeys and Reserved Keystroke Combinations" (http://www.wats.ca/show.php?contentid=43).

As you can see, a lot of accessibility gotchas of links and menus are common sense. Avoiding the more obvious errors will ensure that your site is easy to maintain and, if need be, localized to other languages.

Different layouts for different needs

There are no rules for laying out a web site. Instead, there are many options and you have to be sure to pick what works best for your site and your intended audience. You can position the menu to the top, the left, the right, the bottom, or even in the page—whatever floats your boat. Each of these approaches has different issues and virtues:

- The more or less de facto standard of a web site layout calls for a header, a left-hand menu, a content slot with a right-hand extra slot for advertising or contextual navigation, and a footer.

- Many blog layouts break that convention by offering a header with a very short horizontal menu, a large content block, and a right-hand menu, thus making the content of the page the center of attention and offering the other menu options as alternatives to explore further.

- A lot of e-commerce web sites (with Amazon taking the lead) use a tabbed menu, giving visitors the option to go directly where they intend to go while offering lists of products in the main slot with contextual second-level menus on the left and promotions on the right.

Creating a complex layout in HTML can be a tiring and annoying process, mainly due to browser inconsistencies and some misconceptions of what web design is (we will come back to this in a second). Once again, you can use a library or CSS solutions other developers created and tested for you.

As discussed in an earlier chapter, the CSS Grid section of YUI allows you to create almost any layout with a single CSS file, but you need to know your HTML to make use of it. Thanks to Dav Glass, this is a lot easier now as he created the CSS Grid Builder (http://blog.davglass.com/files/yui/grids/), which is a tool that allows you to define the layout you want to create and gives you the HTML compatible with the YUI Grid as a last step to copy and paste. Figure 8-13 shows what it looks like.

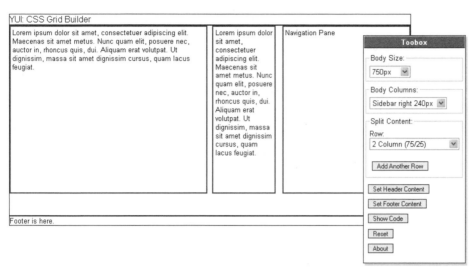

Figure 8-13. Using the YUI Grid Builder makes it easy to create CSS-based layouts that work across all modern browsers without having to know CSS or a lot of HTML. Simply copy and paste the final HTML and add your content where the comments in the generated code tell you to.

You can make your layout as complex as you want to with the CSS Grid, but don't forget that not all visitors will be able to experience the site the same way you do. Make sure that the order of the content still makes sense when CSS is not available or that you experience the page like a sight-impaired person using a screen reader would. To test your layout, you can turn off CSS in your browser; there are several toolbars available that help you with that, such as the Firefox web developer toolbar (`https://addons.mozilla.org/firefox/60/`) or the Web Accessibility Toolbar (`http://www.visionaustralia.org.au/ais/toolbar/`) for IE. Or you can use a text-only browser like Lynx, available at `http://www.subir.com/lynx/binaries.html`, for a hard-core check.

In any case, you should always be aware that you will not be able to define or to demand anything your visitors can or cannot see, and there will be cases where a visitor needs a certain setting on her browser that will break your layout. A pixel-perfect one-for-all layout and design is an archaic view of web design, and you are better off saving yourself a lot of frustration by not expecting it.

The need for flexibility

When the Web came to be and HTML was invented, nobody ever considered a visual Web that allows for the richness print layouts offer. Therefore, HTML has no such thing as a COLUMN element. HTML is not meant to define the look of a document but its semantic structure.

However, that didn't stop print designers having a go at screen design, applying a lot of design mantras that work in print and leaving it to the web developer to come up with solutions to make it happen. Until relatively recent times, we used tables to try to make the browser do what the screen design demands. Tables are part of HTML, as you could have data that is tabular by nature (for example, a calendar). However, they were never meant for layout and are a hack at best—after all, you have rows and columns in a table but not necessarily the option to size them easily.

What table layouts meant, though, was that it was hard to change a layout once it was defined. If you weren't clever enough to cut the whole layout up into several tables (and includes), moving a menu from the top to the left (as the site's information architecture outgrew the horizontal menu model) meant hours, if not days and weeks, of changing every single HTML document in the whole site rather than one CSS file.

This does not mean that layouts created with CSS are necessarily easier to maintain, but it means that they are a step in the right direction—we realized that the layout and the look and feel of a site can change over time and use a technology that is less rigid and allows for quick changes.

When you work as a web developer, you will spend a lot of time arguing with designers who have the best intentions but don't quite understand the nature of web design: you offer a certain look and feel and hope for the best that the visitor will be able to experience it the way you defined it. You cannot demand anything and you cannot expect anything. There are a lot of unknowns you have to be aware of when you offer a web site to the world.

You have no idea about the following:

- The ability of your visitor
- The technical setup of your visitor (connection speed, hardware, operating system, display unit, sound system)
- The browser and configuration of your visitor (how many toolbars are enabled? what are the settings for colors and sizes? does the visitor allow scripting/CSS/ Flash/sound?)
- The font size the visitor is using (people with visual impairments or very high resolutions will resize the fonts to enable them to read)
- The viewport size of the visitor's setup

You might not have encountered the term *viewport size* before. It describes the amount of screen estate a visitor has at their disposal. This is dependent on several variables:

- The resolution of the operating system/video card/display unit (800×600, 1024×786, 1280×800...)
- The chrome (toolbars, scrollbars, plug-ins) of their browser
- The current font size
- The size of the browser window
- The zoom value of the browser (in the case of very modern browsers such as Opera 8 and IE 7) or the screen magnification software of the operating system

All of this makes predicting the experience visitors get very tough indeed. Figure 8-14 shows what a blog looks like with different settings of only one operating system.

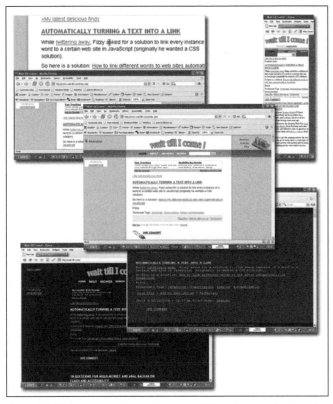

Figure 8-14. The same web site, but many different ways of seeing it

With this in mind, it is time to take a quick look at several myths about web design that still refuse to die. These may not be of much value to you right now, but it is interesting to be aware of them should you hire a professional designer to help you with your web site in the future.

The "above or below the fold" myth

Many a time you will encounter articles, tutorials, and speeches talking about the mythical fold of a web page and that everything that is above it will be found and everything below it discarded by visitors. The term *fold* stems from newspaper layout and publishing. The fold is where the newspaper is folded as publishers don't want to waste the whole table or rack space for one newspaper and any headline below the fold is not visible any longer. Web pages, however, don't have a predefined size like newspapers have, which means that the fold is a moving target. Depending on the screen resolution, the browser chrome, and the font size, the location of the fold can vary vastly and you don't have a chance to define what is above or below the fold.

It is also not that important, assuming your content and wording is engaging enough to make the visitor scroll the page. With faster connection speeds and higher resolutions becoming more and more common, getting a small amount of content and having to go to a different page every few paragraphs can be more annoying than scrolling down to get more of the content you came for.

The "fixed font" myth

One of the biggest thorns in the side of designers with a print background is that typography on the Web is hard to get right. Browsers render font sizes differently, and the differences of operating systems in terms of DPI settings make it almost impossible to define a font size that works consistently. The YUI Reset CSS (http://developer.yahoo.com/yui/reset/) and Fonts CSS (http://developer.yahoo.com/yui/fonts/) widgets do all that is possible, but there is still no way to define a font size for the whole page and all possible browser settings out there.

Your visitors want and need to resize the font when it is necessary, and every browser but IE earlier than version 7 also allows them to. If your initial font size is too small for the needs of the current visitor, they should be able to change that or you'll have lost them.

Therefore, it is very important that any design allow for a bit of breathing space around text (for example, in tabs) and allow borders and backgrounds to grow and change with the font size. Make sure you change the font size in your browser up and down when you get a design. If the design fails to accommodate changes at least two sizes up or down, you cannot consider it usable.

The "screen resolution" myth

Many times you get asked what screen resolution the design should be optimized for with 800×600, 1024×768, or 1280×800 as the options. As mentioned earlier, the resolution of the operating system is only a small part of what the available screen space for the user is. It is always easier for users with larger viewports to resize the browser window than it is for those with small or highly zoomed viewports to scroll around vertically and horizontally.

When asked, the decision to expect a certain resolution normally gets backed up with statistics that prove that "most users have a 1024 resolution these days." These statistics mean nothing, as they are from other sites with other users, and yours are the really interesting ones. As you can only read out the screen resolution and the viewport size using JavaScript, these studies also omit those users who don't have JavaScript enabled.

Summary

We hope this chapter has given you an insight into the very large world of the navigation and layout considerations of web design. A lot of research has gone into these matters, and they are critical when it comes to having a successful web site.

Advertising, snazzy copywriting, and cool imagery can only go so far; if you want to have people come to your site, stay there, and come back, you need to make sure that it is easy for them to find what they are looking for, get to know what else you're offering, and come back to exactly where they were on their last visit.

Especially with navigation it is crucial that you keep reminding yourself that it is not a technological but a psychological matter. Adding fancy menus to a site is simple, but what you want to spark is that feeling of security in your visitors. They need to know where they are and how to return to where they came from, and you need to make it fun for them to explore what else is available—in the same way shopping centers do.

8

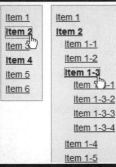

By Chris Heilmann

In this chapter we'll talk about using JavaScript libraries to add some extra zing to your web site. To make this as easy as possible we'll use JavaScript libraries. We've already touched on the subject of JavaScript libraries in Chapter 4, but now we'll go into more examples on how to use them. Specifically we'll pick two common JavaScript tasks and use one library at a time to fulfill them.

> *This chapter contains code examples. Do **not** type these in yourself, as there is no need for that. You'll find these examples in the code download zip file for this chapter at* `http://www.friendsofed.com`; *simply unpack it to your local server in a folder called "libraries" or something similar, and try the examples out by double-clicking the HTML files.*

Originally we meant to add readymade scripts to put into a WordPress installation with these examples. However, seeing that some libraries are still in the process of changing in a very short period of time, it would not be helpful to give a plug-and-play solution. Instead, we want to encourage you to take a look at the library pages themselves and browse the scripts generated there. Before we go on to these examples, let's remind ourselves about the why of JavaScript and the why of libraries.

The why of JavaScript

First things first: you don't need JavaScript to have a good web site. Even more to the point: a good web site should not require JavaScript to work and make sense, but JavaScript should make some things easier for you when and if it is available.

JavaScript was invented as users demanded web sites to be more responsive. Long ago, when reading web sites meant spending a lot of money every minute and loading a page took several minutes, it was simply a necessity.

There is nothing more frustrating even today than having to load a form 10 times because you forgot to enter something or you entered something in the wrong format. Now imagine a scenario where you have to wait about 2 minutes for each reload and see your bill increasing with each of them—you have a recipe for people to bang their keyboard in frustration (no wonder the office guy doing exactly that became one of the first "funny web videos"—see `http://youtube.com/watch?v=5oTZXUI-L8s`).

Browser vendors realized that they needed to offer their impatient users something better to stay in the game and turn the information superhighway into a medium worth exploring for the mass market and not mere science fiction.

They first started with Java and applets—a technology that meant you had to load a large file first, wait for it to initialize and run, and then you'd have a richer user interface. The richer interface also meant that you didn't have to reload the page but data could be retrieved in the background.

Java didn't make it, though—the applets were large to load and very hungry when it came to system resources. First you had to wait a lot and then your computer got slow. Not really a good experience, which is why clever minds shut the door, put their thinking hats on, and came up with a concept that would revolutionize the Web: a language that was embedded in a web document or in its own file that could be loaded and executed by the browser.

Java had the problem that you needed to install the Java engine to make things run, because Java needs to be converted to code that can run on your computer. That got sus-picious minds wondering why they'd need to install an outside program to improve their web experience (Flash used to suffer from the same problem). Furthermore, applets included a lot of code since they contained the user interface.

The new language wouldn't need that: the interface was already there, namely the HTML document with its links, forms, and buttons. All the language needed was the interpreter to translate JavaScript and allow it to work its magic with these interface elements, and browser vendors simply shipped that one as part of the browser code itself.

JavaScript was born—a lightweight language that allowed developers to write programs that could be downloaded in seconds, executed on your computer, and even cached (kept in a temporary file on your hard drive). You had to load the programs only once and could run them over and over again (unless you cleared your cache in between or turned caching off).

And this is what JavaScript is meant to be: a lightweight helper technology that turns web sites into more responsive interfaces. You can use it for good, but a lot of times it is used for evil—more on that later.

What JavaScript can do for you

JavaScript allows for changes to the HTML document after it has been downloaded and ini-tially displayed by the browser. This means you can help your visitors by avoiding unnec-essary page reloads and making the interface appear less cluttered. JavaScript can

- Validate user input on forms and give immediate feedback if there is an error.
- Flag changes that happen asynchronously in the background by giving messages without requiring a page reload. (Normal page requests are *synchronous*—you click something and the page reloads. *Asynchronously* means that you load data in the background and display the results when the data is loaded without leaving the main document.)
- Create modular windows and page elements that the visitor can open and close or expand and collapse.
- Allow for keyboard access to functionality, such as enabling a user to move around a menu using the cursor keys.
- Fix inconsistencies in CSS rendering.
- React to changes to the document such as the visitor clicking elements, scrolling, focusing on a text field, or dragging an item around.

9

You can embed JavaScript anywhere in the document enclosed by SCRIPT tags. If you add the JavaScript after the main document you can already access its elements (as they've already been sent to the browser and therefore exist) and change them. For example, the following script embedded in the HTML document hides all nested lists:

```
<!DOCTYPE HTML PUBLIC "-//W3C//DTD HTML 4.01//EN" ➡
"http://www.w3.org/TR/html4/strict.dtd">
<html dir="ltr" lang="en">
<head>
  <meta http-equiv="Content-Type" content="text/html; charset=utf-8">
  <title>JavaScript Test - Hiding Lists</title>
</head>
<body>
<ul>
  <li>Item 1</li>
  <li>Item 2
    <ul>
      <li>Nested Item 1</li>
    </ul>
  </li>
  <li>Item 3</li>
  <li>Item 4
    <ul>
      <li>Nested Item 2</li>
    </ul>
  </li>
</ul>
<script type="text/javascript">
  function hideStuff(){
    var lists = document.getElementsByTagName( 'ul' );
    for(var i = 0, j = lists.length; i < j; i++){
    if(lists[i].parentNode.nodeName.toLowerCase() === 'li'){
        lists[i].style.display = 'none';
      }
    }
  }
  hideStuff();
</script>
</body>
</html>
```

If you wanted to use this functionality on every page in the site, you'd need to copy and paste the code into each page, which mean the documents would become unnecessarily large; in addition, the JavaScript would not be cached. And it would mean that any future change to the script would have to be replicated in every document. This is why you can put the code in its own file instead and give it a file extension of .js. For example, you could call it hideNestedLinks.js and give it the following content:

```
function hideStuff(){
  var lists = document.getElementsByTagName( 'ul' );
  for(var i = 0, j = lists.length; i < j; i++){
  if(lists[i].parentNode.nodeName.toLowerCase() === 'li'){
    lists[i].style.display = 'none';
    }
  }
}
hideStuff();
```

You add this script to the document by setting the src attribute of the SCRIPT element:

```
<!DOCTYPE HTML PUBLIC "-//W3C//DTD HTML 4.01//EN" ➥
"http://www.w3.org/TR/html4/strict.dtd">
<html dir="ltr" lang="en">
<head>
  <meta http-equiv="Content-Type" content="text/html; charset=utf-8">
  <title>JavaScript Test - Hiding Lists</title>
</head>
<body>
<ul>
  <li>Item 1</li>
  <li>Item 2
    <ul>
      <li>Nested Item 1</li>
    </ul>
  </li>
  <li>Item 3</li>
  <li>Item 4
    <ul>
      <li>Nested Item 2</li>
    </ul>
  </li>
</ul>
<script type="text/javascript" src="hideNestedLinks.js"></script>
</body>
</html>
```

The most appropriate section of the document to embed scripts into is the head, though, because doing so makes it easier for maintainers to know where your JavaScript is embedded and where to change it without having to scan the whole document.

The impractical upshot of this is that browsers download scripts linked in the head before they start showing the document, which could result in a slight delay the first time the scripts are loaded (afterwards they will be cached and loaded from your hard drive, effectively eliminating the delay). Embedding the script in the head also means that it gets executed when the document—and the items you want to affect, in this case the lists—is not yet available for alteration, which will cause this example script to fail. You can avoid this problem by executing the script when the window has finished loading:

```
function hideStuff(){
    var lists = document.getElementsByTagName( 'ul' );
    for(var i = 0, j = lists.length; i < j; i++){
    if(lists[i].parentNode.nodeName.toLowerCase() === 'li'){
        lists[i].style.display = 'none';
      }
    }
  }
window.onload = hideStuff;
```

The problem with this basic solution is that you will have only this script executing when the window has loaded. In reality you might have several scripts, all of them having to execute when the window has loaded. This is why there are several helper scripts that allow you to add your script to a queue to be executed when the window has loaded. Probably the first script to do that was Simon Willison's addLoadEvent() (http://simonwillison. net/2004/May/26/addLoadEvent/):

```
function addLoadEvent(func) {
  var oldonload = window.onload;
  if (typeof window.onload != 'function') {
    window.onload = func;
  } else {
    window.onload = function() {
      oldonload();
      func();
    }
  }
}
```

Using this function you can add the hideStuff() function to the window load event queue with addLoadEvent(hideStuff). You can add as many functions as you want to this queue and they won't overwrite the other call. You'll find an example of that in the code archive. Probably every library out there comes with a similar function to connect functions with events.

Notice that the simple task to hide nested list elements appears quite complex in JavaScript:

1. You retrieve all the lists in the document with getElementsByTagName().

2. You loop through these lists one by one with a for loop.

3. You test if the parent element of the current list is a li (and you need to use toLowerCase() as browsers inconsistently report the name of this parent element either as li or LI).

4. If that is the case, you set the list's display style property to none.

In CSS, all you'd have to do is to use ul ul {display:none;}, which is why clever JavaScript developers don't bother using a loop for this task but instead apply a CSS class name to the body of the document.

```
window.onload = function(){
  document.body.className = 'dynamic';
}
```

That way, you can define any visual changes to the document in CSS with a body.dynamic selector before your others—for example, body.dynamic ul ul {display:none;}. These changes will only be applied when JavaScript is available. There will be a slight delay before the styles get applied, though, as the onload event only fires when the whole document, images, and scripts have finished loading.

The why of JavaScript libraries

In the end, all browser vendors agreed that JavaScript is a great thing to have and that people should use it. What was missing for browser vendors was a selling point—a unique identifier why one browser would be better than the other one, and this is when the whole JavaScript thing went awry. Instead of following a common standard, every browser vendor came up with its own implementations and interfaces to the language to gain an advantage over the competitor.

The big competition was between Microsoft and Netscape, with Microsoft offering a lot of options that were Windows-specific (as IE is part of the Windows operating system and not a standalone application) and Netscape offering the layer element, which allowed for embedding other documents into the current one and positioning or animating the content. This part of web development history—known as the browser wars—still affects us now, partly because you will find a lot of scripts on the Web that were developed during that time that took only these two browsers into consideration and break in more modern browsers. If you find a document.all or document.layers in a script, you should be very suspicious.

These days most modern browsers support the W3C standards, at least to a large degree, which means you don't need to know that many browser-specific extras any longer. However, developing JavaScript is still a tricky subject. Browser bugs and JavaScript architecture limitations mean you need to know a lot of different environments your scripts will be executed in and all their faults and problems. This is where JavaScript libraries come in.

Libraries are collections of functions that take away the random element and provide you with shorter and more precise methods that do all the "browser normalization" for you. In other words, you don't need to know the problems of differing support between browsers and JavaScript itself as the developers of the libraries took on this job for you.

These are the pragmatic libraries that allow you to create web applications and dynamically enhanced web sites that work in different browsers on different operating systems without you having to know the twists and turns a developer needs to take to make these do their bidding.

9

> *There are several issues with JavaScript itself, especially with the DOM interface. For example, there is an* `insertBefore()` *method to add something before something else, but there is no* `insertAfter()`. *You also cannot change the text in any given element using a simple construct such as* `element.text`; *instead you need to modify* `element.firstChild.nodeValue` *to change the text content of the element when it already has some content or* `element.appendChild(document.createTextNode('text'))` *when it doesn't. Truly not one of the most convenient interfaces.*

A different kind of library goes beyond that and does more than fix browser inconsistencies and provide shorter methods to achieve a certain goal. These libraries try to enhance or replace the language itself and use a different syntax. For example, they could be mimicking the behavior and style of higher programming languages like Java, C#, or Perl. Or perhaps the goal is to make it easier for nontechnical web designers to use JavaScript by, for example, providing methods that allow you to retrieve page elements by CSS selector or other means of retrieving nodes in a document such as XPath (http://www.w3.org/TR/xpath).

In essence, using JavaScript libraries is a good idea if you don't want to learn about browser bugs and differences, or if you want to be able to do something quickly without having to know a lot of JavaScript yourself.

The dangers of JavaScript libraries

There is a flipside to the benefits JavaScript libraries bring with them. Probably the biggest problem is that you rely on a third party and their skills to achieve a goal. If a certain part of a library causes issues in a new browser coming out, you won't know how to fix the problem. You'll have to make sure that you keep up-to-date with the library itself and upload any patches or upgrades as they get released. It also means that the library developers must offer upgrades and patches in the future.

Depending on the quality of the library and the dedication of its developers, the library may not be applicable to your site any longer if it becomes bigger or gets a wider audience of users with different browsers and needs. It is good to know which browsers the library code supports, and to what degree, in case people contact you about bugs on your site. Make sure that the library has a dedicated developer team, good documentation, and a community to ask for advice. A lot of one-man-show libraries that look great at first can become a nuisance when the library developer becomes too busy delivering more lucrative jobs than releasing a free JavaScript library.

The other big issue with libraries is that they cloak the code. Any library function will result in native JavaScript code under the hood as this is the only way it can be executed. This is especially the case when it comes to libraries that reinvent JavaScript syntax or offer "get elements by XPath or CSS selectors" shortcut methods. These methods in themselves are not a real problem, but when you start using them inside a loop it is quite interesting to see how much work the JavaScript parser really has to do. Take a pseudo-command like this, for example:

```
var active = getElementsByCssSelector('div ul li a.active');
```

Translated to standard JavaScript, this will result in the following code:

```
var active = [];
var divs = document.getElementsByTagName('div');
for(var i = 0; i<divs.length; i++){
  var uls = divs[i].getElementsByTagName('ul');
  for(var j = 0; j<uls.length; j++){
    var lis = uls[j].getElementsByTagName('li');
    for(var k = 0; k<lis.length; k++){
      var as  = lis[k].getElementsByTagName('a');
      for(var l = 0; l<as.length; l++){
        if(as[l].className === 'active'){
          active.push(as[l]);
        }
      }
    }
  }
}
```

Every for loop in JavaScript takes a lot of time and resources (as in memory). When you nest loops you multiply this issue, and depending on how large the document and how complex the CSS selector is, you could end up with a really slow web site—although it has already loaded.

> *This is a very basic way of achieving this functionality, and there are cleverer ways using recursive functions. However, the underlying problem stays the same—you simulate in JavaScript what the CSS parser of the browser was built for.*

Having easier access to the document and easier ways to manipulate it is a great thing. However, what you need to be aware of is that under the hood you expect a lot of the browser and the JavaScript parser. In the end, successful web sites are fast web sites and what helps your visitors is much more important than what is handy or easy for you as the developer.

There is another aspect of JavaScript that you should be aware of: avoiding the trap of creating effects for the sake of having effects.

Fighting the temptation

Dynamic effects on web sites are great. A panel that slides in and out smoothly, text that fades in, and a photo frame that grows smoothly before showing the photo are fun things to see and give the impression of a much more sophisticated user interface than a web page that simply shows and hides parts of it.

9

There is such a thing as overkill, though. There is also a thing called "not wanting to wait." If you ever sat through a presentation of a bad public speaker who tried to make up for this by applying a lot of transition and animation effects to their PowerPoint (or Keynote) slides, you know what we mean.

If you want to use animation and dynamic JavaScript changes on your web site, think about the following:

- An elaborate effect is cool the first time, but may become a nuisance when the same visitor comes back to your site to get some information they found the last time.

- Using animation in JavaScript (which has to be converted by a browser running inside an operating system) is incredibly hard to get smooth. Any other processing the computer has to do will interfere with your animations, and because there is no direct access to the video hardware (like OpenGL or ActiveX components have), there is no buffering to gloss over timing problems. In other words, if you use several animations that are dependent on each other, don't rely on timing to execute them. Instead, make sure that one animation initiates the next one once it has finished animating.

- Animation may pose an accessibility barrier as people with learning disabilities or epilepsy might not be able to cope with it. Make sure that if you use animation heavily, or you need animation that is very hectic, you also offer an option to turn it off.

- Don't rely on the animation to work when it comes to crucial elements of your site—like the menu. If an animation fails for some reason and the visitor cannot access your menu, you have lost them.

- While there are many examples where hiding and showing different page elements is beneficial to the usability of the page, don't get overly excited about this trick. First, the interface you created is not necessarily what the visitor sees (they might have JavaScript disabled, only see part of the screen in a magnifying tool, or have CSS turned off), and they'll have to download and deal with all the content (hiding something in CSS doesn't make it disappear from the document; it just hides it). Second, it can become very annoying to have to click and expand elements repeatedly to reach what you came for. This is especially annoying when the state is not stored and you have to do it all again on your next visit.

- Although it is easy to validate user data entry with JavaScript, it is not a foolproof method. If your only means of blocking out invalid data entry is JavaScript, all a malicious attacker needs to do is to turn it off. The other handy part for evildoers when it comes to JavaScript validation is that they can simply analyze your JavaScript and see what the rules are.

In essence, if you use animation and dynamic effects, be sure to use them in moderation and only when they benefit the user. There are not many things left you can do to amaze people on the Web with JavaScript bells and whistles. Advertisers and enthusiastic developers have done this for years already, and people got thoroughly fed up with waiting for animations to finish and trying to figure out how a menu works.

The two tasks

Let's now go through three examples of libraries with different approaches to the whole theme of what a library should do: jQuery by John Resig, MooTools by Valerio Proietti, and the Yahoo! User Interface Library (YUI).

The tasks we will try to achieve are

- Creating a hierarchical navigation
- Animating page elements

Creating a hierarchical navigation

We'll use the libraries to turn the following HTML list into a hierarchical and collapsible menu:

```
<ul id="nav">
  <li><a href="#">Item 1</a></li>
  <li><a href="#">Item 2</a>
    <ul>
      <li><a href="#">Item 1-1</a></li>
      <li><a href="#">Item 1-2</a></li>
      <li><a href="#">Item 1-3</a>
        <ul>
          <li><a href="#">Item 1-3-1</a></li>
          <li><a href="#">Item 1-3-2</a></li>
          <li><a href="#">Item 1-3-3</a></li>
          <li><a href="#">Item 1-3-4</a></li>
        </ul>
      </li>
      <li><a href="#">Item 1-4</a></li>
      <li><a href="#">Item 1-5</a></li>
      <li><a href="#">Item 1-6</a></li>
    </ul>
  </li>
  <li><a href="#">Item 3</a></li>
  <li><a href="#">Item 4</a>
    <ul>
      <li><a href="#">Item 4-1</a></li>
      <li><a href="#">Item 4-2</a></li>
      <li><a href="#">Item 4-3</a></li>
    </ul>
  </li>
  <li><a href="#">Item 5</a></li>
  <li><a href="#">Item 6</a></li>
</ul>
```

9

The idea is that a nested list structure like this is the semantically correct way to mark up (turn into HTML) a menu. The script should hide all the nested lists and add a CSS class to the li elements that contain a nested list. Furthermore, it should show and hide the nested lists when the visitor clicks the links in these parent list elements. All the other links should work as expected. When there is no JavaScript available, the list should not collapse at all, as shown in Figure 9-1.

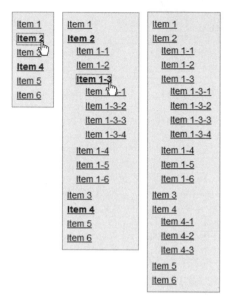

Figure 9-1. Turning a nested list into a hierarchical dynamic menu with JavaScript and how it looks without JavaScript

Animating page elements

One task JavaScript libraries are constantly used for is animation of page elements. We've covered this earlier in the chapter and will create a small example that slowly shows and hides a menu, as shown in Figure 9-2. You may remember that we advised against using animation in something crucial like a menu; however, this example will work without JavaScript because the link to show and hide the menu is generated via JavaScript and the DOM. When JavaScript is disabled, the show and hide link is not generated at all—the user does not get the promise of functionality that will not work. If you add the link in HTML and make it dependent on JavaScript to make sense, this wouldn't be the case.

A natural animation does not work in linear fashion, but either accelerates at the start and gets slower or starts slower and accelerates toward its end value (imagine a ball running out of momentum or a metal ball being dragged by a magnet). That is why some JavaScript libraries use Easing (http://www.robertpenner.com/easing/), which is a collection of premade animation algorithms that simulate these more natural movements. Not all libraries support this, but it is a nice way to make animations look more "real life."

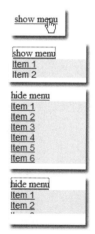

Figure 9-2. Animating the showing and hiding of a menu

Understanding and using jQuery

Probably one of the most aspiring libraries out there is John Resig's jQuery, available at http://jquery.net. The idea and goal of it becomes apparent in the introduction:

> *jQuery is a new type of JavaScript library. It is not a huge, bloated framework promising the best in Ajax—nor is it just a set of needlessly complex enhancements—**jQuery is designed to change the way that you write JavaScript**.*

One of the main goals of jQuery is to keep the library itself and your code as small as possible. In order to achieve this it uses a technique called chainable methods, which means you can attach any of its functions to the other and create one logical stream of functionality. For example, the native JavaScript for calling a function called example() when any link in the document gets clicked is as follows:

```
var as = document.getElementsByTagName('a');
for (var i = 0; i < as.length; i++){
    as[i].onclick = example;
}
```

Using jQuery, this would be

```
$('a').click(example);
```

All the available functions of jQuery are explained and can be navigated at Visual jQuery (http://www.visualjquery.com/index.xml), as shown in Figure 9-3.

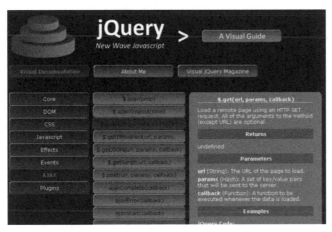

Figure 9-3. Visual jQuery is a visual representation of all the methods you have at your disposal with a quick explanation.

9

Hierarchical navigation in jQuery

The code to turn our demo list into a hierarchical navigation in jQuery looks like this. You can see that it is quite short, but also not that easy to understand if you don't adhere to a clean coding style with proper indentation. We won't go into details about the script, since there are many comments in this example explaining what each line does. Comments in JavaScript start with a double slash, //.

```javascript
// when the document has finished loading
$( document ) . ready (
  function() {
    // add a class called "dynamic" to the element with the ID nav
    $( '#nav' ).addClass('dynamic');
    // loop through all UL elements inside the "nav" element
    $( '#nav ul' ).each(
      function(){
        // add a class called "parent" to the parent element
        // of the current UL
        $(this.parentNode).addClass('parent');
      }
    );
    // if the visitor clicks on any link inside the "nav" element
    $('#nav a').click(
      function(){
        // get all lists inside the parent node of this link
        var uls = this.parentNode.getElementsByTagName('ul');
        // if there is at least one
        if(uls.length>0){
          // check its style display attribute and toggle it from
          // block to none
          uls[0].display=uls[0].style.display=='block'?'none':'block';
          // don't follow the link
          return false;
        }
      }
    );
  }
);
```

Animation in jQuery

Animation of objects in jQuery is either done with the animate() method or with preset permutations of it, namely fadeIn(), fadeOut(), fadeTo(), hide(), show(), slideDown(), slideUp(), and slideToggle(), each of which do what their name says.

Most of these methods take parameters such as the speed of the animation, which can be defined either in milliseconds or as slow, medium, or fast. Some methods also need a final value of the element's property; for example, fadeTo() needs the speed of the animation and the final opacity as a value between 0 and 1 as parameters.

The animate() method itself has the handy option to define parameter values with text like hide, show, or toggle, which makes it easy to show and hide elements in a smooth fashion without having to know their initial measurements (something you have to do if you wanted to create the animation sequence with your own JavaScript methods).

```javascript
// when the document has finished loading
$( document ) . ready (
  function() {
    // hide the navigation element
    $('#nav').hide();
    // create a link to show and hide the navigation
    $('#nav').before('<a href="#">show menu</a>');
    // define the states to execute alternately when the visitor
    // clicks the link
    $('#nav').prev().toggle(
      // set the text of the link to "hide menu" and show the menu
      function(){
        $(this).html('hide menu');
        $('#nav').slideToggle('medium');
      },
      // set the text of the link to "show menu" and hide the menu
      function(){
        $(this).html('show menu');
        $('#nav').slideToggle('medium');
      }
    );
  }
);
```

The animation capabilities of jQuery are easy to use and give you some shortcuts other libraries don't give you. On the other hand, at the time of this writing there is no option of changing the animation speed throughout the animation because jQuery does not feature Easing.

Understanding and using MooTools

MooTools (http://MooTools.net/) is a library with a bit of a confusing history. Originally MooTools was a visual effect library called moo.fx (http://moofx.mad4milk.net/) that was built on top of what may be the biggest JavaScript framework, Prototype (http://prototype.conio.net/).

The developers soon realized that Prototype is a bit too much to use for small effects, reengineered moo.fx, and started to create their own base library to use rather than Prototype. Thus, MooTools was born. The core of MooTools and the main idea was to allow classical object-oriented programming like you'd use in other languages such as Java or C#. On top of that, the effect libraries of moo.fx have been incorporated; all this together makes up quite a nice library to use. In the words of the developers:

9

MooTools is a very compact, modular, object-oriented JavaScript framework. Its unique design makes it extremely cross browser, easy to use, and a snap to extend with your own code. It comes with a choice of more than fifteen scripts, plugins and add-ons, including Effects, based on (moo.fx) Ajax, based on (moo.ajax), Dom Navigator, based on (moo.dom), Drag and Drop, Sortable lists, cookies Manager and many more. All the previous moo scripts have been made better, reorganized and extended to fully take advantage of the new OO architecture. One of the big differences is The Element Extension: MooTools makes it possible for you to extend HTML elements with your own methods, to make your life easier and your coding style way cooler.

In other words, just like jQuery, MooTools disregards the current style of JavaScript and tries to improve and change the way we write scripts for the Web.

Undoubtedly the coolest thing about MooTools is the accompanying web site and especially the download section at http://MooTools.net/download/release, shown in Figure 9-4. The download section allows you to customize your version of MooTools to make sure you only get what you need instead of a really large library with lots of elements you'll never use.

Figure 9-4. The MooTools download section allows for a customizable download that only gives you what you need in either a readable format or optimized and packed for size. The interface also recognizes dependencies and every download will be a working chunk of the whole library.

MooTools also comes with extensive documentation (which you'll find at http://docs. MooTools.net/) listing all the options you have. The problem with the documentation is that there is no offline version available at the moment, which can be frustrating if you wanted to use MooTools on the go and you needed to look up something.

MooTools is a library that makes it appear easy to create dynamic interfaces that can be animated to fade in and out or slide around. The whole site is built with MooTools and is a case study for the things MooTools is capable of.

However, there are still some inconsistencies in the library that (we hope) will be fixed by the time you are reading this. The most obvious fault is that MooTools has no method to stop a link from being followed or a button from submitting a form. Most of the time you need this, though, as you make a link or a button call a JavaScript function instead of loading a new document or submitting a form. As best practices when it comes to scripting dictate that you don't rely on JavaScript, this makes it a real pain to develop to these practices. It is easy to create an inaccessible web application in MooTools, but if you want to enhance an already working web site that uses HTML and server-side scripting means you need to extend MooTools with a function that allows you to stop the default event from happening. There is a function like this in the code that follows soon.

Generally there is a lot of work going into MooTools, and many communication channels such as the MooTools forum (http://forum.MooTools.net/) are available where you can ask for help. The fresh look and feel of the site makes it interesting to dig around and find out more.

Hierarchical navigation in MooTools

MooTools approaches JavaScript much the same way jQuery does. Instead of using and extending existing DOM methods like getElementsByTagName() or getElementById(), it offers you shortcut methods like $() and allows for chaining of methods.

The example script of the hierarchical navigation therefore looks rather similar to the jQuery example, except for some differences in naming and syntax. Information about what each line does is provided as inline comments (the lines starting with //).

```
// when the DOM of the page is ready
Window.onDomReady(
  function(){
    // add the CSS class "dynamic" to the element with the ID "nav"
    $('nav').addClass('dynamic');
    // get all LI elements inside the element with the ID "nav"
    $lis = $('nav').getElements('li');
    // loop through all the list items
    $lis.each(
      // the each() method parses each list item as the parameter o
      function(o){
        // if the list item contains UL elements
        if($(o).getElements('ul').length>0){
          // add a CSS class to the list item with the name "parent"
          o.addClass('parent');
          // get the first link inside the list item
          var trigger = $E('a', o);
          // execute a function when the visitor clicks the link
          trigger.addEvent('click',
            function(e){
              // get the first nested UL element and toggle its display
              var nest = o.getElements('ul')[0];
```

9

```
                        nest.style.display=nest.style.display==➥
'block'?'none':'block';
                    // don't follow the link
                    return Window.stopEvent(e);
                }
            )
        }
      }
    );
  }
);
// Hack extension to allow links not being followed when the user
// clicks them, this is not part of MooTools yet, but should be.
Window.extend({
  stopEvent: function(e){
    if (e.stopPropagation){
      e.stopPropagation();
      e.preventDefault();
    } else {
      e.returnValue = false;
      e.cancelBubble = true;
    } return false; }
});
```

Animation in MooTools

With moo.fx as its ancestor, MooTools comes with an impressive set of predefined animation sequences and effects. You can create effects with the Fx object, and each effect has
different methods to control it such as show(), hide(), or toggle().

```
// when the DOM of the page is ready
Window.onDomReady(
  function(){
    // add the CSS class "dynamic" to the element with the ID "nav"
    // thus hiding it
    $('nav').addClass('dynamic');
    // create a new link element, set the href attribute to # (to make
    // it appear as a link) and add text inside the link
    // saying "show menu"
    var trigger = new Element('a');
    trigger.setProperty('href','#');
    trigger.appendText('show menu');
    // add the new link before the menu to the document
    $(trigger).injectBefore('nav');
    // define a new slide effect for the menu
    var slideeffect = new Fx.Slide('nav');
```

```
        // hide the menu initially
        slideeffect.hide();
        // make the newly added link execute a function when a visitor
        // clicks it
        $(trigger).addEvent(
        'click',
           // function to toggle the menu state
           function(e){
             // alternately show and hide the menu and slide it open or
             // closed
             slideeffect.toggle('vertical');
             // change the text of the trigger link accordingly
             if($(trigger).innerHTML === 'show menu'){
               $(trigger).innerHTML = 'hide menu';
             } else {
               $(trigger).innerHTML = 'show menu';
             }
             // don't follow the link
             return Window.stopEvent(e);
           }
        )
      }
   );
   // Hack extension to allow links not being followed when the user
   // clicks them
   Window.extend({
     stopEvent: function(e){
       if (e.stopPropagation){
         e.stopPropagation();
         e.preventDefault();
       } else {
         e.returnValue = false;
         e.cancelBubble = true;
       } return false; }
   });
```

Understanding and using YUI

The Yahoo! User Interface Library (YUI), which you'll find at http://developer.yahoo.
com/yui, was developed primarily to ease the development process of web sites inside
Yahoo!. Instead of each development team consistently having to face and fix browser issues
and create scripts that do the same things over and over again, YUI (shown in Figure 9-5) acts
as a central repository for these tasks. Developers feed problems they encounter back to the
YUI team and those problems get fixed in the next version of the library.

Figure 9-5. The Yahoo! User Interface Library web site

The idea behind the different YUI components is that they help developers with one issue at a time rather than offering an all-encompassing approach the way that jQuery or MooTools does with methods like $(). To this end, YUI is separated into several components, each of which is designed to help with one part of web scripting:

- Animation—Allows you to animate parts of a document, cross-browser and securely

- Connection—Allows you to connect to the server to retrieve data via Ajax

- Dom—Allows you to retrieve, alter, and add elements from and to the document

- DragDrop—Allows you to create drag-and-drop interfaces

- Event—Allows you to get informed and react to happenings in the browser and to the document (for example, a user clicking a link)

- Fonts/Grids/Reset—CSS components that allow you to create layouts that work consistently across browsers

The library is separated into library components and widgets. While the components mentioned earlier allow you to easily create your own scripts, widgets are interface elements that can be used as they are and customized to your needs. At the time of this writing, YUI has the following widgets:

- Logger—Allows you to debug an application while developing it independent of the browser

- Menu/TreeView—Allows you to create menus for your site or application ranging from simple static menus via dynamic hierarchical menus up to contextual menus

- Slider—Provides you with a method to create slider controls or color pickers

- Tabs—Allows you to develop tabbed interfaces

- Autocomplete—Allows you to create text boxes that offer possible values to go in them while you are typing

- Calendar—Provides you with an out-of-the-box calendar widget to make date picking in a form a lot easier for the visitor

- Container—Allows for overlays, tooltips, modular windows, and dialog boxes

YUI may have the most extensive documentation and set of code examples of all the libraries. However, the examples can be a bit exhaustive as they try to show every option a component or widget has rather than explain step by step what the options are. A couple of really good companions if you want to use YUI are the Cheatsheets (which are available as PDFs) and the mailing list, which you can use to find help and search for instances where your problem has already been solved.

Because YUI code is meant to work in large web sites and applications, its main focus is to be stable across all modern browsers (what modern browsers are and how Yahoo! defines support is explained in the browser support grid at http://developer.yahoo.com/yui/articles/gbs/gbs.html) and safe to implement together with other scripts. The latter is achieved by adding namespaces to the code. This means that every function developed using YUI has to start with the word YAHOO followed by what it is and its name. This might appear verbose at first sight, but it ensures that no Yahoo! script overwrites other functionality. Here are some examples:

- YAHOO.example.createDynamicMenu() is an example script using YUI that will create a dynamic menu.
- YAHOO.util.Event is the event utility component.
- YAHOO.widget.Calendar is YUI's calendar widget.

Following this convention and sticking to a standard JavaScript syntax rather than allowing for shortcuts like jQuery and MooTools does mean that scripts using YUI tend to be larger. What it also means, though, is that the scripts don't need to be converted back to something the JavaScript parser understands.

Hierarchical navigation using YUI

The easiest option for creating the example of a collapsible hierarchical navigation is to use either the Menu (http://developer.yahoo.com/yui/menu/) or the TreeView widget (http://developer.yahoo.com/yui/treeview/). However, to demonstrate how to use the different components of the library in your own script, let's give it a go. Notice once again that the explanations of what the script does are in the inline comments starting with a double slash.

```
// use the example namespace and call the main object "tree"
YAHOO.example.tree = {

    // the init function to hide elements and add the "parent" classes
    init:function(){

        // add a class called dynamic to the element that was sent as a
        // parameter (stored in this)
        YAHOO.util.Dom.addClass(this,'dynamic');
```

```
                      // add an event listener that calls the toggle method when a
                      // visitor clicks anywhere inside the tree element
                      YAHOO.util.Event.addListener(this, 'click', ➥
                YAHOO.example.tree.toggle);

                      // grab all UL elements inside the element and loop through
                      // each of them
                      var uls = this.getElementsByTagName('ul');
                      for(var i=uls.length-1;i>-1;i--){

                        // add a class called "parent" to each LI that contains a UL
                        YAHOO.util.Dom.addClass(uls[i].parentNode, 'parent');

                      }
                    },

                    // the method to show and hide the nested lists
                    toggle:function(e){

                      // use the Event component to find out which element was clicked on
                      var t = YAHOO.util.Event.getTarget(e);

                      // compare if the element had the name "a", thus being a link
                      if(t.nodeName.toLowerCase()==='a'){

                        // check if the link is inside an LI that has a nested UL element
                        var nestedLists = t.parentNode.getElementsByTagName('ul');
                        if( nestedLists.length > 0 ){

                          // toggle the display of the nested UL
                          nestedLists[0].style.display = nestedLists[0].style.➥
                display === 'block'?'none':'block';

                          // don't follow the link
                          YAHOO.util.Event.preventDefault(e);
                        }
                      }
                    }
                  }

                  // as soon as the element with the ID 'nav' is available, call the
                  // init method
                  YAHOO.util.Event.onAvailable('nav', YAHOO.example.tree.init);
```

The structure of a script using YUI does not differ much from any other traditional JavaScript, which makes it look a bit cumbersome compared to the slicker "new" way of scripting that jQuery or MooTools offer. However, the practical upshot of this is that you don't need to learn about the library itself to use it. In a professional or distributed development environment, this can be a very important asset, as you normally don't have the time and budget to train people on systems that should make their job easier.

Animation using YUI

Animation is a component of YUI that uses the aforementioned Easing methods to allow you to create natural-looking animations. Unlike the other libraries we've mentioned, YUI does not provide premade methods to show and hide or toggle elements; you are expected to create your own instead. This seems a less practical approach, but on the other hand you have much more control over the outcome. There are lots of examples on the homepage (http://developer.yahoo.com/yui/animation/) and inside the YUI download zip to get you going. The overall structure of creating an animation is pretty straightforward. You define an animation with this constructor:

```
var anim = new YAHOO.util.Anim(element, { properties }, duration, ➡
Easing method );
```

- The properties define how you want to animate the element; for example, width: {from:100, to: 500}.
- The duration is the length of the animation in seconds.
- The easing method specifies which one of the preset methods for natural animation you want to use (for example, easeIn).

You start the animation by calling the method animate(), and you could stop it prematurely with the stop() method. You can also execute different functions before, during, and after the animation using the onStart, onTween, and onComplete custom events, respectively.

9

> *Custom events are a specialty of YUI. Normal JavaScript events are interesting moments in the life cycle of a web page. Examples are when the page was loaded (the load event), when a user clicks an element inside the page (the click event), or when the browser window is resized (the resize event). You can listen for these events and do something when they occur. YUI also allows you to define your own events for the current document that are not part of the normal browser toolset. You can define functions that get executed when these events are fired (listeners) and make the event happen any time you want to. This is extremely handy if you have a complex application or you want to make sure that several page elements change when something happens to another one. If you go to Yahoo! Maps in Europe (http://uk.local.yahoo.com/maps) you can see custom events in action; we used about 20 different ones to make this interface work smoothly.*

Putting all of this together, we once again have a script that does look a lot bigger than the jQuery or MooTools equivalents, but also makes it easy to debug and find your way even if you don't know YUI. Explanations are once again in comments (the lines starting with //).

```
YAHOO.example.animateMenu = {
  // predefine a property to store the visibility status of the menu
  menuvisible:false,
  // initialization method
  init:function(){
    // store the height of the menu in menuheight
    YAHOO.example.animateMenu.menuheight = this.offsetHeight;
    // add a CSS class called dynamic to the menu, thus hiding it
    YAHOO.util.Dom.addClass(this, 'dynamic');
    // create a new link element and give it a href to make it display
    // as a link
    YAHOO.example.animateMenu.trigger = document.createElement('a');
    YAHOO.example.animateMenu.trigger.setAttribute('href', '#');
    // add the text "show menu" to the link
    YAHOO.example.animateMenu.trigger. ➡
appendChild(document.createTextNode('show menu'));
    // insert the link before the menu
    this.parentNode.insertBefore(YAHOO.example.animateMenu.trigger, ➡
this);
    // call the method togglemenu when a user clicks the link
    YAHOO.util.Event.addListener(YAHOO.example.animateMenu.trigger, ➡
'click',
    YAHOO.example.animateMenu.togglemenu );
  },
  // method to show and hide the menu
  togglemenu:function(e){
    // if the menu is hidden
    if(YAHOO.example.animateMenu.menuvisible === false){
    // set the menu height to zero (to avoid it flashing up before the
    // animation starts)
      YAHOO.util.Dom.setStyle('nav', 'height', '0');
      // remove the CSS class to show the menu
      YAHOO.util.Dom.removeClass('nav', 'dynamic');
      // define the end value of the animation as the original height
      // of the menu
      var end = YAHOO.example.animateMenu.menuheight;
      // animation attributes - animate until the height is the
      // original height
      var attributes = {height:{to:end}};
      // set the property to state that the menu is visible
      YAHOO.example.animateMenu.menuvisible = true;
      // change the text of the link to "hide menu"
      var linktext = 'hide menu';
    // if the menu is visible...
    } else {
      // define the end value of the animation as 0
      var attributes = {height:{to:0}};
      // set the property to state that the menu is hidden
      YAHOO.example.animateMenu.menuvisible = false;
```

```
        // change the text of the link to "show menu"
        var linktext = 'show menu';
    }
    // define a new animation to change the element with the ID nav
    // using the defined attributes, a duration of one second
    // and start and end slower using the Easing methods.
    var anim = new YAHOO.util.Anim('nav', attributes, 1, ➡
YAHOO.util.Easing.easeBoth);
    // start the animation
    anim.animate();
    // when the animation is finished
    anim.onComplete.subscribe(
      function(){
        // change the text of the link
        YAHOO.example.animateMenu.trigger.firstChild.nodeValue = ➡
linktext;
      }
    );
    // don't follow the original link
    YAHOO.util.Event.preventDefault(e);
  }
}
// execute the initialization method as soon as the element
// with the ID "nav" is available.
YAHOO.util.Event.onAvailable('nav', YAHOO.example.animateMenu.init);
```

The animation component of YUI is massive in terms of features and functionality and allows for a lot of different effects and ideas. It does mean, however, that you need to write these effects yourself based on a set of tools. This is harder to do than, say, using jQuery's show('fast'), but it also gives you a lot more options.

9

Summary

We hope this chapter has given you some insight into the process and the concept behind using special effects in web sites and blogs. We've deliberately tried to keep the examples to a bare minimum and didn't delve too much into details about the various libraries. After all, this is not a JavaScript book (there are other books to teach you the basics of this language), and the JavaScript library environment is such a fast-moving target that any book written on it will be outdated in a month's time. By the time this one comes out, some of the things explained even in these short introductions might have changed.

Our intention was to make sure that if you are going to use special effects on your site, you do so for a reason and you understand the implications of it. Far too many web sites out there go heavy on JavaScript for the sake of using it or to try to draw visitors' attention away from lack of content or updates. This only works for a very short period of time and is nothing to build your network of contacts or visitors on.

10 WHAT TO DO AND WHERE TO FIND HELP WHEN THINGS GO WRONG

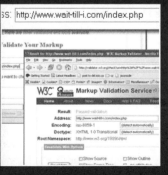

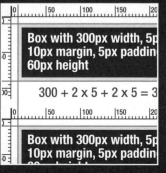

By Chris Heilmann

In this chapter we'll talk about online resources you can contact when you are stuck with a certain web development problem. We'll also go into details on how to ask questions the right way so that they result in helpful answers rather than one-liners or no answers at all. We'll list several channels where you can get help and their pros and cons.

It has always been this author's credo to question any authority—it keeps them on their toes. So here is why you can trust the findings here: the information you find in this chapter is based on my own experiences in different communication channels, collected in the last 10 years (I used to connect to IRC on my Commodore 64 with a 2400-baud modem). I've published about 30 different articles online, written more emails and forum posts than I'd like to remember, and worked as an editor for books and an online editor for evolt.org. *Before I worked on the Internet I was a radio journalist spending my days writing interviews and news. In order to back up my assumptions, I conducted a survey on several mailing lists asking about the biggest nuisances for both information seekers and information givers, and incorporated the findings here.*

Of egos and altruism

Getting stuck with a problem about web development is, strangely enough, a good thing. It encourages you to ask other developers for help, and it may even be that you've discovered a problem or bug that others haven't yet experienced. Asking for help about this problem and getting a solution means one more issue sorted for the web development community as a whole.

Coming into the web development community as an outsider is an interesting experience. If you access the right channels for information you'll find out quickly that the sharing of information and collaborative finding of solutions is much more important than advertising products. You may get some replies that tell you to buy a specific product that will be the end to all your problems, but you'll also get immediate information about how much truth lies in that statement. Other participants of the chat or the mailing list or forum thread will tell you flat out if they can verify the quality and usefulness of the product, and pure advertisers will get scrutinized and mercilessly told to stop spamming.

Danger, incoming egos

The flipside of that is that not products but egos are the main annoyance. A lot of times collaboration doesn't work properly because every new member of a certain community is eager to share their knowledge and resources exclusively and generally make a name for themselves in the community. Instead of adding solutions to a collaborative resource like a wiki (http://en.wikipedia.org/wiki/Wiki), they end up on the person's web site or blog. This can be a good thing, and many great online resources started that way. In most cases, however, the initially eager developer soon gets bored of dealing with questions and their resources deteriorate into yet another car wreck on the information superhighway.

Another ego problem is that a lot of developers who just started a small agency try to get endorsement and their names high up on the search engines' results by publishing articles on as many "webzines" as possible. This wouldn't be a problem if their articles contained sound information and were well researched, but in many cases it is a dog and pony show stating that a currently hot topic in web design is easy to solve by trusting an expert (i.e., the writer) and not having to do anything yourself. This is never the case—if you don't look at what you get and at least grasp the ideas behind it, you will get bad service. Smoke and mirrors is a lot easier to do than providing thorough, well-researched information. The biggest example is search engine optimization (SEO) articles. If they are connected to a new and upcoming agency, you might as well not bother reading them.

The other ego problem is that a lot of participants in these communication channels have pet peeves and are likely to attack anyone who dares to ask about them (font sizing being one of them). Another related problem is not very experienced developers attacking anyone who does not comply with their current ideal of quality or who ask for shortcuts and hacks because time is essential in getting something fixed. Be aware of these types when you post on a forum, send an email or join a chat. It is not about you; it is about the quality of web development as a whole.

Human communication is very much neutered when you only see what other people type—moods don't easily come across when you don't hear the voice or see the person. Therefore, it is easy to misunderstand someone or not recognize humor or irony in an answer. Again, don't be miffed or discouraged by seemingly harsh answers. Nobody attacks you personally—if that were the case, the community would deal with it as that person would be considered out of line. Even if that were to happen, you can be relatively sure that the person is not worth the hassle. I have sometimes had people attack me personally on mailing lists, and on every one of these occasions I got several private emails from list members apologizing and telling me not to take it personally. Negative feedback is an opportunity to get better, not a smack in the face or a sign stating you have to stay outside.

Friendly advice, given for free

While you will encounter some annoyances like these, you can avoid a lot by recognizing what you are getting: free advice. Many participants in online help systems do it in their free time (or when the boss isn't watching) and there is nothing more frustrating than lending a helping hand just to get it slapped or bitten. You are asking for free advice from people who work toward a common goal—making web development easier and higher quality—so here are some points you should remember:

- People tend to help you to help yourself, and are not there to solve your problems for you without you putting some effort into solving them.

- As you don't pay people, don't expect immediate answers and their full attention; good answers might take a while as people research what you have asked or test it themselves.

10

- Your setup and environment is not the world. Although something might work for you, it might break horribly on other setups. Listen to this advice and don't tell people you don't care about their "odd" operating system or browser.

- If someone was helpful to you, a simple "thank you" email doesn't take much of your time but sparks a nice subconscious memory the next time that person reads your name. Over time, this may even turn into a fruitful professional relationship. This author has several contacts whose web design knowledge is very basic and they sometimes ask questions that may seem trivial to more experienced web developers, but their personality makes it fun to help them out—and their enthusiasm is addictive!

You'll be surprised how much help you can get when you approach people and different communication channels the right way. You'll also be amazed at how many negative vibes you'll spark when you do it the wrong way.

Things to do before asking for help

In this section we'll discuss how to make sure you've done everything you need to before you go asking for help. All of these were mentioned in our survey as main annoyances by people who are willing to help but feel as if they'd be wasting their time if they did.

Search the Web for solutions

The top spot of "annoying habits of newbies" according to the survey was people asking to fix problems that are known "in the community" and have been fixed over and over again. It is frustrating to give help in a certain community and see it stagnating as the discussion revolves repeatedly about the same issues and there is never time to tackle new problems. Therefore, it is a good idea to check on the Web if there is any article, blog post, or even forum post that already explains what you are trying to fix. Places to look for solutions are

- Search engines (Yahoo!, Google)—but make sure that you search for keywords, not for full questions. An entry like "hotel paris" will most likely get you a better result than "where can I find a hotel in paris". Search engines are working on bridging this gap between humans and machines, though, and human-to-human knowledge search systems like Yahoo! Answers (http://answers.yahoo.com) are a better place to find information if you want to pose real questions.

- Webzines (and their archives) that deal with web development issues, such as http://www.alistapart.com, http://www.evolt.org, http://www.sitepoint.com, http://www.digital-web.com, and http://www.thinkvitamin.com. Most of these also provide a comment facility to every article—make sure you read the comments and the article, as the article is the view of one person but comments were made by many. In many cases, the article solution has flaws or didn't cover a certain aspect and somebody other than the writer found a solution and commented on it.

- Forum archives such as http://www.builder.com, http://www.sitepoint.com, and the friends of ED forums at http://friendsofed.infopop.net/2/OpenTopic/.

- FAQ sites such as http://www.siteexperts.com.

- Bug-fixing libraries such as http://www.positioniseverything.net and http://www.communitymx.com.

- Blogs such as http://www.quirksmode.org, http://www.456bereastreet.com, http://www.stuffandnonsense.com, and http://www.wait-till-i.com.

Once you've looked through these, there is a high possibility you won't have to ask for help, and if not, you will at least have an insight into what others have already tried while searching for a solution.

> *Just like with groceries, make sure you check the date of publication before digesting. Fixes that were all the rage in 1999 might not necessarily be a clever option today.*

Validate your code

Probably the most important step to take is to validate your code before asking for help. A lot of times you simply made a small mistake and fixing it will make your problem disappear. Often you will also find that an error earlier in the document can cause many more subsequent errors and fixing the first one will make the whole document show up correctly. This is a step that any good developer giving you advice will take anyway, and you can spare them having to take it.

Code validation is a means to an end, not necessarily a quality control mechanism. You can write HTML that validates and yet semantically makes no sense whatsoever. However, validating your code and making sure that it is standards-compliant makes debugging a lot easier because there will be no surprises. You know how it should render and what the code should do, and any deviation from that means that there is a browser bug that needs attention or a workaround. Since you simply cannot know all these bugs and their workarounds (very few people do), you can safely say you need help, as you've successfully validated your code, so it can't be your code that is the issue.

Validating HTML

Many layout glitches and even script errors are caused by invalid HTML, which is easy to avoid if you validate and fix your code. You can validate HTML documents in many ways, and many editors have validation tools built in. For web pages that are already on a publicly available server, there is the W3C online validator at http://validator.w3.org. You simply copy and paste a URL in it and click the validate button. Figure 10-1 shows how validation looks and works using this approach.

10

Figure 10-1. Validating with the W3C online validator

This example shows a valid page; however, when you enter an invalid page you get a warning and a list of errors, as shown in Figure 10-2.

Figure 10-2. A failed validation result listing all the HTML errors

The great thing about the online validator is that it is always up-to-date (unlike validation tools that are embedded into a desktop application, which can get outdated or may have bugs that never get fixed). The problem with the online validator is that it is annoying to test each page by copying and pasting the URL.

To this end, the W3C also offers a free tool called Tidy to download and use offline to validate HTML documents. You can download Tidy at http://tidy.sourceforge.net/ and use it as a *command-line tool* (this means that Tidy is a developer tool and does not come with a graphical interface).

A much easier way of using Tidy is via available browser plug-ins. Examples are the HTML Validator extension for Firefox (http://users.skynet.be/mgueury/mozilla/) or the Safari Tidy plug-in (http://zappatic.net/safaritidy/). There is no plug-in for Internet Explorer, but there are toolbars that have shortcuts to the validators, like the Web Developer Toolbar (http://www.microsoft.com/downloads/details.aspx?FamilyID= e59c3964-672d-4511-bb3e-2d5e1db91038&displaylang=en) or the Web Accessibility Toolbar (http://www.visionaustralia.org.au/ais/toolbar/).

The Firefox HTML Validator extension sits in the bottom of the browser window and shows when there is an HTML validation error on the page (instead of a green icon there is a red one). When you hover the mouse over the icon you get a tooltip explaining how many errors there are.

If you double-click the icon, a new window shows the source of the HTML document with all the errors highlighted. On the bottom left is a list of errors that occurred, and clicking each of them scrolls the upper area to the erroneous part of the code. On the bottom-right side you get explanations as to what this error means. Figure 10-3 shows the different states of the plug-in and the source code window.

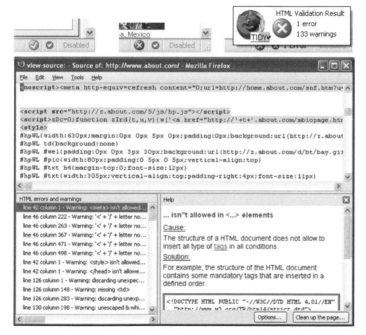

Figure 10-3. The Tidy validator plug-in in action. The top shows the different states of the icon in the bottom of the browser, and the bottom shows the validator pop-up window with the highlighted source code, the list of warnings and errors, and their explanation on the right.

10

Be aware that any validator shows both warnings and errors. Warnings are not likely to cause issues with the rendering of the page, while errors do. Furthermore, one error early in the document may cause a lot of follow-up warnings and errors, which means that once you fix it, the overwhelming list of hundreds of errors will probably shrink down to two or three main problems.

A large amount of display problems can be fixed by validating and amending the HTML. The most likely mistakes that cause rendering issues are

- Unclosed or mismatched tags (`<p> some text` rather than `<p>some text</p>`, or `<tr><td></tr></td>` instead of `<tr><td></td></tr>`)

- Unclosed quotation marks around attributes (`<div id="header>` instead of `<div id="header">`)

Validating CSS

The W3C also offers a validation service for CSS files at `http://jigsaw.w3.org/css-validator/`. While this is handy to debug obvious typos and syntax errors, most CSS problems are actually caused by other issues like browser bugs or by choosing a wrong or an invalid DOCTYPE (which causes the browser to show pages in a wrong rendering mode).

Of DOCTYPEs and rendering modes

Browser developers are stuck with a dilemma every time they release a new version of their software: how to ensure that web sites developed for the older browsers will still render correctly although they use invalid CSS, hacks, and incorrect settings to accommodate for bugs in the old version. Although it would be incredibly handy if browsers just flat out refused to display invalid code—or at least show a warning message—it is not good advertising as web surfers who don't know or care about code or web standards would blame the browser and expect it to be faulty.

To accommodate invalid code and keep old hacks working, browser vendors have included different rendering modes. You trigger these rendering modes by choosing different DOCTYPEs—more modern and stricter ones for the standards-compliant rendering mode and others that are more forgiving for the faulty rendering mode.

As an example, the faulty rendering mode causes IE 6 to show pages as if it were IE 5. Switching between these modes is called *DOCTYPE switching* and the modes are called Standards mode and Quirks mode. To create standards-compliant web sites and allow other people to help you debug your sites, you should always try to enforce Standards mode. You can do this by choosing one of the following DOCTYPEs in your HTML documents, like we did in the earlier examples. Using any other DOCTYPE or simply omitting it will make the browser automatically go into Quirks mode.

```
HTML 4.01 Strict:
<!DOCTYPE HTML PUBLIC "-//W3C//DTD HTML 4.01//EN"
"http://www.w3.org/TR/html4/strict.dtd">
HTML 4.01 Transitional:
<!DOCTYPE HTML PUBLIC "-//W3C//DTD HTML 4.01 Transitional//EN"
"http://www.w3.org/TR/html4/loose.dtd">
HTML 4.01 Frameset:
<!DOCTYPE HTML PUBLIC "-//W3C//DTD HTML 4.01 Frameset//EN"
"http://www.w3.org/TR/html4/frameset.dtd">
XHTML 1.0 Strict:
<!DOCTYPE html PUBLIC "-//W3C//DTD XHTML 1.0 Strict//EN"
"http://www.w3.org/TR/xhtml1/DTD/xhtml1-strict.dtd">
XHTML 1.0 Transitional:
<!DOCTYPE html PUBLIC"-//W3C//DTD XHTML 1.0 Transitional//EN"
"http://www.w3.org/TR/xhtml1/DTD/xhtml1-transitional.dtd">
XHTML 1.0 Frameset:
<!DOCTYPE html PUBLIC "-//W3C//DTD XHTML 1.0 Frameset//EN"
"http://www.w3.org/TR/xhtml1/DTD/xhtml1-frameset.dtd">
XHTML 1.1 DTD:
<!DOCTYPE html PUBLIC "-//W3C//DTD XHTML 1.1//EN"
"http://www.w3.org/TR/xhtml11/DTD/xhtml11.dtd">
```

> *You can find out more about DOCTYPE switching at the Community MX web site, where Holly Bergevin provides more in-depth information and has collected several more resource URLs:* http://www.communitymx.com/content/article.cfm?cid=85FE.

Quirks mode is—as the name may suggest—quirky and, in terms of being able to predict how something should be rendered, somewhat unreliable. Using it throws web development some years back where developers had to create different versions of the same web site to support different browsers. The modern web developer should aim to be browser agnostic and concentrate on supporting the standards defined by the W3C instead—thus making sure that browsers that will be developed in the future know what to do with the document.

The difference in the modes becomes obvious when you define a box with a width, height, padding, margins, and border and check it with one of the previously listed DOCTYPEs and without any in Internet Explorer. Figure 10-4 shows the difference.

10

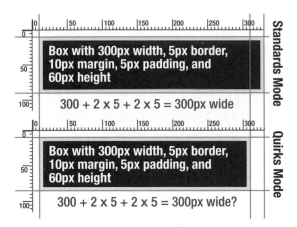

Figure 10-4. Internet Explorer does not add padding and borders to the dimensions of a box when it isn't in Standards mode.

The top example in Figure 10-4 is how the W3C defines how a box should be rendered (http://www.w3.org/TR/REC-CSS2/box.html): both padding and border should add to the overall width of the box. The bottom example shows how older versions of IE calculated a box: neither the border nor the padding adds to the overall width or height of the box. In W3C CSS2-compliant browsers, this box should be 320 pixels wide. As IE 6 is in Quirks mode in the bottom example, the box is 300 pixels wide. This can cause endless frustration when trying to debug a CSS layout.

Using the developer toolbar to check the rendering mode

One amazingly helpful tool for testing and web development is a Firefox extension called Web Developer Toolbar, created by Chris Pederick and available at http://chrispederick.com/work/webdeveloper/. Once installed, it adds a toolbar to Firefox that allows you to do a lot of things with the current document. You can, for example, edit the CSS of the site by pressing Ctrl+Shift+E and see the effect on the live site (although the changes are not saved on the live site). This is handy for quickly working out how to fix a problem without having to make changes locally, upload the CSS, and then refresh the browser. The toolbar also indicates which rendering mode is currently active by showing an icon on the top right either as colored (Standards mode) or grayed out (Quirks mode). Figure 10-5 shows the two different states with their tooltips.

Figure 10-5. Firefox Web Developer Toolbar indicating the rendering mode—Standards or Quirks mode

Validating JavaScript

To validate JavaScript, you need to find out what went wrong by reading the output of the error console, something most browsers offer these days (IE 6 does not have one, though). When reporting a JavaScript problem, you can send the output of the console to the people willing to help.

Although some error console messages are very detailed and helpful (the output of Opera is probably the best), others are quite cryptic. Internet Explorer tends to report things like undefined is not defined or object does not support this property or method for almost any error.

Debugging and validating JavaScript requires that you know it, and you may not be interested that much in learning JavaScript. Therefore, it is good to have a preliminary check reading the output of the error console and check the lines in the script that are reported to have an obvious error like an unclosed quotation mark.

You can reach the error console in Firefox by selecting Tools ➤ JavaScript Console or, if you have the Web Developer Toolbar installed, by clicking the icon next to the rendering mode indicator. If there is no error, the icon is a speech bubble with an "I"; otherwise it is a red error marker—both are visible in Figure 10-5.

If you want to know about everything that is going on in the document, you can install yet another extension for Firefox called Firebug, which is available at http://joehewitt.com/software/firebug/. If you visit the site you can see what Firebug does, and it is simply amazing. Anything that happens in and to the document can be checked in most cases, and even altered when you have this extension. Figure 10-6 compares the Firefox JavaScript Console and Firebug.

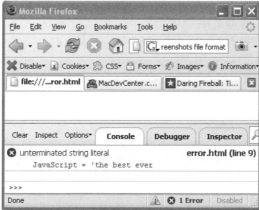

Figure 10-6. The Firefox JavaScript console and Firebug extension displaying the same error

10

235

Wrapping up validation

In order to get good (and fast!) help, make sure that you have

- Validated your HTML—unclosed elements and quotation marks can cause rendering errors
- Chosen a DOCTYPE that forces the browser to use standards rendering mode—there is no way to predict cross-browser results in Quirks mode
- Validated your CSS and checked the JavaScript console to make sure there isn't a simple problem with your JavaScript such as a typo that is causing the issue

Make your problem reproducible

Once you've taken the preliminary validation steps, make sure that potential helpers can reach what you want them to help you to debug. Have a URL handy where they can reach the site and see the issue for themselves, and tell them what configuration you are seeing the problem in. This includes

- The browser you use (name and version—if you are not sure, go to any browser's Help ➤ About menu option)
- The screen resolution you are running
- The operating system (Windows, Mac, Linux, etc.)

Also include any other software you have installed that might interfere with the browser or the Internet connection, like firewalls, browser extensions, extra toolbars, or virus or spyware protection software. Classic cases are Norton Internet Security, which adds JavaScript to web sites to protect you from malicious code and pop-ups, or the Google Toolbar for Internet Explorer, which colors fields with available data yellow.

If the problem requires a certain interaction to take place, provide a step-by-step explanation of how to reproduce the issue and provide screenshots of how the problem shows itself on your end. It is a good idea to upload these screenshots to a convenient URL (for example, a photo-hosting service) so they can be seen by would-be helpers. Ensure that your web site does not need any authorization, and if it does, provide a temporary login and password.

Make sure that you use test URLs for your problem and not a live site. There are a couple of reasons for that. First, the live site is likely to change, and second, URLs provided on mailing lists and forums will be indexed by search engines and found by spammers. Therefore, it is very important not to have a real URL that needs removing from an old email or forum post. If you cannot create a test copy of your code, you can also use URL redirection services like http://www.tinyurl.com *or* http://www.snipurl.com *to point to your problem site.*

Taking screenshots on Mac OS X Tiger

The easiest option to take a screenshot on Mac OS X Tiger is to press Command+Shift+3. This will take a screen capture of the whole screen and save it to your Desktop as a PNG file. Another key combination is Command+Shift+4, which allows you to select the part of the screen you'd like as a screenshot. The drawback of this approach is that it does not include the mouse cursors. If you want the mouse cursor to be captured, you need to use a utility called Grab from the Applications\Utilities folder. This tool allows for much more functionality, including a timed grab process in case you need to open some menus or follow some other interaction steps before taking the screenshot.

If you need to capture a whole document, you can create a PDF of it. You can achieve this by selecting Print from the File menu. Select the Preview option at the bottom of the Print dialog box and you will get a PDF version of the document in the Preview application. Simply select Save as PDF from the File menu to store it on your computer. This does not necessarily work if the page has a dedicated print style sheet. Be sure to deactivate those before you take a screenshot using this trick.

> You can learn more about the ins and outs of screenshots on Macs by checking out this article: http://www.macdevcenter.com/pub/a/mac/2003/02/28/screenshot.html.

Taking screenshots on Windows XP

Windows XP does not come with as many handy applications to take screenshots. All you can do is press the PrtScrn or Print key on your keyboard and that will store the current screen in the Clipboard. You won't get any cursor, and there is also no way to create a screenshot of a whole document without resorting to commercial software, like TechSmith's SnagIt (http://www.techsmith.com). You also have to find out how to store the data in the Clipboard as an optimized file. The OS-given choice is to use Microsoft Paint, which you can find in Programs\Accessories. The snag is that although you can choose JPG or GIF to store the screenshot as a file, you can't change the settings to improve the file's quality and reduce its size.

A free alternative is IrfanView, available at http://www.irfanview.com. Not only is this tool an amazing image converter that reads and writes almost any image format out there, but it also is a basic screen-capturing tool. Pressing the C key will get you to the capturing options shown in Figure 10-7. You can choose to set a hotkey combination that you can press to take the screenshot (by default, Ctrl+F11), or set it to automatically take a shot after a certain amount of time. You can choose to take a screenshot of the whole screen, the current window, or the client area of the current window (which means omitting the toolbars). You can choose to include the mouse cursor and whether you want to store the images automatically or open them in IrfanView to perform some more alterations and choose different optimization settings.

10

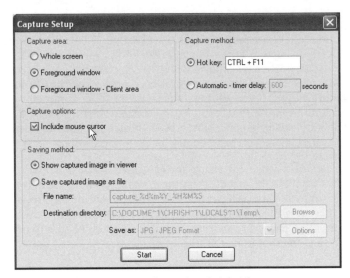

Figure 10-7. The screen-capturing options in IrfanView

Screen capturing with a Firefox extension

You might have guessed it already—there is a great Firefox extension that allows you to take screenshots of the current document, either the currently visible section or the whole document. Called Pearl Crescent Page Saver, this extension adds a small camera to the top right of your browser that allows you to save the current document as a PNG file. The same options are also available in the context menu when you right-click the document. You can download the extension at http://pearlcrescent.com/products/pagesaver/.

Reproduction wrap-up and example

In summary, you should provide a lot of information to make sure you get a quick, relevant, and detailed solution for your problem:

- Give detailed information about the circumstances that led to the problem.
- Provide details about your setup and configuration.
- Make sure your problem can be reproduced—provide URLs with screenshots or temporary login/password combinations.
- Use temporary web locations for your examples, never a live system or one that might make data available to search engines and spammers that you don't want to be accessed in the future.

Here are some examples of how requests should look:

Subject: Odd bold character on MSIE when using fading in animations

Hello there, I have a problem with the following example: http://tinyurl/xxxx.

When you click the "more information" link I want the following text to fade in smoothly. I am using the Yahoo! User Interface Library (http://developer.yahoo.com/yui) for this.

Now, on MSIE 6 on Windows XP the fading in works nicely, but the characters are somehow distorted and look bold during animation. A screenshot is available at http://tinyurl/xxxx.

Can anybody tell me what is going on?

(FYI: It is bug in Windows XP's font-smoothing technology and you need to set a background color on the element to avoid it. The xxxx in this example is also only an example; you don't necessarily want to enter this URL to check.)

Subject: List items double the height in MSIE compared to Firefox

Can you please take a look at http://tinyurl/xxxx? I am trying to create a menu from a nested list and need the links to occupy the whole width, which is why I set the display of the links to block.

Now, on my system (Windows XP2, Norton Internet Security 1024x768) everything looks fine in Firefox, but in MSIE 6 the menu items are twice as high (screenshot at http://tiniyurl/xxxx).

What is the reason for this, and is there a solution?

(FYI: It is about line breaks in the code. IE has a bug that shows them as padding. Remove the white space and all is fine.)

You should get the idea from these examples, which are applicable to both forums and mailing lists. To make it clearer, just check the following request. Would you feel like answering and helping the writer of the following email?

Hello I have a problem with my site. I have not much time and could you check what is wrong? I don't really want to change anything on the page but somehow it is wrong. Please contact me and I can send you a zip file with the page.

10

Different help channels and their best practices

In this section we'll explore some of the most common channels of communication you can take to ask for help online. We'll also list examples and what to avoid doing when you use them.

Mailing lists

Mailing lists are email lists you can send a message to once you have signed up for them. Emails you send to the list are sent to all the subscribing members and archived on a web site. Depending on the list software in use, you can get a copy of your email sent to yourself and define the mode of your subscription (*digest mode*, which sends one email a day or week that contains all the postings to the list, or *email mode*, which sends every mail immediately when it gets sent to the list). List examples are

- **The CSS Discuss List**: Created by CSS guru Eric Meyer, this list (http://www.css-discuss.org/) is probably the one with the most subscribers (thousands) and the highest traffic (about 50 emails a day). It deals with CSS exclusively and has a wiki (an online archive anyone can contribute to) as well as an archive.

- **Evolt's thelist**: Deals with web development as a whole, including server-side problems like Apache setup and database questions (http://lists.evolt.org/mailman/listinfo/thelist).

- **The Web Standards Group list**: Deals with web standards and how to implement them (http://webstandardsgroup.org/mail/).

- **Web Accessibility in Mind (WebAiM)**: Deals with web accessibility matters (http://www.webaim.org/discussion/).

- **WebDesign-L**: About web design as a whole (http://www.webdesign-l.com/).

Things to keep in mind about mailing lists

Some rules to keep in mind about mailing lists are

- No matter how basic—and in some cases outright appalling—the web site accompanying the list is, there will be a lot of people signed up to it. These are people who want to learn and share information about a certain topic and who do so in their precious free time (or while hiding from their boss in the office).

- The traffic on mailing lists is high and longtime subscribers take pride in having given their share to make it better. Don't waste their time with unnecessary emails.

- Your email goes out to a lot of people and will be archived for even more people to access. Read it and check your tone and facts before you send it out. A badly phrased or factually dubious email can and will reflect badly on you and will be stored for the future.

- Almost every mailing list comes with a searchable archive and sometimes even an extra wiki or FAQ/tips list. Check these to avoid asking things that have been answered dozens of times before.

- Every mailing list comes with posting guidelines; most of the time these are explained as part of the signup process.

- There are moderators on almost every mailing list who will chastise you or even ban you for violating these guidelines.

- Even worse, a lot of subscribers are protective about the list they spent a lot of time on and will tell you off in less-sophisticated ways than moderators (usually referred to as "flaming").

- If your post is off-topic, it might still spark a lot of answers and heated debates until a moderator intervenes. Read the FAQ/posting guidelines of the list to avoid these "hot topics" or "holy war materials."

Things not to do on mailing lists

And now for some things to avoid:

- Don't sign up with a company email, as you are requested to set "out of office" replies when you go on vacation. You don't want thousands of people to know that your house is empty and give away company internal telephone numbers and contacts. People have lost their jobs because of this—a clever hacker can use this information for social engineering. You also don't want to torture thousands of subscribers with long and unnecessary "this email does comply with XYZ and represents the views of ABC and not the company DEF..." email footers. You can get free emails with lots of storage at Yahoo!, Gmail, or Hotmail these days.

- Don't post questions about your login details or about how to unsubscribe from the list. All this information is on the signup or the list's homepage.

- Don't send personal emails to the list. If you have issues with someone, or you want to give personal advice, send it to the person directly.

- Be careful when replying directly to a sender if you are going to say something controversial about them or another list member—many mailing lists will *automatically* send the reply to the list rather than the original sender, which can be the cause of much embarrassment!

- Don't add overly elaborate email footers to your mails and avoid ASCII art.

- Be yourself in your email name. Things like ...:::\\\cooldesign///:::... make you appear arrogant and ignorant before people even start reading your mails. Also, if you are a one-man shop nobody will believe you any more if you talk about "XYZ consultants." Another irritant is people using their company or product name as their email identity. This can go in your footer instead.

- Don't hijack an email thread with your request; start a new one instead (don't reply to an email with yours but send a new one to the list instead).

- If some answers take the discussion in a different direction, don't keep the same subject but change it instead to "New Topic [was] old topic." This allows subscribers to stop following the thread when the new direction it takes doesn't interest them.

- Don't leave people guessing—if an answer satisfied your needs, thank the person who responded and change the email subject to "[solved] Your Topic." This allows for easy search of the archive.

- Don't use HTML email, attachments, or inline stationery/images in your email. Almost every mailing list disallows both HTML mail and attachments to protect list subscribers from viruses and spamming attempts (spammers insert images into emails pointing to scripts on their server to ensure that the email arrived and was read—once you open the email and load the picture, it will show up in their server logs and they know yours is a valid email to send spam to).

- Don't top-post (add your own answer on top of the unchanged original email) or quote whole emails. Only quote what is absolutely necessary to maintain the context and delete the rest. It makes it a lot easier to follow a thread without losing it or spending hours scrolling. Figure 10-8 shows the differences in quoting styles.

10

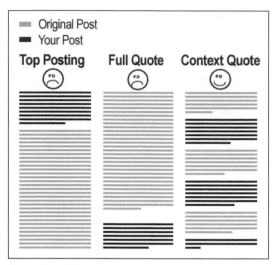

Figure 10-8. Different styles of posting. It is neither advisable to post before a whole quote or after one. Instead, only quote what is necessary to keep things in context.

Mailing lists are a great opportunity both to get information from a lot of knowledgeable people simultaneously, but also to get in contact with them over a period of time. While the community focus is stronger in forums or on chat systems (probably due to the different access levels), mailing lists mean that you already know the person's email, and, as most subscribers to lists advertise their URLs in their email footers, their work. Add a clever email system like Google's Gmail, and you quickly have a network of people you helped and who helped you.

Forums

Forums can be easily compared to mailing lists insofar as they work with threads: someone posts a question and people answer. The difference is that instead of using emails and storing them in a searchable archive, you post them in a form directly on the forum web site. The benefit is that you don't have to give away your email information (most forums keep those secret to avoid spamming). The drawback is that you cannot keep an offline archive on your computer; instead you need to go to the forum site every time you want some information.

Because web forums mean a lot of users and hits, they are also a lot more in danger of being abused. Some people try to advertise their latest products or services, and many a fake "Can you help me with this problem?" post is generated that doesn't showing any problem at all but instead lures many people to go to a freshly created web site. Clients are easily impressed by counter statistics, so this is an easy way to give the impression of being a web developer who really knows how to do web sites: "Wow, 450 hits on the first day, and we haven't even advertised!"

Despite these anomalies, there is still a lot of great information in forums. Some forum admins are rather strict about these things and are ruthless about dealing with spam postings. Most forums are also searchable and are a great resource to come back to. In order to get some money in to pay for the high amount of file traffic, a lot of forums will display advertising and only allow signed-up members to search for information in the forum. This is necessary but can be annoying if it is done in an obtrusive way.

Things to keep in mind about forums

Some rules to keep in mind about forums are

- Forums have fewer users than mailing lists and generally tend to become much closer-knit communities.

- While "becoming known" on mailing lists is more or less erratic and happens through other people mentioning and remembering you, a lot of forums have a hierarchical structure: you become a power user, mentor, guru, or whatever other titles the forum owners come up with for your attendance, both in quality and quantity. This can be a great thing—if done correctly—but can also result in a competition that is unhealthy for quality. If there is a compensation for becoming a guru, people are likely to try to become popular by providing quick-fix solutions rather than telling you what really is wrong with your approach and how to fix the cause rather than the symptom.

- As there is an immediate search function, you are less likely to be forgiven for asking questions that have been answered dozens of times already. Use the search before you post.

- Forums are normally organized in different sections (CSS, JavaScript, Design, Accessibility, and so forth), so make sure you pick the right one when asking a question.

- A lot of forums have "sticky messages" listed on top, although they are not the last-posted ones. These are hot topics or frequently asked questions with lots of user participation (dozens of posts), and it is a good idea to check those before asking the same question again. Administrators take the extra step to make those available without you having to search for them, so have a look.

- As forums are web based and cause a lot of traffic (both the posting and the reading, while mailing lists only cause reading traffic), they tend to be more commercial. You will have advertising to deal with, and in some cases you may even be forced to click or wait for some seconds to get to post a message or reach an answer.

Things not to do on forums

And now for some things to avoid:

- Many of the mailing list rules apply to forums as well:
  - Do quote sensibly and not fully with a one-liner below it (known as top posting).
  - Do not hijack threads; instead, start new ones when you change the subject.
  - Go easy on your footer signature (most forum systems allow you to create one—even using HTML—but usually limit the amount of characters you can use).
  - Don't post questions about your login or the forum itself on the forum. There is either a forum section for that or a different way to contact the maintainers.

10

- Be sure to post in the right subsection of the forum.
- Don't post the same question in different sections—even if it covers more than one topic. Pick the one that causes you the most problems.

Forums are a great communication channel if you want to delve deeper into a particular subject, and their community nature makes it fun to spend days and days answering and posting questions. They can be rather addictive and need a lot of attention to keep up. While mailing lists will make you automatically aware when there is an answer to your problem—an email with the right subject comes in—you'd have to check the forum site frequently to make sure there is one. Although some forums allow you to set up alert emails, most of the time these won't have the answer, and you are asked to visit the site instead—it is all about coming back and reloading the page—since this means advertising revenue. Forums are a great resource for collected knowledge, and it may be worthwhile signing up for that—a lot of them prevent you from searching unless you're a member.

Chat systems

Chat systems like IRC (Internet Relay Chat: http://www.irc.org/) or even online chats on web sites or in Instant Messenger conferences are the Formula One of help systems. They are the fastest and easiest way to get information.

The flipside is that the information may not be very thorough and is not likely to be retained for the future. Some chat channels do keep log libraries and FAQ web sites, which may be a good idea to consult before you dive right in asking your question. These sites also tell you who is likely to be on the channel and who is not a person but a "bot."

> A bot *is a program that runs on a server and shows up as a name in the chat. These programs automatically respond to commands or happenings in the channel and are useful, but they make a terrible conversation partner. Typical tasks for bots are to prevent people from posting too much text, or using all uppercase or other typographical abominations; to recognize moderators and automatically change their status when they join the chat; to ban other users from joining; or to keep a history of who was on the channel and keep messages to show them next time they join.*

Chat—as the name suggests—is all about quick communication and short-lived conversations. Don't expect people on chat systems to have much time or want to deal with your problem exclusively. In most cases several discussions are going on in parallel and as a newcomer you might find it hard to follow what is going on. If that is the case, just lean back a bit, read the discussions without interfering, and try to spot who knows what and how busy the different chat participants are.

Things to keep in mind about chat systems

Some rules to keep in mind about chat systems are

- It is all about speed and quick responses. Just state your problem and people will respond by asking you to give more details.

- There is a hierarchy—several to be exact. Some chat participants are operators (on IRC they have an @ in front of their name), and others are just local gurus. Operators can kick people out of the channel and ban them from reentering. Some channels won't allow you to post until an admin gives you the right to do so (a + in front of your name on IRC).

- People on chat systems seem to abbreviate a lot. A list of common acronyms in use can be found at http://www.gaarde.org/acronyms/.

- Quick answers may not necessarily be good answers; on the other hand, if someone takes the time to explain to you in detail why a certain symptom appears and what you need to do to prevent it, take this as a compliment.

- Every channel on IRC has a topic that will be shown to you when you join the channel. Be sure to read the topic as it contains information about the ground rules of the channel and helpful URLs to check before asking.

Things not to do in chats

And now for some things to avoid:

- Don't start private queries without being invited to do so. Discussions take place on the channel as more people can give their input and attack a problem from several angles. Directly approaching someone has a creepy feel to it and makes you appear to be arrogant enough to consider your problem the most important of all the ones discussed at that time.

- Don't ask generic questions but plunge right into it. A question like "Can someone help me?" will either result in sarcastic remarks about trying a shrink instead or silence. Nobody is willing to commit to the unknown. "Hi, I have a problem with MSIE not showing list elements correctly, can someone have a look?" is much more likely to get you attention and help.

- Don't paste large amounts of text in the channel. This is called flooding and is used by malicious attackers to "take over" the channel. If you have to show a bit of code, provide a URL or use a tool site like http://www.nomorepasting.com.

- Don't stray away from the topic. While people in the JavaScript channel are likely to know something about CSS and HTML, too, it is not the right place to ask an exclusive CSS question.

- Don't accept any software or executable attachments for download. Chat systems are not only full of helpful people, but also those with mischief in mind, sending out Trojans and viruses.

10

- Don't click links that you get offered automatically by someone when joining a channel. Notify an admin that this happened. These links are very likely spam and the sender will get banned from the channel.

- Don't give out any personal data, passwords, or—worst-case scenario—credit card numbers in the channel. There is a big chance that people you don't want to have them will get them.

Chats are fun to take part in but can take up a lot of your free time as the speed of questions and responses makes it amazingly easy to spend hours without noticing it. I've got a lot of brilliant connections and met a lot of savvy people on IRC over the years.

Summary

As you can see, there is a lot you can do before asking for help on the Web. It might appear a bit too much reading it here, but remember that this is a "best idea" concept. You don't need to take *all* the steps explained here, but it'll make it more likely to get good and fast information when you do. Generally the best results for beginners are joining a forum and getting to know it well by following the information flow for a while before participating.

To get good answers you have to ask good questions—it is as easy as that. People are happy to help, but they are not there to do your job for you (and the "but you can do it so much quicker and better" argument doesn't work). Always remember that a negative response is not necessarily a bad thing—see it as a challenge to either find out more yourself or change your approach next time.

So here's a quick review of what to do and where to look:

- Search the Web first—a lot has been researched, published, and answered already and many problems are common obstacles for new web developers.

- Make sure you explain your problem in detail and add the circumstances the issue appears in (your setup, the URL, what to do to reproduce the error).

- Make the problem reproducible—provide a URL and show screenshots.

- Pick the channel of communication most suitable for you at that time: mailing lists when you are not afraid to get emails, forums if you need in-depth help but don't want to give out your email address, and chat systems when you need quick help right here and now.

INDEX

W

friendsofed.com/forums

Join the friends of ED forums to find out more about our books, discover useful technology tips and tricks, or get a helping hand on a challenging project. *Designer to Designer*™ is what it's all about—our community sharing ideas and inspiring each other. In the friends of ED forums, you'll find a wide range of topics to discuss, so look around, find a forum, and dive right in!

- ### Books and Information
  Chat about friends of ED books, gossip about the community, or even tell us some bad jokes!

- ### Flash
  Discuss design issues, ActionScript, dynamic content, and video and sound.

- ### Web Design
  From front-end frustrations to back-end blight, share your problems and your knowledge here.

- ### Site Check
  Show off your work or get new ideas.

- ### Digital Imagery
  Create eye candy with Photoshop, Fireworks, Illustrator, and FreeHand.

- ### ArchivED
  Browse through an archive of old questions and answers.

HOW TO PARTICIPATE

Go to the friends of ED forums at **www.friendsofed.com/forums**.

Visit **www.friendsofed.com** to get the latest on our books, find out what's going on in the community, and discover some of the slickest sites online today!

friendsof
DESIGNER TO DESIGNER™
an Apress® company

   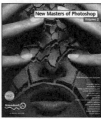